Commonsense Methods for Children with Special Educational Needs – 5th Edition

The worldwide trend towards inclusive education has made it even more necessary for mainstream teachers to develop an understanding of the learning characteristics of children with special educational needs. Not only must all teachers understand and accept students with disabilities and learning difficulties or behavioural problems, but they must also possess a wide range of teaching and management strategies to meet the needs of these students in the classroom. This book offers sound practical advice on suitable intervention methods.

This fully revised and updated fifth edition includes expanded chapters on:

- learning difficulties
- students with intellectual, physical or sensory disabilities
- behaviour management
- self-regulation
- the teaching of literacy and numeracy skills
- adapting curriculum and instruction

In addition, the book includes a new chapter offering a description and critique of mainstream teaching methods, with particular reference to their suitability for specific purposes and their efficacy in addressing students' special needs.

The practical advice the author gives throughout the book is embedded within a clear theoretical context supported by current research and classroom practice.

Commonsense Methods for Children with Special Educational Needs is essential reading for practising teachers and student teachers worldwide.

Peter Westwood is currently an education consultant working in south China.

D0315415

Commonsense Methods for Children with Special Educational Needs – 5th Edition

Peter Westwood

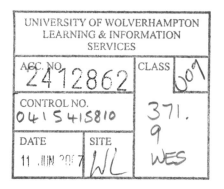

Routledge
Taylor & Francis Group
LONDON AND NEW YORK

First edition published 1987
Second edition published 1993 by Routledge
Third edition published 1997 by Routledge
Fourth edition published 2003 by RoutledgeFalmer
This edition published 2007 by Routledge
2 Park Square, Milton Park, Abingdon, Oxon OX14 4RN

Simultaneously published in the USA and Canada
by Routledge
270 Madison Ave, New York, NY 10016

*Routledge is an imprint of the Taylor & Francis Group, an informa
business*

© 2007 Peter Westwood

Typeset in Times by
HWA Text and Data Management, Tunbridge Wells
Printed and bound in Great Britain by
The Cromwell Press, Trowbridge, Wiltshire

British Library Cataloguing in Publication Data
A catalogue record for this book is available from the British
Library

Library of Congress Cataloging-in-Publication Data
A catalog record for this book has been requested

ISBN10: 0–415–41581–0 (hbk)
ISBN10: 0–415–41582–9 (pbk)
ISBN10: 0–203–64330–5 (ebk)

ISBN13: 978–0–415–41581–1 (hbk)
ISBN13: 978–0–415–41582–8 (pbk)
ISBN13: 978–0–203–64330–3 (ebk)

For Chan Wing Yan (Carol)
My constant support and inspiration

Contents

Introduction

This book is primarily about learning and teaching, rather than the philosophy and ideology of inclusive education. The material comes from my own experience as a teacher and educational psychologist, but I have also drawn extensively on the most recent international literature relating to classroom research and practice.

In this fifth edition of *Commonsense Methods for Children with Special Educational Needs* I have continued to provide generic information and practical advice that can be applied in any country and under any education system. I have avoided, as far as possible, relating the content of the chapters closely to the special education administrative procedures, legal mandates, regulations, codes and terminology used in any one country. Where reference to a particular system has been necessary I have usually compared the situation under discussion with similar situations in other countries, particularly Britain, Australia, New Zealand and the US. Children with special needs, no matter where they are in the world, display remarkably similar learning characteristics and therefore require similar forms of effective intervention. It is also my experience that high-quality teaching can be identified anywhere in the world by a set of generic competencies. It is of great interest to me that earlier editions of this book have been translated into Japanese and Chinese languages, thus supporting my view that practical ideas have international relevance and appeal.

This new edition has retained the same scope and sequence of topics as the previous edition, but all chapters have been revised and updated to include the latest ideas and methods for teaching and managing children with special educational needs. A new final chapter has been added, providing a critical overview of mainstream teaching methods, with particular reference to their suitability for specific purposes and their efficacy for children with learning difficulties. At the present time, in Britain, Australia and the US, there has been a public demand that teachers must employ instructional methods that have been thoroughly evaluated for their effectiveness, rather than using untested approaches based on the latest fad or on teachers' own idiosyncratic beliefs and styles. This urgent call for research-based methods is reflected, for example, in recent government reports dealing with the teaching of literacy in Britain and Australia, cited later within this text.

In Chapter 2 I have added new information on methods that are evolving for children with intellectual disability and with autism. The chapter on physical and sensory disabilities has also been expanded. One unfortunate effect of the focus on 'inclusion' over the past decade seems to have been a significant reduction in the amount of attention given to creating new teaching methods for students with disabilities. For a while it appeared that special education journals had ceased reporting practical teaching approaches in favour of publishing only philosophical and rhetorical papers debating the concept of 'inclusive education'. Fortunately, we seem to be moving back now to more practical concerns and more balanced reporting.

In Chapter 5, I have included new approaches to behaviour management, with a focus on proactive intervention and support. Chapters covering self-regulation in learning and social skills development have been thoroughly revised. The chapters on teaching basic academic skills (literacy and numeracy) contain several new teaching strategies described for the first time. The important topic of adapting instruction to meet students' special needs is addressed critically and realistically in Chapter 13.

The extensive list of references – including for the first time many online resources – should be of value to teachers and researchers wishing to pursue any of the topics in greater depth. The *Further reading* sections at the end of chapters will also be of assistance.

I hope this new edition will help all teachers understand better their students' special educational needs – and at the same time, increase their repertoire of planning, assessment, management and instructional strategies.

I express my very sincere thanks to Mona Wong and Lam Hiu Chi (Denise) for assistance in accessing relevant print and electronic resources necessary for preparing this edition.

Peter Westwood
Education Consultant
China
2007

Chapter 1

Special educational needs and learning difficulties

> Children with special educational needs all have learning difficulties or disabilities that make it harder for them to learn or access education than most children of the same age. These children may need extra or different help from that given to other children of the same age.
>
> (DfES 2006a: n.p.)

The above definition of 'special educational needs' (SEN) provides a simple but accurate description of the children and students whose education is the main focus of this book. It is believed that approximately 15 to 20 per cent of children will have some form of special educational need at some time during their time at school, with about 3 per cent requiring ongoing high-level educational support (DfEE 2001).

Some children with SEN have significant difficulty learning effectively within the mainstream curriculum, due in some cases to below-average cognitive ability, an emotional or motivational problem, poor school attendance, or a behaviour disorder. Others may have difficulty, not in learning, but in accessing resources within the school environment due to a physical or sensory disability (DfES 2006b). In addition, it is now recognised that *any* student may have 'additional educational needs' (AEN) arising from other factors such as English as an additional language, family difficulties, health problems, or social disadvantage (Soan 2004).

Most developed countries share very similar views of what constitutes a 'special educational need'; but countries vary in the extent to which their education policies embody a categorical perspective specifying the particular disabilities that enable a child to be eligible for special education and related services. Countries such as Australia and New Zealand, for example, adopt a fairly non-categorical approach, and identify special educational needs more in terms of the amount of additional support a child or student may require, rather than by the nature of the individual's disability. In the US, by way of contrast, the amended *Individuals with Disabilities Education Act* (IDEA) of 1997 identifies specific disabilities and impairments such as mental retardation (intellectual disability), problems with hearing, vision, speech or language and health, emotional disturbance, orthopaedic impairments, autism, traumatic brain injury, and specific learning disabilities (US Congress 2002). To this long list one can also add children who have been described in the past as 'slow learners', children with attention-deficit hyperactivity disorder (ADHD) and children who are at risk of developing learning problems due to second-language difficulties (Friend and Bursuck 2006). Many writers point out that gifted and talented students also have special educational needs – but not many countries include the category of gifted in their policies for special education services.

In an attempt to clarify definitions and descriptions of students with special needs the OECD (2000) suggested three broad categories:

- students with identifiable disabilities and impairments;
- students with learning difficulties not attributable to any disability or impairment;
- students with difficulties due to socio-economic, cultural or linguistic disadvantage.

For most children in all three categories (other than those with severe and complex disabilities) the worldwide trend is toward placement in mainstream classes. In the UK for example, documents such as *Every Child Matters* (HMSO 2003) and *Removing Barriers to Achievement* (DfES 2004a) make it clear that all teachers can expect to teach children with special educational needs in their regular classes, and all schools must strive to be inclusive by educating the full range of children from the local community.

The policy of inclusion has had a major impact on the role of regular class teachers, who are now required to cater for a much wider range of ability than ever before. The population of students with special educational needs is extremely diverse, and the education of these children in the mainstream presents a major challenge to teachers everywhere. Ellis (2005: 2) has remarked that, 'The inclusion of students with diverse educational needs in the regular classroom is proving to be an extremely difficult and complex task for many teachers'. The move toward inclusive schooling has created a situation where all teachers must now acquire additional knowledge about students with special needs and how best to meet those needs in regular classrooms.

Inclusion has also changed the role of special education and remedial teachers, who must now work much more closely with regular class teachers to provide support. It is clear that teachers themselves need support in meeting the challenges of inclusive education (Atkinson *et al.* 2006).

Inclusive schooling and special educational needs

Prior to the 1970s, most SEN students, particularly those with moderate intellectual disability or with significant physical or sensory impairments, were routinely placed in special classes or special schools to receive an adapted form of education. In recent years the situation has changed, and students with mild to moderate degrees of disability or difficulty are usually retained in mainstream classes and given any necessary support in that setting. This change reflects, to some extent, a shift in thinking from a medical 'separate treatment' model to a 'social model', where differences among learners are recognised, respected and addressed within the context of mixed-ability teaching (Soan 2004).

The move toward inclusion began tentatively in the 1970s under the banner 'integration' or 'mainstreaming', and gained momentum in the late 1980s and 1990s under the influence of policies of social justice and equity. The inclusion ideal was given additional impetus by *The Salamanca Statement and Framework for Action on Special Needs Education* (UNESCO 1994), a document advocating strongly for students with special educational needs to be taught within the regular education system. In 2004, UNESCO defined inclusive education in these terms:

> Inclusive education is a developmental approach seeking to address the learning needs of all children, youth and adults with a specific focus on those who are vulnerable to marginalisation and exclusion.
>
> (UNESCO 2004: n.p.)

Underpinning inclusive education is the principle that every child, regardless of gender, ethnicity, social class, ability or disability, has the basic right to be educated in the regular classroom. It is believed that inclusive schooling paves the way for a more inclusive society. This principle has been accepted to varying degrees in most developed countries, and has influenced education policy-making in the United States, Canada, Britain, Australia, New Zealand, Scandinavia, and much of Europe and Asia. However, in many of these countries the implementation of inclusive classroom practice is still lagging behind the stated policies – and often the rhetoric of 'inclusion' is far ahead of the reality in schools (DfES 2004a; Rustemier and Vaughn 2005). Some countries have been slow to promote inclusion, in part because teachers and principals were not strongly in favour of teaching children with SEN in the mainstream. Studies have shown that teachers' attitude toward inclusion and toward students with disabilities is a powerful influence on the success or failure of inclusion (e.g. Skidmore 2004; Ostrosky *et al.* 2006). In the UK, the Department for Education and Skills (DfES 2004a: 32) states:

> Effective inclusion relies on more than specialist skills and resources. It requires positive attitudes toward children who have difficulties in school, a greater responsiveness to individual needs and critically, a willingness among all staff to play their part. The leadership of the head-teacher is a key factor in making this happen.

Sometimes there is opposition from parents of both disabled and non-disabled children, concerned that classrooms containing a very wide range of ability may end up failing to meet the needs of any of the children (Leyser and Kirk 2004). Other obstacles have been a lack of funds for providing an adequate system of support to children with special needs and their teachers, and difficulties in providing sufficient additional training for teachers to enable them to manage and teach students with special needs more effectively (Rose 2001).

Although there is fairly general acceptance of the principle that students with mild disabilities should be included in the regular classroom, policies that advocate the inclusion of *all* students with disabilities ('full inclusion') are not without their critics – with some educators arguing that regular class placement is not the least restrictive learning environment for some children (e.g. Dymond and Orelove 2001; Kauffman *et al.* 2005). Many tensions still remain between those who advocate inclusion for all and those who believe strongly that some children with special needs can have those needs met most effectively in separate settings with alternative curricula and readily-available support services. For this reason it is often argued that the full range of placement options, including special schools and special classes, must be retained, thus allowing for responsible choice to be made concerning the most appropriate educational setting for each individual with a disability. Many educators believe that the right of parents to make the choice between mainstream and special setting should be preserved. However, the more vocal of the inclusive education advocacy groups are still calling for the closure of all special schools and segregated units.

The practical problems surrounding inclusion are most obvious in the case of individuals with severe and multiple disabilities or with challenging behaviour, since many of these students require a high degree of physical care and management over and above their educational needs. By comparison, the inclusion of students with milder forms of disability and with general learning difficulties presents fewer problems. It is believed that regular class teachers can adopt teaching approaches that are more adaptive to the specific needs of such students (Janney and Snell 2004). Regardless of whether a child with SEN is placed in a mainstream class or in a special setting, the aim is always to address the child's needs through the provision of a broad and balanced education, together with any additional support and special methods or resources that may be required (DfES 2006a: n.p.).

Factors associated with successful inclusion

Research is still investigating which models of school organisation and which classroom practices result in the most effective inclusion for all students (e.g. Johnson 2006; Kauffman *et al.* 2005; Rea *et al.* 2002). It seems that as a very minimum the following ingredients are required if students with significant learning or adjustment problems are to be successfully included in the regular classroom with appropriate access to the general curriculum:

- strong leadership on the part of the school principal;
- development of a whole-school policy supportive of inclusion;
- positive attitudes in staff, parents and children towards students with disabilities;
- commitment on the part of all staff to work collaboratively and to share expertise;
- development of mutual support networks among staff;
- regular assistance from paraprofessionals (classroom aides and assistants);
- adaptation of curriculum and teaching methods (differentiation);
- effective links with outside agencies and services;
- adequate resourcing in terms of materials and personnel;
- ongoing training and professional development for staff;
- close liaison with parents;
- direct parental involvement in a child's educational programme, where possible.

In recent years many books and articles have been written on the theme of inclusive education, mainly from philosophical, political and managerial perspectives. Gradually, more books are addressing the classroom practicalities of inclusion. Inclusive education – and how best to achieve it – will be the topic of debate for many years to come.

How many students have special educational needs?

When mainstream teachers are asked to identify the number of students with special needs in their own classes they tend always to identify significantly more children than the official prevalence figures would predict (McKinnon and Gordon 1999; Westwood and Graham 2000). This may be because teachers have a vested interest in reporting high prevalence rates in order to gain additional resources or support for the school; on the other hand, official figures may be underestimating the true number of children with disabilities, learning difficulties or behaviour problems. An OECD report on inclusive education states that it has been widely accepted in many countries that 15 to 20 per cent of students will have special needs at some time in their school careers (OECD 1999). Some studies have suggested a much higher figure – even as high as 32 per cent if all students with general learning difficulties, low achievement, and behaviour problems are included (Westwood and Graham 2000). Very significant emotional and behavioural difficulties are reported in approximately 9 per cent of the school population (Croll and Moses 2000). The percentage of children with significant intellectual, physical, or sensory disabilities is relatively small, possibly no more than 3 per cent of the school population (Colbert and van Kraayenoord 2000), with just over 1 per cent enrolled in special schools (DfES 2004a).

The remaining sections of this chapter address the characteristics and needs of students with general and specific learning difficulties. In later chapters the characteristics and instructional needs of children with various types of disability will be discussed.

Learning difficulties: confusing terminology

It must be noted here that the terms 'moderate learning difficulties' (MLD) and 'severe learning difficulties' (SLD) are used very differently in the UK from their use in most other countries. In the UK these terms are applied to students with *intellectual disability* (mental handicap or mental retardation). In the UK, students with intellectual disability are also sometimes described as having 'a learning disability' (see for example British Institute of Learning Disabilities 2004). In most other countries the terms 'learning difficulty' and 'learning disability' are not used to describe intellectual disability. This inconsistent terminology gives rise to confusion when reading the international literature on special education, particularly since the abbreviation SLD has traditionally been used in most countries to denote '*specific learning disability*' in students of normal intelligence. In this book, the terms 'learning difficulty' and 'learning disability' will not be used to refer to students with intellectual disability; and the abbreviation SpLD will be used to denote specific learning disability, as described below.

Students with general and specific learning difficulties

The largest single group of students with special needs in any country comprises those with general and specific learning difficulties that are not related to any intellectual, physical or sensory impairment. Estimates suggest that this may involve 15 to 20 per cent of the school population (Smart *et al.* 2005). These learning difficulties most frequently manifest themselves as problems in acquiring literacy and numeracy skills. Difficulties with reading, writing and numeracy then impact adversely on a child's ability to learn across the curriculum (Hay *et al.* 2005).

The term 'learning difficulties' is a very general one, used widely and without much precision. Usually the term is applied to students whose difficulties are not directly related to a specific intellectual, physical or sensory disability. Students who have been referred to as 'slow learners', 'low achievers', or simply 'the hard to teach', certainly fall within the category 'learning difficulties'. So too does the very much smaller group of children described as having a specific learning disability (SpLD) – those of at least average intelligence who for no obvious reason experience chronic problems in learning basic academic skills (APA 2000). It is estimated that this group represents approximately 3 per cent of the school population.

It is vitally important to identify students who are experiencing general or specific problems in learning and to provide support and skilled teaching to improve their achievement level and restore their confidence. Kirby *et al.* (2005: 123) suggest that: 'There is evidence that difficulties experienced at school, if not addressed, may persist into adulthood with a greater risk of psychological problems such as anxiety, depression and lowered self-esteem'.

Possible causes of general learning difficulty

The cause of a learning difficulty usually cannot be attributed to a single factor. Most learning problems arise from a complex interaction among variables such as curriculum content, learners' prior knowledge and experience, learners' cognitive ability and task-approach strategies, teachers' instructional methods, complexity of teachers' language, suitability of resource materials, learners' confidence and expectation of success, and the perceived relevance or value of the learning task. Until recently, curricula, teaching methods, and materials were rarely investigated as possible causes of a learning difficulty, but now it is acknowledged that:

> Difficulties in learning arise from an unsuitable environment – inappropriate grouping of pupils, inflexible teaching styles, or inaccessible curriculum materials – as much as from individual children's physical, sensory or cognitive impairments.
>
> (DfES 2004a: 28)

Many additional factors may also contribute to a failure to learn, such as distractions in the learning environment, the health or emotional state of the learner, the interpersonal relationship between teacher and learner, and relationships with the peer group.

Despite the many and varied possible causal factors associated with learning difficulty, it seems that most teachers, psychologists and researchers still tend to focus almost exclusively on so-called 'deficits' or weaknesses within the learner to account for children's problems in coping successfully with the school curriculum. Even parents tend to assume that there is something 'wrong' with their child if school progress is unsatisfactory.

Many researchers have attempted to summarise characteristics of students with learning difficulties, resulting in lists similar to the one below – often referred to as the 'deficit model' or 'blame the victim'. The deficit model suggests that learning problems are due to:

- below average intelligence;
- poor concentration;
- problems with visual and auditory perception;
- difficulties in understanding complex language;
- limited vocabulary;

- low motivation;
- poor recall of previous learning;
- inability to generalise learning to new contexts;
- lack of effective learning strategies;
- deficient self-management skills;
- poor self-esteem;
- learned helplessness, or diminished belief concerning self-efficacy;
- behavioural and emotional reactions to failure.

While these weaknesses do exist in many students with learning difficulties, they should not be viewed as obstacles too difficult for teachers to overcome, but rather as clear indications of the students' need for high-quality teaching. The deficit model does at least highlight specific difficulties that need to be taken into account when planning and implementing classroom programmes.

Rather than blaming the victim it is usually much more productive to examine factors outside the child such as quality and type of instruction, teacher expectations, relevance of the curriculum, classroom environment, interpersonal dynamics within the class social group, and rapport with the teacher. These factors are much more amenable to modification than are factors within the child or within the child's family background or culture. Trying to identify how best to help a student with general learning difficulties involves finding the most significant and alterable factors that need to be addressed, and providing students with high-quality instruction.

Students with specific learning disabilities (SpLD)

Specific learning disability (SpLD) is the term applied to approximately three children in every 100 whose difficulties cannot be traced to any lack of intelligence, sensory impairment, cultural or linguistic disadvantage or inadequate teaching. This disability manifests itself as a marked discrepancy between intellectual ability and academic achievement (APA 2000). This small group exhibits chronic problems in mastering the basic academic skills of reading, writing, spelling and mathematics. Some students with SpLD also have problems with social relationships (Pavri 2006) and a few have minor difficulties with physical skills.

Perhaps the most comprehensive and widely accepted definition of SpLD comes from legislation in the US, where it is stated that:

The term 'specific learning disability' means a disorder in one or more of the basic psychological processes involved in understanding or in using language, spoken or written, which disorder may manifest itself in imperfect ability to listen, think, speak, write, spell, or to do mathematical calculations. Such term includes such conditions as perceptual disabilities, brain injury, minimal brain dysfunction, dyslexia, and developmental aphasia. Such term does not

include a learning problem that is primarily the result of visual, hear.
motor disabilities; of mental retardation; of emotional disturbance; o,
environmental, cultural, or economic disadvantage.
(US Public Law 108-446, cited in Lerner and Kline 2006: 7)

Over the years, children with learning disabilities have been described as
possessing some of the following characteristics:

- a history of late speech development; continuing immaturities in articulation and syntax;
- visual perception problems resulting in frequent reversal of letters and numerals; some individuals reporting distortion or blurring of print when reading;
- auditory perception problems, including difficulties in developing phonemic awareness;
- difficulty in recalling words, or quickly naming familiar objects;
- minor signs of possible neurological dysfunction;
- hyperactivity and/or attention deficits;
- poor motor co-ordination;
- inefficient learning strategies and poor self-management;
- secondary emotional and behavioural problems due to persistent failure;
- diminished motivation;
- learned helplessness, anxiety and depression.

It must be noted that almost all of the problems listed above may also be found
to varying degrees in students who have *general* learning difficulties rather than
SpLD, so the list does not really help to differentiate between those who have a
genuine learning disability and those who are often referred to as having 'garden
variety' learning difficulties. To add to the problem of identification it is also the
case that any one child with SpLD may exhibit only a few of the characteristics
in the list.

Identification of SpLD

It is often argued that the difficulties of many students with learning disability are
not recognised early enough in school, and unfortunately many SpLD students
are considered simply lazy or unmotivated. Some of these students will go on
to develop social and emotional problems and some will present with major
behaviour difficulties (Hallahan and Kauffman 2006). Studies have shown that a
significant number of students with SpLD leave school at the earliest possible date
and do not pursue studies later as adults (Sabornie and deBettencourt 2004).

The traditional method for identifying SpLD is to assess the student's level
of intelligence using a standardised intelligence test, then to obtain standardised
measures of attainment in academic skills such as reading, spelling, and

mathematics. Any marked discrepancy between level of intelligence and level of attainment (an indication of so-called 'significant under achievement') might indicate the presence of a learning disability. There have been many objections raised to the rigid use of this discrepancy approach to identification, since it might exclude some students who have obvious learning difficulties from receiving additional remedial support, simply on the basis of IQ (Sternberg and Grigorenko 2001).

It has been suggested that the best indication of SpLD, as opposed to a general learning difficulty, is the child's lack of positive response to high-quality intervention (Kavale 2005). Under this 'response to intervention' (RTI) model, students with learning difficulties would first be given regular additional intensive tutoring in small groups, and only those who fail to respond within a reasonable period of time are then referred for in-depth psychometric assessment and ongoing one-to-one tuition (Bradley *et al.* 2005; Vellutino *et al.* 2006). This model sits well with the 'multi-tiered' or 'multi-wave' intervention systems currently being adopted for remedial reading and mathematics (e.g. DfES 2002; 2005). Under this system, Tier 1 represents 'primary prevention', with all students exposed to systematic and high-quality first teaching of reading and maths in the regular class. Tier 2 represents 'secondary prevention', with additional small-group tutoring and practice provided for up to 20 per cent of children. Tier 3 (termed 'Third Wave Intervention' in the UK) provides daily intensive tuition for poor responders, with children taught in pairs or individually. Children who are still making very poor progress even with Tier 3 support are possibly those with a genuine learning disability (Reschly 2005).

Dyslexia and other learning disabilities

The most widely recognised learning disability is *dyslexia*. This form of reading problem is thought to be present in approximately 1 to 2 per cent of the school population – although some reports place the prevalence rate very much higher. Dyslexia is often defined as a 'disorder' causing difficulty in learning to read despite conventional instruction, adequate intelligence, and opportunity.

The oral reading performance of dyslexic students tends to be very slow and laboured, with maximum effort devoted to identifying each individual word, leaving minimum cognitive capacity available for focusing on meaning. The student tires easily and avoids reading if possible. The dyslexic student typically has great difficulty in:

- understanding and applying phonic decoding principles;
- building a vocabulary of words recognised by sight;
- making adequate use of contextual cues to assist word recognition;
- developing speed and fluency in reading;
- understanding what has been read.

Other forms of learning disability described in the literature include *dysgraphia* (problems with writing), *dysorthographia* (problems with spelling), *dyscalculia* (problems with number concepts and arithmetic) and *dysnomia* (inability to retrieve words, names, or symbols quickly from memory). It is doubtful, of course, that these pseudo-medical terms have any real value, particularly in determining an intervention programme for an individual child. The *Diagnostic and Statistical Manual of Mental Disorders* (APA 2000) describes the same problems under the categories: 'reading disorder', 'mathematics disorder', and 'disorders of written language'.

Possible causes of specific learning disability

Some authorities in the learning disability field tend to attribute the learning problem to neurological deficits or to developmental delay (see for example discussions in Lerner and Kline 2006, or Lyon *et al.* 2003). Bender (2004) on the other hand, points out that the neurological perspective, although capturing researchers' keen attention for nearly 70 years, remains controversial and has failed to produce any useful treatment strategies or teaching interventions.

Although much emphasis has been placed on possible organic and biological causes of learning disability, interest has also been shown in other possible causes. In particular, attention has been directed towards students' learning styles and learning strategies (Gregory and Chapman 2002). In many cases of learning disability the children do not appear to have an effective system for approaching a task such as phonic decoding, writing a story, or completing an arithmetic problem. Their lack of effective strategies produces a high error-rate and rapid frustration. It has become popular in recent years to say that these students need to 'learn how to learn' so that they can tackle classroom activities with a greater chance of success. The important thing to note is that current evidence suggests that children can be taught to use more efficient learning strategies and can then function at significantly higher levels (Ellis 2005; Paris and Paris 2001). What is also clear is that attempts at matching the method of instruction to students' so-called natural and 'preferred learning style' is not effective, although the notion appeals intuitively to many teachers (Coffield *et al.* 2004; Mortimore 2005).

One particular factor considered to cause learning problems typical of students with a specific reading disability is a lack of awareness of the phonological (speech–sound) aspects of oral language. This difficulty in identifying component sounds within words also impairs their ability to master phonic principles and apply the decoding strategy for reading and spelling (Muter and Snowling 2003; Stahl and McKenna 2006). It is now believed that in the most severe cases of reading disability this poor phonological awareness is often accompanied by a 'naming-speed' deficiency in which the student cannot quickly retrieve a word or a syllable or a letter-sound association from long-term memory (dysnomia). These combined weaknesses create what is termed a 'double deficit' and together make it extremely difficult for the child to develop effective word recognition skills or become a fluent reader (Vukovic and Siegel 2006).

Is the concept of 'learning disability' useful?

Learning disability remains a controversial topic. Stanovich (1999: vii) remarked: 'The field of learning disabilities is littered with dead ends, false starts, pseudo-science, and fads.' While some experts argue strongly that, for example, a severe reading disability is qualitatively and etiologically different from any of the more general forms of reading failure, others regard it as merely a different point on the same reading-difficulty continuum.

It is fairly clear that the study of SpLD has not resulted in any major breakthrough in tailored teaching methods or instructional resources. In terms of pedagogy, it is difficult to visualise that any teaching method found useful for children with general problems in learning to read or calculate would not also be highly relevant for other children identified as dyslexic or dyscalculic – and vice versa. If one examines the literature on teaching methodology for children with SpLD (e.g. Lerner and Kline 2006; Lewis and Doorlag 2006; Pierangelo and Giuliani 2006) one usually finds not a unique methodology applicable only to SpLD students but a range of valuable teaching strategies that would be helpful to all children. Any child with a learning problem requires assistance, and there seems little to be gained from seeking to differentiate between SpLD and 'non-SpLD' students; the need for high-quality, effective instruction is equally strong in both groups. All children who find learning to read and write difficult are best served by designing and delivering intensive high-quality instruction, rather than by identifying them with a label.

Correlates of learning difficulty: reduced motivation and learned helplessness

Teachers often blame a student's learning problems on his or her lack of motivation. They believe that this lack of motivation is the underlying reason that students avoid class work, refuse to become fully engaged in a learning task, fail to complete work they could easily do, or are willing to complete a task only for some extrinsic reward it may bring. It is almost as if teachers believe motivation to be an innate trait of learners, rather than a variable that is significantly influenced by outside factors.

For many students with learning difficulties the problem is certainly not an innate lack of motivation but rather a marked reluctance to take risks or make any new commitment in a learning situation. This reluctance is due chiefly to prior experiences of failure. There is abundant evidence that obtaining poor outcomes from personal effort to learn can have lasting negative effects on the students' self-esteem, and perceptions of self-efficacy (Westwood 2004a). If students come to believe that they lack the ability ever to succeed they may try to avoid participating in achievement-oriented activities simply to protect their feeling of self-worth – believing that if they don't attempt the task they will not be seen by others to have failed.

Students who encounter continual failure and disapproval may regress over time to a state of learned helplessness, with a very significant decline in motivation and effort (Burden and Snowling 2005). Learned helplessness is the situation in which an individual never expects to succeed with any task he or she is given, and feels totally powerless to change this outcome. Observation of young children suggests that, even at an early age, they can begin to regard themselves as failures in certain learning situations. If, for some reason, a child finds that he or she cannot do something that other children are doing easily, there is a loss of confidence. This loss of confidence leads to deliberate avoidance of the type of activity associated with the failure, and sometimes even avoidance of any new or challenging situation. Avoidance leads to lack of practice. Lack of practice ensures that the individual does not gain in proficiency or confidence, while other children forge ahead. The effects of early failure are thus cumulative, and may contribute later to many instances of learning difficulty in school.

While there are different individual thresholds of tolerance for failure among students, it must be acknowledged that failure is not a pleasing experience, and given sufficient exposure to it almost any student will develop avoidance strategies and learned helplessness. One of the ways of remedying this situation is through attribution retraining (Brophy 2004; Horner and Gaither 2004), an approach to be discussed later. The main challenge for teachers is to try to use teaching methods and learning activities in the classroom that will lead all students to feel successful. Prevention of a learning difficulty in this way is so much more effective than remedial support provided after failure has become well established.

Impact of students' learning difficulties on teachers' motivation

Unfortunately, children's learning problems can have a negative impact on teachers' attitude and motivation. The poor learning habits, low achievement, and reduced motivation seen fairly frequently in students with learning difficulties can influence the attitude teachers develop towards such students (Berry 2006; Feldman and Denti 2004). According to studies reviewed by Eggen and Kauchak (2004), teaching students with learning problems, particularly if the students are in low-stream classes, can have a very negative effect on teachers' own enthusiasm and motivation. Researchers have suggested that teachers' expectations for students' progress and improvement are lowered in the case of bottom-stream classes (Chang and Westwood 2001). This is one of the reasons why grouping students by ability has become a less popular model of organisation within schools.

Teachers' negative beliefs and attitudes are extremely significant because they are communicated all too easily to students. When teachers' attitudes towards the students are perceived as negative they often exert detrimental influences on students' self-esteem and willingness to work. Students' self-esteem and self-efficacy are built out of the way that teachers behave towards them; and as Biggs (1995: 98) remarked, 'Any messages that suggest incompetence are damaging.' The everyday actions and reactions of teachers when teaching low-ability classes may add to students' own perceptions of being incompetent. Even unintentional cues from teachers – such as providing simplified materials, easier tasks, too much praise, too much help – may cause students to believe they are lacking in ability or that teachers believe them to be so. Brophy (2004) has summarised many ways in which teachers, albeit unwittingly, communicate reduced expectations to students they perceive as having low ability. The end result is a lowering of the students' feelings of self-efficacy. When students believe their teachers regard them as 'dull' or 'no-hopers', the development of learned helplessness becomes more likely.

In terms of students' progress and motivation it is important to consider which teaching approaches tend to produce the most successful learning. This theme is developed more fully in Chapter 14.

Teaching approaches

Due to the fairly disappointing standards achieved by too many students in recent years there have been demands in several countries for schools to adopt teaching methods that have been carefully evaluated for their efficacy – rather than employing methods based on teachers' personal intuition, style, or preference (Carnine 2000; DEST 2005; DfES 2004a; Moran 2004). This clarion call for 'research-based instruction' has focused mainly on the teaching of literacy and numeracy, where there are concerns that child-centred approaches have not been effective with some students; but its impact is also being felt in other areas of the curriculum such as science and social studies (Tweed 2004).

In the past, some educators have suggested that child-centred constructivist approaches such as project work, resource-based learning, activity methods, and whole-language approach to literacy have most to offer children with special educational needs (e.g. Goddard 1995; MacInnis and Hemming 1995). These 'process-oriented approaches' – which often seem to emphasise social and emotional development rather than mastery of curriculum content – are thought to be more accommodating of student differences. However, research evidence suggests that students with disabilities and learning problems frequently do best in more tightly structured programmes where direct teaching methods and guided practice are employed (Swanson and Deshler 2003; Vaughn et al. 2000).

It is firmly believed now that the most effective teaching methods for developing basic academic skills are those that provide a balance between explicit instruction from the teacher on the one hand, and student-centred application and practice on the other (Ellis 2005). In general, effective teaching methods are those that provide students with the maximum opportunity to learn by increasing 'academic engaged time' and maintaining high levels of on-task behaviour. Academic engaged time refers to the proportion of instructional time in which students are actively focused on their work. This active involvement includes attending to instruction from the teacher, working independently or with a group on assigned academic tasks, and applying previously acquired knowledge and skills. Studies have shown that students who are receiving instruction directly from the teacher attend better to the content of the lesson than students who are expected to find out information for themselves. Effective lessons, particularly those covering basic academic skills, tend to have a clear structure, with effective use made of the available time. Effective teaching not only raises the attainment level of all students but also reduces significantly the prevalence of learning failure.

According to Foorman *et al.* (2006) the features most commonly found in effective classrooms that distinguish them from less effective classrooms in terms of student achievement include:

- teachers display good classroom management;
- more time is devoted to instructional activities;
- students are more academically engaged;
- more active and explicit instruction is used;
- a good balance between teacher-centred and student-centred activities;
- teachers provide support and 'scaffolding' to help students develop deeper understanding;
- tasks and activities are well matched to students' varying abilities (differentiation);
- students are encouraged to become more independent and self-regulated in their learning.

Swanson (2000), using meta-analyses of learning outcomes from different types of teaching approach, drew the conclusion that the most effective approach for teaching basic academic skills to students with learning difficulties combines the following features:

- carefully controlling and sequencing the curriculum content to be studied;
- providing abundant opportunities for practice and application of newly acquired knowledge and skills;
- ensuring high levels of participation and responding by the children (for example, answering the teacher's questions; staying on task);
- providing frequent feedback, correction and reinforcement;
- using interactive group teaching;
- modelling by the teacher of effective ways of completing school tasks;
- teaching children how best to attempt new learning tasks (direct strategy training);
- making appropriate use of technology (e.g. computer-assisted instruction);
- providing supplementary assistance (e.g. homework; parental tutoring, etc.).

In summary, explicit instruction appears to achieve most in the early stages of learning basic academic skills. The use of direct teaching methods in no way precludes the student from ultimately developing independence in learning; indeed, direct teaching in the early stages facilitates greater confidence and independence in later stages. Over many decades, despite the popularity of student-centred, activity-based approaches, clear evidence supports the value of appropriate direct teaching, often delivered through the medium of interactive whole-class lessons (Dickinson 2003).

Wilen *et al.* (2000: 283) remarked:

> As to which types of learners benefit most from this systematic approach, research tells us that it is helpful for young children, slower learners, and students of all ages and abilities during the first stages of learning informational material or material that is difficult to learn.

Further reading

Guerin, G. and Male, M.C. (eds) (2006) *Addressing Learning Disabilities and Difficulties*, Thousand Oaks, CA: Corwin Press.

Jorgensen, C.M., Schuh, M.C. and Nisbet, J. (2006) *The Inclusion Facilitator's Guide*, Baltimore, MD: Brookes.

Lewis, A. and Norwich, B. (eds) (2005) *Special Teaching for Special Children: Pedagogies for Inclusion*, Maidenhead: Open University Press.

Lewis, R.B. and Doorlag, D.H. (2006). *Teaching Special Students in General Education Classrooms* (7th edn), Upper Saddle River, NJ: Pearson-Merrill-Prentice Hall.

Loreman, T., Deppeler, J. and Harvey, D. (2005) *Inclusive Education: A Practical Guide to Supporting Diversity in the Classroom*, London: Routledge-Falmer.

Mastriopieri, M.A. and Scruggs, T.E. (2007) *The Inclusive Classroom: Strategies for Effective Instruction* (3rd edn), Upper Saddle River, NJ: Pearson-Merrill-Prentice Hall.

Pierangelo, R. and Giuliani, G. (2006) *Learning Disabilities: A Practical Approach to Foundations, Assessment, Diagnosis and Teaching*, Boston, MA: Pearson-Allyn and Bacon.

Topping, K. and Maloney, S. (eds) (2005) *The RoutledgeFalmer Reader in Inclusive Education*, London: Routledge.

Vaughn, S., Bos, C.S. and Schumm, J.S. (2006) *Teaching Exceptional, Diverse and At-risk Students in the General Education Classroom*, Boston, MA: Allyn and Bacon.

Chapter 2

Students with intellectual disability and autism

Mental retardation [intellectual disability] is a disability characterized by significant limitations both in intellectual functioning and adaptive behavior as expressed in conceptual, social, and practical adaptive skills. This disability originates before age 18.

(Luckason *et al.* 2002: 1)

In the early days of 'integration', teachers often expressed grave doubts about the feasibility of placing children with intellectual disability in regular classrooms, particularly in relation to their own competence to meet the needs of these students. Teachers' doubts and negative attitudes could be attributed in part to their limited knowledge of disabilities and their lack of first-hand experience working with atypical children (Weisel and Tur-Kaspa 2002). However, the trend toward inclusion has made it essential now for all teachers to possess a working knowledge of the effects a disability can have on a student's development, learning and social adjustment. Teachers also need to develop strategies for helping these children participate in the mainstream curriculum.

Guiding principles for the mainstream teacher

It is essential first to stress two basic principles that should underpin teachers' beliefs and actions in relation to students with disabilities:

- Students with disabilities are *more like* all other children than they are *different from them*. A lack of awareness of this fact is what contributes to teachers' fear of the unknown.
- Students with a particular disability (e.g. Down's Syndrome) as a group are *just as diverse* in their personal characteristics, behaviour, interests, and learning aptitudes as any other group of students. The assumption that they are all the same leads to negative stereotyping of particular disability groups.

The following statement should be read in conjunction with the main sections in this chapter and the next:

> The student with disability in your class is first and foremost another student – just like all the others in your class. As far as possible, treat him or her in exactly the same way that you treat all other students. He or she has the same basic need for your friendship, respect, assistance, stimulation and good quality teaching as every other student in your class. Don't lower your expectations. It is particularly important to remember that students with disabilities are not necessarily lacking in ability or motivation, and often they can learn effectively if they can gain access to the normal curriculum through appropriate support. Some students may need assistive technology and some may require a modified curriculum; but in general students with disabilities need the same experiences as are encountered by all other students in your class. Many of the following suggestions to support students with disabilities will also be helpful to some of the other students with learning problems.

Students with intellectual disability

Individuals with intellectual disability (previously referred to as mental handicap or mental retardation) comprise a very heterogeneous group, including some very low-functioning individuals who require almost complete and continuous care and management, through to others (the majority) with only mild difficulties often not detected until they are required to learn in school.

Children with *mild* intellectual disability tend to be indistinguishable in many ways from children who have been described in the past as 'slow learners'. In most countries where inclusive education practices have been established, many children with mild intellectual disability attend mainstream schools and receive additional support in that setting. To assist these students in the mainstream, teachers will usually need to make modifications to the learning activities and to the content of the curriculum (Cushing *et al.* 2005). In Chapter 13, strategies for adapting curriculum and teaching methods are discussed. Students with intellectual disability can and will learn if provided with an appropriate instructional programme, adequate support, and teaching methods oriented to their individual needs (Wehmeyer and Agran 2005).

Children with *moderate to severe* intellectual disability are more commonly accommodated in special schools or special classes – although in America, Britain, Canada, Australia and some parts of Europe there is a belief that children with even this degree of intellectual impairment should be integrated in mainstream schools. In these countries, some students with moderate intellectual disability are already integrated, mainly in preschool and early primary years. It is argued that this degree of disability should not act as a barrier to children attending their local schools, and should not be a reason for forcing them into segregated education.

Many individuals with severe intellectual disability also have additional difficulties (physical, sensory, emotional, behavioural) and are frequently described as having 'high support needs' (Orelove *et al.* 2004). In particular, intellectual disability often results in significant limitations of development in the following seven areas. These areas thus become the priorities within the curriculum for students with intellectual disability (Ee and Soh 2005):

- communication;
- self-care and daily living skills;
- social skills;
- basic academic skills (literacy and numeracy);
- self-regulation and self-direction;
- independent functioning in the community;
- employability.

The great dilemma facing those who wish to educate all children with severe disabilities in the mainstream is how to meet their basic needs for training in self-care, daily living skills and communication once they are placed in an environment where a standard academic curriculum prevails. Kauffman *et al.* (2005) have queried whether the potential benefits of socialisation and normalisation in the mainstream can outweigh all the problems involved in supporting these children in a curriculum that is not necessarily very relevant to them. Dymond and Orelove (2001: 111) warn that, 'Functional skills, which were once widely accepted as the basis for curriculum development, have received limited attention as the field has moved to a more inclusive service delivery model'. For some students with disabilities a special education setting may still offer the best environment to meet their needs. The purpose of having special schools and special classes was – and still is – to create a situation in which curriculum content, resources, and methods of instruction can be geared appropriately to the students' needs and abilities (Wolraich 2003).

Identification of intellectual disability

In the past, for an individual to be identified as having an intellectual disability he or she had obtained a measured intelligence quotient (IQ) below 70 and exhibited delays in acquiring normal adaptive behaviours or independent functioning. In recent years attention in many countries has moved away from the rigid use of IQ for the identification of intellectual disability, and now the emphasis is more on assessing how well the individual can function independently and what additional support is needed (Cuskelly 2004).

The most obvious characteristic of most individuals with intellectual disability is that they experience significant difficulty learning almost everything that others can learn with ease. From a practical viewpoint, intellectual disability presents itself as an inability to think as quickly, reason as deeply, remember as easily, or adapt as rapidly to new situations, when compared with so-called normal children. Children with intellectual disability usually appear to be much less mature than their age peers, exhibiting general behaviours typical of much younger children. Their behaviour patterns, skills and general knowledge are related more closely to their developmental age than to their chronological age.

Learning characteristics of students with intellectual disability

Children who are developmentally delayed are slower at acquiring cognitive skills. For them, interpreting information, thinking, reasoning and problem solving are very difficult. In most aspects of conceptual development and reasoning, school-age children with mild to moderate intellectual disability tend to be functioning at what Piaget (1963) referred to as the 'concrete operational' level. They understand and remember only those things and situations that they can directly experience; teaching for them has to be *reality-based*. Students with severe to profound disability may be at an even earlier Piagetian cognitive stage of 'sensori-motor' or 'pre-operational'. It is generally accepted that children with intellectual disability pass through the same sequence of stages in cognitive development as other children (from sensori-motor, through pre-operational to concrete operational, and finally formal operational) but at a much slower rate. It is also clear that some intellectually disabled individuals even as adults never reach the highest level of formal operational thinking and reasoning.

The main messages that educators need to take from Piaget's work are these:

- Cognitive development comes from action – students 'learn by doing'.
- Children need someone to interact with who will interpret (or *mediate*) learning experiences.

These principles must guide the teaching and design of curricula for students with intellectual disability, whether in special or mainstream schools (Ee and Soh 2005).

Specific difficulties

Attention

Individuals with intellectual disability appear often to have problems in attending to the relevant aspects of a learning situation (Hardman *et al.* 2005). For example, when a teacher is showing the student how to form the numeral 5 with a pencil, or how to use scissors to cut paper, the student is attracted perhaps to the ring on the teacher's finger or to a picture on the paper, rather than the task itself. This tendency to focus on irrelevant detail, or to be distracted easily from a learning task, is potentially a major problem for the child with intellectual disability when integrated into mainstream programmes without close supervision. The teacher will need to think of many ways of helping a child with intellectual disability to focus on a learning task. Without adequate attention to task, any student will fail to learn or remember what the teacher is trying to teach.

Memory

Many students with intellectual disability also have difficulty in storing information in long-term memory (Pickering and Gathercole 2004). This problem may, in part, be linked with the failure to attend closely to the learning task as discussed above. It also indicates that the lower the intellectual ability of the student the greater the amount of repetition and practice required to ensure that information and skills are eventually stored. Many students with intellectual disability do not develop effective strategies to aid memorisation, so the message for the teacher is to provide even more opportunities for guided and independent practice in every area of the curriculum. Frequent revision and overlearning are also needed.

Generalisation

For any learner, the final and most difficult stage of acquiring new learning is that of *generalisation*. In order to master information, skills or strategies, a stage must be reached when the student can apply that learning to new situations not directly linked with the context in which it was first taught. It is typical of many students with intellectual disability that they do not generalise what they learn (Meese 2001); they may learn a particular skill or strategy in one context but fail to transfer it to a different situation. It is generally recommended that teachers consider ways of facilitating generalisation when planning lessons for students with special needs by, for example, re-teaching the same skills or strategies in different contexts, gradually increasing the range of contexts, challenging students to decide whether a skill or strategy could be used to solve a new problem, and reinforcing any evidence of students' spontaneous generalisation of previous learning.

Language delay in children with intellectual disability

Language ability is important for cognitive and social development. In particular, language serves the following functions:

- It enables an individual to make his or her needs, opinions and ideas known to others.
- It is important for cognitive development; without language one lacks much of the raw material with which to think and reason.
- Concepts are more effectively stored in memory if they have a mental representation in words as well as in sensations and perceptions.

- Language is the main medium through which school learning is mediated.
- Positive social interactions with other persons are heavily dependent upon effective language and communication skills.
- Language is important for regulating one's own behaviour and responses (self-talk).

One of the main characteristics of children with moderate and severe intellectual disability is the very slow rate at which many of them acquire speech and language. Even the child with mild retardation is likely to be behind the normal milestones for language development. Some individuals with severe and multiple disabilities never develop speech – so for them alternative or augmentative methods of communication may need to be developed (e.g. sign language; picture or symbol communication systems) (Heller and Bigge 2005).

The development of communication skills in students with intellectual disability is given high priority in special school curricula. Language stimulation will continue to be of vital importance for these students in mainstream settings. While language is best acquired naturally – through using it to express needs, obtain information, and interact socially – for some disabled students a more direct instructional approach may also be necessary (Beirne-Smith *et al.* 2006). Where possible, naturally occurring opportunities within the school day are used to teach and reinforce new vocabulary and language patterns. This 'milieu approach' is found to be more productive in terms of generalisation and transfer of learning to everyday use than are the more clinical approaches to teaching language in isolation (Kaiser and Grim 2006). Two obvious benefits of placing a child with intellectual disability in a mainstream class are immersion in a naturally enriched language environment and the increased need for the student to communicate with others.

Many students with intellectual disability require the services of a speech therapist; but improvement can be very slow indeed. This is because the individuals receiving help may not appreciate the need for it and may therefore have no motivation to practise what is taught. There is also the usual problem of lack of generalisation – what is taught in a clinical setting does not necessarily transfer to the person's everyday speech.

Social development of students with intellectual disability

The presence or absence of social skills in students with intellectual disability tends to be related to the extent to which they have had the opportunity to socialise in the home and other environments. Within the family, the social interactions between the child and others are likely to be mainly positive, but the same assumption cannot be made for contacts within the community and at school (Norwich and Kelly 2004). Although community attitudes toward people with disabilities are changing, there is still a likelihood that some children with intellectual disability will experience difficulty making friends and gaining acceptance – particularly if they have some irritating or challenging behaviours. In such cases a child may experience rejection and teasing from others. Some students with intellectual disability are rejected by their peers more on the basis of their irritating behaviour than because they are disabled. For example, the presence of inappropriate responses such as aggression, shouting, or temper tantrums makes it difficult for a few of these children to be socially accepted. Intervention is needed to eliminate these negative behaviours and replace them with pro-social behaviours. If the student with a disability is to make friends and be accepted in the peer group, social skills training may need to be given a high priority in the programme. Strategies for developing social skills are described in Chapter 6.

While stressing the need to increase social interaction with others, students with intellectual disability (male and female) also need to be taught *protective behaviours* to reduce the possibility that they become the victims of sexual abuse. The lack of social judgement of some teenagers and young adults with intellectual disability causes them to be rather naïve and trusting. They may not really comprehend right from wrong in matters of physical contact and are therefore at risk. For their own protection they need to be taught the danger of going anywhere with a stranger, accepting rides in a car, or taking gifts for favours. They need to know that some forms of touching are wrong, and they also need to know that they can tell some trusted adult if they feel they are at risk from some other person. These matters must be dealt with openly in schools and also stressed as important by parents.

Teaching approaches for students with intellectual disability

The main priority in teaching children with intellectual disability is to make the curriculum *reality-based*. It has already been mentioned that for cognitive development and for the acquisition of skills, these children need to experience things at first hand, and have others help them interpret these experiences. For children at the concrete operational stage in terms of cognitive development, the age-old principle of 'learning by doing' certainly applies. If they are to learn important number skills, for example, they should learn them not only from books, computer games and instructional materials but also from real situations such as shopping, stocktaking, measuring, estimating, counting, grouping, recording data and comparing quantities (Xin *et al.* 2005a). Reading skills should be developed and practised using real books, real instruction cards, real recipes, real brochures and real comic books, as well as through graded readers, games and flashcards. As far as possible the '4 R Test' should be applied when selecting curriculum content – is the content you are going to teach *real, relevant, realistic* and *rational*?

In addition to reality-based learning, children with intellectual disability also need some high-quality direct teaching, with the content broken down into very simple steps to ensure high success rates. It has been found that direct instruction using these principles is extremely effective for students with disabilities, particularly for teaching basic skills and functional academics (Carnine *et al.* 2004; Turnbull *et al.* 2007). Lessons that employ direct instructional methods aim to use a fast pace of teaching with as many successful responses from the students as possible in the time available. There is heavy emphasis on practice and reinforcement, but lessons are made enjoyable and entertaining. Direct instruction is among the most extensively researched teaching methods and has consistently proved more effective for some types of learning than student-centred, independent learning approaches (Carnine 2000). The method is discussed fully in Chapter 14.

Other basic principles to consider when working with students with intellectual disability include the following:

- Provide plentiful cues and prompts to enable the learner to manage each step in a task.
- Make all possible use of cooperative group work, and teach children the necessary group-working skills.
- Frequently assess the learning that has taken place against the child's objectives in the curriculum.
- Use additional helpers to assist with the teaching (aides, volunteers, parents).
- Involve parents in the educational programme when possible.
- Most importantly, do not sell the students short by expecting too little from them.

In recent years, much emphasis has been placed on trying to increase self-regulation and self-monitoring strategies in students with intellectual disability by using cognitive methods and metacognitive training (Dixon *et al.* 2004). While this approach is proving very useful for students with mild disabilities, it is very difficult indeed to employ cognitive training with low-functioning students for reasons that will be discussed later in connection with autism. The topic of self-regulation is addressed in Chapter 4.

Decision-making and self-determination are also areas attracting greater attention in the education of individuals with intellectual disability. It is recognised that too much of the life of a person with severe disability is determined by others; so in recent years educators and caregivers have been encouraged to find many more ways of ensuring that persons with disabilities have opportunities to exercise choice and make decisions for themselves (Holverstott 2005; Stafford 2005).

Approaches for individuals with severe and complex disabilities

A method known as '*intensive interaction*' has been developed for use with children who have severe and complex disabilities and who lack verbal communication.

The method has also been used with low-functioning autistic children. The interactive approach tries to ensure that much of the teaching that takes place is based directly on a student's own self-initiated actions and reactions, rather than on a pre-planned curriculum imposed by an adult. In many ways the method is similar to the natural approach used instinctively by mothers or fathers when responding to a baby's actions. For example, the parent may smile, reach out, touch, stroke, hug and speak. Something the child does spontaneously leads the adult to react, rather than the other way around. The adult responds, and by doing so reinforces the child and the behaviour. A vital ingredient of warm social interaction and communication is involved. Often playing simple games or using sensory equipment will create a context for this to happen. For more information on intensive interaction, see Caldwell (2006), Kellett and Nind (2003), or visit the website at www.intensiveinteraction.co.uk.

Another approach that is currently emerging for students with severe disabilities – 'preference-based teaching' – has fairly similar underpinnings to intensive interaction. It is based on the belief that students enjoy engaging in learning activities much more if the modes of teaching and the materials used are compatible with the individual's personal preferences. Attention is more effectively gained and maintained, and there are fewer behaviour problems (Reid and Green 2006).

In the case of young children with severe and multiple disabilities or with challenging behaviour, sensory stimulation is important (Chilvers and Cole 2006). Great interest has been shown in an approach called 'Snoezelen' developed in Holland (Cuvo et al. 2001; Hutchinson and Kewin 1994). The approach is being adopted in a number of special schools in Europe and Australasia and provides both sensory stimulation and relaxation for severely or profoundly disabled individuals. The approach is therapeutic and educational, using structured multi-sensory environments containing lights, textures, aromas, sounds and movement. Snoezelen is reported to have particular benefits for individuals who have emotional and behavioural problems combined with their intellectual disability, and also for helping autistic children. In some cases Snoezelen has proved useful in reducing self-injurious behaviour (SIB) and self-stimulating behaviour (SSB) (Shapiro et al. 1997). While Snoezelen rooms are unlikely to be developed in mainstream schools, teachers in preschools and special schools do need to note the potential value of sensory stimulation for young children with intellectual disability.

Students with autistic spectrum disorders (ASD)

Children with autism remain among the most difficult students to place successfully in mainstream classrooms (Turnbull et al. 2007). Those with severe autism are usually functioning intellectually at a level too low even to cope with the demands of an adapted mainstream curriculum. Coupled with lowered intellectual functioning are the added problems of poor social development and significant lack of communication. In the US, Australasia, and Britain only about 12 per cent of children with diagnosed autism receive their education in mainstream classes. However, most of the higher-functioning students with *Asperger Syndrome* do attend mainstream schools.

Autism is a low-incidence disability with approximately 4 to 10 cases per 10,000 in the population (but the rate is said to be increasing). The lower figure represents the more severe cases; the upper figure includes those children with mild autistic tendencies. The ratio of males to females is 4 or 5 to 1. Autism is one of several disorders referred to under a general category of *Pervasive Developmental Disorders* (PDDs); Asperger Syndrome and Rett Syndrome are other examples. Autistic children have been identified in all parts of the world and the disorder does not appear to be in any way culturally determined. Although autism has been found in individuals at all levels of intelligence, a degree of intellectual disability ranging from mild to severe retardation is found in many cases. As many as three-quarters of children with autistic disorders have IQ scores below 70, and on-going intensive special education is usually required to address their learning needs.

Characteristics of students with autism

Autism is a severe form of developmental disorder in which the most obvious characteristics are:

- major impairment of social interactions – lack of normal emotional relationship with others;
- impairment of communication;
- reduced ability to learn, particularly through observation and imitation;
- the presence of stereotyped behaviour patterns (e.g. rocking, hand flapping, spinning);
- obsessive interests, ritualised activities, and the desire to preserve 'sameness' in surroundings and daily routines;
- lack of imaginative and creative play.

Current thinking on the nature of autism embodies the notion of a *continuum* of autistic characteristics, implying that there is no clearly defined single syndrome (Magnusen 2005). Included at the upper level within this continuum are all the atypical children who are difficult to diagnose and do not necessarily conform to the typical pattern of autism. Individuals with autism vary greatly – and any single child diagnosed as autistic may not show all the above characteristics. Some students with 'autistic tendencies' are close to normal in many facets of their behaviour, but others are very low functioning in terms of cognition, self-regulation, and social development. Some children with moderate to severe degrees of autism often sit for hours, engaging in unusual repetitive habits (*stereotypic behaviours*) such as spinning objects, head banging, flapping fingers in front of their eyes, or just staring at their hands. Many autistic children exhibit self-injurious behaviours, such as biting or scratching their hands. Such stereotypic behaviours need to be reduced as far as possible, in order to make the child more available for new learning and to increase social acceptance by peers (Conroy *et al.* 2005).

Diagnosis of autism

To be diagnosed as autistic a child must show symptoms of abnormal social and interpersonal development before the age of 3 years, and must meet at least 6 of the 12 criteria listed in the *Diagnostic and Statistical Manual of Mental Disorders* (APA 2000). The list helps to delineate in more detail the key areas of abnormal development typical of children with autistic spectrum disorders. The 12 diagnostic criteria are:

- marked impairment of nonverbal behaviours used in social interaction (e.g. eye contact, facial expression, posture, use of gestures, etc.);
- failure to develop peer relationships;
- no spontaneous interest in, or enjoyment of, other persons;
- no desire to return social or emotional contacts;
- delay (or total lack) of verbal communication skills;
- in individuals with speech, no obvious ability or desire to converse with others;
- the use of stereotyped and repetitive language (often echolalic);
- absence of imaginative play;
- preoccupation with one or more stereotyped patterns of behaviour or interest;
- inflexible adherence to specific rituals and routines;
- repetitive movements such as hand flapping, body rocking;
- obsessive preoccupation with tiny parts or details of objects.

Interventions for autism

Many different approaches have been used to reduce the negative behaviours often associated with autism, including pharmacological treatments, diet control, psychotherapy, behaviour modification, and cognitive self-management training. Of these approaches, behaviour modification has produced the best results (Dempsey and Foreman 2001). Cognitive approaches are problematic with low-functioning children because they require self-monitoring and a degree of metacognition not usually found in severely autistic children.

Many other approaches have been tried, including sensory-integration training, music therapy, play therapy, holding therapy, Snoezelen, facilitated communication, speech and language training, and social skills coaching. Some of the treatments are regarded as highly controversial (Levy and Hyman 2005). For a description of these approaches see Simpson (2005), Waterhouse (2000), or Dempsey and

Foreman (2001). A summary and critique of treatment and management methods is available online at http://www.mousetrial.com/links_treatments.html.

Teaching and training approaches: general principles

While some short-term gains from teaching programmes are reported in studies of autistic children, longer-term benefits are much more difficult to prove. Children with the most severe forms of autism often appear to make minimal gains, despite many hours of careful stimulation and teaching. However, the benefits reported for a number of children with autism are positive enough to make the investment of time and effort worthwhile. Sewell (2000: 23) writes, 'Remember – everything you teach children with autism to do for themselves will be one more skill they will not have to depend on someone else to do for them the rest of their lives.'

There is general agreement that the focus of any intervention programme should attempt to:

- stimulate cognitive development;
- facilitate language acquisition;
- promote social development.

A number of approaches to intervention for children with autism can lead to improved outcomes, even though the underlying causes of the problem cannot be identified or remedied. Evidence has proved that the most effective intervention strategies are *highly structured* and *delivered with intensity* (Waterhouse 2000). Teaching sessions for children with autism generally need to be implemented according to a predictable schedule. They need to teach new information, skills or behaviours in small increments through consistent, systematic and direct methods. Each child's programme must be based on a very careful and detailed appraisal of the child's current developmental level and existing skills and responses. It is essential to assess the strengths of each individual child and to set intervention programme goals that will help build on these strengths. All teachers, parents and other caregivers must know the precise goals and objectives of the programme and must collaborate closely on the methods to be used with the child. It is essential that parents also be trained in the teaching strategies to be used in any intervention programme as the child spends more time at home than at school.

Sewell (2000) suggest the following ten top priorities when working with autistic children:

- Seek early behavioural and educational intervention.
- Be consistent in your management of the child (firmness plus affection).
- Maintain intensity and aid generalisation by extending the teaching into all environments.
- Build up the child's attention to task.
- Speak clearly and concisely to facilitate comprehension.

- Ignore attention-seeking behaviours but reward appropriate and compliant behaviours.
- Be firm but fair in making sure the child carries out requests.
- Ensure that all caregivers are aware of the objectives and targets for behaviour.
- Challenge the child enough to encourage progress towards new learning goals.
- Apply the '3 Ps': planning, patience and perseverance.

Objectives are best achieved by using both direct instructional methods and by maximising the naturally occurring opportunities in the child's daily life. The most effective interventions involve the child's family as well as teachers and therapists. Home-based intervention programmes (or programmes combining both school- or clinic-based intervention with home programmes) produce better results than purely clinical programmes (Lovaas 1993). There is some evidence that collaborative use of a computer at home or in the classroom may help to establish some social responses from autistic children. The research highlighted the social interaction that can occur around the computer, with the child initiating actions that are responded to positively by the teacher (Jacklin and Farr 2005).

For non-verbal autistic children the intensive use of visual cues (hand signing, pointing, pictures, symbols; alternative communication) is usually necessary in most teaching situations. Some programmes have been based on teaching a basic vocabulary of hand signs to autistic children who lack speech. For a few students, picture boards and other forms of communication aids can be useful.

Specific programmes and methods

TEACCH

One approach that has become popular in recent years is TEACCH (Treatment and Education of Autistic and Communication-handicapped Children) (Mesibov *et al.* 2005). This approach stresses the need for a high degree of structure in the autistic child's day, and uses a combination of cognitive and behavioural-change strategies, coupled with direct teaching of specific skills. Importance is also placed on training parents to work with their own children and to make effective use of support services. An important feature of the approach is that it tries to capitalise on autistic children's preference for a visual mode of communication (e.g. sign language or picture cues) rather than the auditory-verbal mode. Several studies have supported the value of using visual cues, prompts, and schedules to hold the child's attention and to represent information in a form that is easily interpreted (Kimball *et al.* 2004). Such systems can also operate at home. In general, TEACCH has proved to be of positive value in the education of autistic children (Simpson 2005).

Lovaas's 'Young Autism Program'

One very intensive programme for autistic children is that devised by Lovaas (1993). The programme begins with the child at age 2 years, and involves language development, social behaviours and the stimulation of play activity. Emphasis is also given to the elimination of excessive ritualistic behaviour, temper tantrums and aggression. The second year of treatment focuses on higher levels of language stimulation, and on cooperative play and interaction with peers. Lovaas claims high success rates for the programme, including increases in IQ. He claims that almost half of the treated group of children reached 'normal' functioning levels. The fact that this programme takes 40 hours per week, using one-to-one teaching over two years, makes it very labour-intensive and expensive. While the general principles are undoubtedly sound, it is difficult if not impossible to replicate the approach in the average special preschool.

Pivotal response training

This approach, developed by Robert and Lynn Koegel and associates (2006), is based on the principle that intervention in autism should focus heavily on strengthening particular behaviours that will simultaneously have a beneficial effect on other associated behaviours. These 'pivotal behaviours' in a child's repertoire are those that have widespread positive effects leading to generalised improvement. An example of pivotal behaviour is the child's response to multiple stimuli. Training would seek to increase selective attention and improve the ability to combine information from different sources. Motivation is another pivotal response, because improved motivation will increase attention to task, participation, and autonomy. Training to improve motivation might include the use of preferred activities and opportunities for the child to make many choices.

Pivotal response training employs basic applied behaviour analysis techniques and has been used effectively in the areas of language skills, play, and social behaviours. More detailed information can be found in the document *How to teach pivotal behaviors to children with autism: a training manual*, online at http://www.users.qwest.net/~tbharris/prt.htm.

The SCERTS model

Detailed information on SCERTS can be found in the two-volume manual by Prizant *et al.* (2005). The acronym SCERTS is derived from Social Communication (SC), Emotional Regulation (ER) and Transactional Support (TS): these are the areas of development prioritised within this approach. The designers of this transdisciplinary and family-centred model stress that SCERTS is not intended to be exclusionary of other treatments or methods. It attempts to capitalise on naturally occurring opportunities for development that occur throughout a child's daily activities and across social partners, such as siblings, parents, caregivers, and other children. The overriding goal of SCERTS is to help a child with autism become a more competent participant in social activities by enhancing his or her capacity for attention, reciprocity, expression of emotion, and understanding of others' emotions. In particular, SCERTS aims to help children become better communicators and to enhance their abilities for pretend play.

DIR/Floortime approach

Details of this approach can be found in the text by Greenspan and Wieder (2006). The letters DIR represent 'developmental, individualised, and relationship-based' – these are the underlying principles of this early-years approach. 'Floortime' refers to the several sessions per day of natural adult–child interaction, play, and close contact through which the approach is implemented, chiefly by parents at home. The aim of floortime sessions is to improve the child's overall ability to relate to others, communicate, and think. Floortime engages the child and adult in developmentally appropriate and enjoyable activities –'on the mat'– that increase attention, two-way communication, initiative, and problem solving.

Social stories

A technique that appears helpful in developing autistic children's awareness of 'normal' codes of behaviour is use of 'social stories' (Crozier and Sileo 2005; Howley and Arnold 2005). Social stories are simple narratives, personalised to suit the child's own needs and behaviours, to which the child can relate. The theme and context of the story help the autistic child perceive, interpret and respond more appropriately to typical social situations – for example, sharing a toy, taking turns, or standing in line.

Social stories are also being used with young children who are not autistic but who have other serious emotional and behavioural problems (Haggerty *et al.* 2005). This application will be discussed in Chapter 5.

Asperger Syndrome

Individuals with Asperger Syndrome have some of the behavioural and social difficulties associated with other degrees of autism but they tend to have language and cognitive skills in the average or even above-average range. Some researchers argue that Asperger Syndrome is simply a subgroup within the autistic disorders spectrum, but others believe it is a different form of disability representing a discrete group of higher-functioning individuals with only a few autistic tendencies (Baker and Welkowitz 2005). Most students with this type of disorder are in mainstream schools. Their unusual behaviour patterns cause them to be regarded as strange by peers and teachers, and they may have difficulty in making friends.

Students with Asperger Syndrome may exhibit the following characteristics:

- unusual features in their oral language (e.g. repeatedly asking the same question of the same person, even though it has been answered; using a strangely pedantic style of speech; the overuse of stereotypic phrases);
- a lack of common sense in their daily encounters with the physical environment;
- naïve and inappropriate social approaches to others;
- narrow, obsessive interests;
- some appear physically awkward and poorly coordinated.

A few high-functioning students with this syndrome may exhibit certain areas of very great talent or knowledge. The areas of outstanding performance have included such things as music, art, mental calculation and recall of factual information with amazing accuracy. Students with these highly developed abilities are sometimes referred to as 'autistic savants'.

The key educational considerations for these students include:

- strategic seating in the classroom so that they can be monitored closely and kept on task;
- great clarity in setting a task for the student to attempt;
- using direct, literal questioning, rather than open-ended questioning;
- avoiding the over-use of complex language that requires deeper interpretation (e.g. metaphors, idioms);
- trying to establish a reasonably predictable routine and structure to all lessons;
- using visual aids during lessons wherever possible;
- if necessary, using a student's obsessive interests as a focus for schoolwork, but at the same time trying to extend and vary the student's range of interests over time.

Some students with this form of autism may benefit from personal counselling to discuss such issues as the feelings of others, social interactions, dealing with their own problems, how to avoid trouble with other students and teachers. The student's own inability to understand the emotional world of others will not easily be overcome, but at least he or she can be taught some coping strategies. Children with Asperger Syndrome are stronger candidates for social-skills training than are autistic children with intellectual disability.

Further reading

Beirne-Smith, M., Patton, J.R. and Kim, S.H. (2006) *Mental Retardation: An Introduction to Intellectual Disabilities* (7th edn), Upper Saddle River, NJ: Pearson-Merrill-Prentice Hall.
Farrell, M. (2005) *The Effective Teacher's Guide to Moderate, Severe and Profound Difficulties*, New York: Guilford Press.

Hallahan, D.P. and Kauffman, J.M. (2006) *Exceptional Learners* (10th edn), Boston, MA: Pearson-Allyn and Bacon.

Harris, J.C. (2006) *Intellectual Disability: Understanding its Development, Causes, Classification, Evaluation and Treatment*, Oxford: Oxford University Press.

Heward, W.L. (2006) *Exceptional Children* (8th edn), Upper Saddle River, NJ: Pearson-Merrill-Prentice Hall.

Smith, D.D. (2007). *Introduction to Special Education: Making a Difference* (6th edn), Boston, MA: Pearson-Allyn and Bacon.

Snell, M.E. and Brown, F. (eds) (2006) *Instruction of Students with Severe Disabilities*, Upper Saddle River, NJ: Pearson-Merrill-Prentice Hall.

Wehmeyer, M.L. and Agran, M. (eds) (2005) *Mental Retardation and Intellectual Disabilities: Teaching Students using Innovative and Research-based Strategies*, Boston, MA: Pearson-Merrill-Prentice Hall.

Zager, D. (ed.) (2005) *Autism Spectrum Disorders: Identification, Education and Treatment* (3rd edn), Mahwah, NJ: Erlbaum.

Chapter 3

Students with physical disabilities and sensory impairments

> It is suggested that young people with physical disabilities need to be considered as individuals and that if schools are to achieve the goal of inclusion they need to develop ways to accommodate each individual's needs.
>
> (Curtin and Clarke 2005: 195)

Unlike the disabilities described in the previous chapter, the difficulties considered in this chapter do not necessarily arise from a student's impaired intellectual functioning. Some students with physical disabilities or with impaired sight or hearing will be of average or better than average intelligence. Many of these students can cope well with the mainstream curriculum if specific teaching approaches are used to motivate and support them. In the case of students with physical disabilities or sensory impairment their greatest need may be help in accessing normal learning environments, instructional resources, and classroom experiences.

Students with physical disabilities

Students with physical disabilities comprise a relatively small but diverse group. Their disabilities can range from those that have little or no influence on learning and development, through to other conditions that may involve neurological impairment affecting both fine and gross motor skills. It is important for teachers to realise that a physical disability does not automatically impair a student's ability to learn. While it is true that some students with physical impairment do have learning problems, assumptions should never be made about an individual's capacity to learn on the basis of a physical disability. Even severe types of physical impairment sometimes have no impact on intellectual ability. The intelligence levels for students with physical disabilities cover the full range from gifted to severely intellectually disabled (Best *et al.* 2005). It has been noted, however, that some students with physical disabilities lack confidence in their own self-efficacy, and present as rather passive learners requiring more than usual extrinsic motivation (Konings *et al.* 2005).

The education of students with physical disabilities needs to focus on providing these individuals with opportunities to access the same range of experiences as those available to students without handicaps. This may require adaptations to be made to the environment, to the ways in which these students move (or are moved) around the environment, and to the teaching methods and instructional resources used (Best *et al.* 2005). In the case of students with milder forms of disability, and those with average or above-average learning aptitude, there is usually no reason why they should not attend ordinary schools and access the mainstream curriculum. For those with more severe disabilities and high support needs, special schools may still offer the best placement (Kauffman *et al.* 2005). The special school can offer a curriculum, resources, methods of instruction and therapies tailored to meet their needs. *confusion around*

The problem for many severely disabled students with normal intelligence is to find ways of communicating with others in order to interact socially. It is also necessary to find alternative ways of accessing the school curriculum. Even those physically disabled students with good learning skills may need a great deal of support in order to achieve their potential. They, like many other students with disabilities, may also need to draw upon outside services in order to function successfully and to maintain a good quality of life (Snell and Brown 2006).

When working with students with physical and cognitive disabilities it is usually necessary for the teacher to undertake not only task analysis (to reduce an activity to simple steps) but also *situation analysis* relating to the learning environment (Best *et al.* 2005). It is essential to consider any modifications needed in the learning environment (e.g. seating, equipment, access routes, movement, use of available supports and resources) to enhance the students' opportunities to participate.

It is beyond the scope of this book to provide details of each and every physical disability or health problem. Readers will find such information in Batshaw (2002), Best *et al.* (2005), Orelove *et al.* (2004), and Pickles (2004). Attention here will be devoted only to cerebral palsy (CP), spina bifida (SB) and traumatic brain injury (TBI).

Cerebral palsy (CP)

Cerebral palsy (CP) is a disorder of posture, muscle tone and movement resulting from damage to the motor areas of the brain occurring before, during or soon after birth (Petersen and Whitaker 2003). CP exists in several forms (e.g. *spasticity*, *athetosis*, *ataxia*) and at different levels of severity from mild to severe. Type and severity of the condition are related to the particular area or areas of the brain that have been damaged and the extent of that damage. CP is not curable, but its negative impact on the individual's physical coordination, mobility, learning capacity and communication skills can be reduced through appropriate intensive therapy, training and education.

Assistive technology (AT) plays a major role in the education of students with physical disabilities by enhancing movement, participation and communication, and to facilitate access to the curriculum. AT ranges from 'low tech' equipment such as slant-top desks, pencil grips, modified scissor grips, specially designed seating, pads and wedges to help position a child for optimum functioning, electric wheelchairs, walking and standing frames, and head-pointers, through to high-tech adaptations such as modified computer keyboards or switching devices. Assistive technology is described well by Best *et al.* (2005).

Students with CP often have additional disabilities. At least 10 to 16 per cent of cases have impaired hearing or vision. Major difficulties with eye-muscle control can lead the children to find close-focus tasks such as looking at pictures or attempting to read print physically exhausting and stressful, and they will tend to avoid engaging in such activity. Epilepsy is evident in up to 30 per cent of cases of CP and a significant number of the children are on regular medication to control seizures. Medication can often have the effect of reducing individuals' level of arousal or alertness, thus adding to their problems in learning.

Some children with CP may not develop speech, although their receptive language and understanding may be quite normal. In their attempts to vocalise they may produce unintelligible sounds and their laughter may be loud and distorted. In addition they may exhibit other symptoms of inability to control their tongue, jaw and face muscles, resulting in drooling or facial contortions. These problems are beyond the individual's control but they can create potential barriers for easy social integration.

It is reported that approximately 60 per cent of individuals with CP also have some degree of intellectual disability (Turnbull *et al.* 2007), but some persons with quite severe CP are highly intelligent. There is a danger that the potential of some non-verbal students is not recognised because of their inability to communicate. One of the main priorities for these individuals is to be provided with an alternative method of communication (Heller and Bigge 2005).

Cerebral palsy is one of the more frequently occurring physical disabilities with a prevalence rate of approximately two cases per 1000 live births. There has been no significant decline in the prevalence rate of CP, even though there have been major advances in prenatal and antenatal care.

The instructional needs of students with cerebral palsy

Academic instruction for children with CP will depend mainly upon their cognitive ability. Students with mild cerebral palsy and normal intelligence may simply be slower at completing assignments and need more time. Allowance may need to be made for large and poorly coordinated handwriting. Some students may need to use a keyboard to type or word-process their assignments. For some, adapted devices such as pencil grips and page-turners may be required. Papers may need to be taped firmly to the desktop. Computers with adaptations such as touch panels, rather than a keyboard or a 'mouse', are useful both for presenting academic work and as a medium for communication with others.

In addition to the problems with movement and speech, many children with CP tend to:

- tire easily and have difficulty in attending to tasks for more than brief periods of time;
- take a very long time to perform basic physical actions (e.g. pointing at or picking up an object; eating). Many need to be fed and toileted by a parent or an aide;
- require special physical positioning in order to make best use of their coordinated movements;
- require padded 'wedges' or other specially constructed cushions to enable them to be positioned correctly for work;
- rely on the teacher or an aide to lift and move them.

There are many suggested 'treatments' for CP, but few of the approaches have been subjected to rigorous evaluation. Even 'conductive education', once hailed as a major breakthrough, produces very mixed results in evaluation studies. Liptak (2005) provides a comprehensive review of the major alternative approaches.

Spina bifida (SB)

Spina bifida is a congenital disorder, possibly of genetic origin, presenting with different degrees of severity. The condition results from a failure of certain bones in the spine to close over and protect the spinal cord before birth. The milder forms of SB have no significant influence on learning and mobility, and it is estimated that approximately 80 per cent of individuals with spina bifida have normal intelligence. However, learning difficulties are common in the remaining 20 per cent, with problems in attention, visuo-spatial ability, memory, and number skills often reported (Jacobs 2003). The likelihood that difficulties in learning will occur increases with severity of the disability.

The most serious form of spina bifida with the greatest impact on the individual's development is *myelomeningocele*. In this condition, a part of the spinal cord itself is exposed at birth and protrudes from a gap in the spine. The cord is often damaged and bodily functions below this point may be seriously disrupted, including no use of lower limbs. The individual may need to use a wheelchair or leg braces. Control of bladder and bowel function may be impaired, necessitating the use of a catheter tube to drain the bladder and the implementation of a careful diet and bowel-emptying routine. The management of incontinence presents the greatest social problem for individuals with SB.

In some cases the individual with spina bifida may have learning difficulties due to minor perceptual problems. Some may have had a restricted range of experiences prior to schooling, and this adds to their difficulty in understanding some aspects of the curriculum. Their lack of mobility may have also reduced their range of social interactions.

Approximately 60 to 70 per cent of children with myelomeningocele may also have some degree of *hydrocephalus*. The normal circulation and drainage of cerebrospinal fluid within the skull is impaired, resulting in increased intra-cranial pressure. Treatment for hydrocephalus involves the surgical implanting of a catheter into a ventricle in the brain to drain the excess fluid to the abdominal cavity. A valve is implanted below the skin behind the child's ear to prevent any back flow of cerebrospinal fluid. Teachers need to be aware that shunts and valves can become blocked, or the site can become infected. If the child with treated hydrocephalus complains of headache or earache, or if he or she appears feverish and irritable, medical advice should be obtained.

Children with spina bifida and hydrocephalus tend to be hospitalised at regular intervals during their school lives for such events as replacing shunts and valves, treating urinary infections or controlling respiratory problems. This frequent hospitalisation can significantly interrupt the child's schooling, with subjects such as mathematics being most affected by lost instructional time. Many students in this situation require intensive remedial assistance with their schoolwork.

Traumatic brain injury (TBI)

The term *traumatic brain injury* (TBI) is used to describe any acquired brain damage resulting from such events as car accidents, falls, blows to the head, unsuccessful suicide attempts, sports injury, 'shaken infant syndrome', and recovery after drowning (Hardman *et al.* 2005). An increasing number of school-age individuals acquire brain injury from falls, car accidents, and partial drowning.

The effects of TBI can include:

- memory problems;
- attention difficulties;
- slowed information processing;
- inability to solve problems and plan strategies;
- speech and language functions disrupted temporarily or permanently;
- impairment of general motor patterns such as walking, balancing;
- onset of epilepsy;
- vision problems;
- severe headaches;
- unpredictable and irrational moods or behaviour (aggressive, restless, apathetic, lacking in self-control).

Hardman *et al.* (2005) state that often students with TBI improve dramatically in the first year following their injury; but after that, progress is often much slower.

It is beyond the scope of this chapter to provide details of all the classroom instructional considerations that may be necessary when working with students with TBI. The book by Best *et al.* (2005) contains a useful section on this subject. The main challenges for the teacher are:

- finding ways of maximising the individual's attention to the learning task (removing distractions; providing cues; limiting the amount of information presented);
- helping to compensate for memory loss and poor recall (presenting visual cues to aid recall of information; encouraging visual imagery; rehearsing information more than would be necessary with other learners; teaching self-help strategies such as keeping reminder notes in your pocket; checking the daily timetable);
- helping the individual plan ahead and monitor own progress, set goals and work towards them;
- keeping instructions clear and simple, and not overloading the student with information or tasks;
- understanding and accepting the student's poor ability to concentrate and to complete set work.

Frequent difficulties with word and information retrieval can slow down the individual's speech and cause great frustration. Many children with TBI express great irritation in knowing an answer to a question in class but being unable to retrieve the necessary words at the right time (Hardman *et al.* 2005).

Augmentative and alternative communication

It has been mentioned that many students with severe and multiple disabilities, whether congenital or acquired, may have no oral–verbal method of communication. This can lead others to judge them wrongly as functioning at a low cognitive level. The priority need for severely disabled persons without speech is to develop an alternative method of communicating (Hegde and Maul 2006). The ultimate aim of any augmentative or alternative communication system is to allow the child to 'talk' about the same range of things that other children of that age would discuss.

Alternative communication modes include:

- sign language, finger-spelling and gesture;
- the use of a picture and symbol system that the person may access by pointing, or in some cases by eye glance;
- computer-aided communication.

The simplest form of alternative communication is the communication board, comprising a small set of pictures or symbols that are personally relevant to the child's life and context. For example, the board may have pictures of a TV set, a glass, a knife and fork or plate, a toilet, a toy, and a cross for 'no' and a tick for 'yes'. The child can communicate his or her wishes or needs by pointing to or looking at the appropriate picture.

General points for the mainstream teacher

For students in wheelchairs or walking with leg-braces and sticks, it may be necessary to rearrange the classroom desks and chairs slightly to give easier access (wider corridor for movement).

Some students with physical disabilities may have a high absence rate due to (a) the need to attend therapy or treatment appointments during school hours; (b) frequent health problems. Frequent absence means that the teacher may need to provide the student with work to do at home, and may need to enlist the help of the support teacher to provide some short-term remedial assistance for the student.

Some students with physical disabilities (especially cerebral palsy) may also have epilepsy. To control the epilepsy the student may be on medication that tends to lower their level of arousal and responsiveness in class.

While applying all commonsense safety procedures, teachers should try not to overprotect students with physical disabilities. Whenever possible these students should be encouraged to take part in the same activities enjoyed by other students. Teachers of PE and sport need to get practical advice on ways in which these physical activities can be modified to include students with disabilities. Physically disabled students should never be left on the sidelines as mere spectators.

Some students with physical disabilities will need to use modified desks or chairs. It is the teacher's responsibility to ensure that the student makes use of the equipment.

Some students with physical disabilities will have great difficulty in writing and taking notes. Their fine-motor movements may be slow and their coordination very poor and inaccurate. The teacher needs to establish a peer support network and also allow the student to photocopy the notes of other students or use a tape recorder to record lessons. Sometimes the teacher may need to allow the student to submit an assignment as an audiotape rather than an essay.

Additional information on teaching and management of students with physical disabilities will be found in Best *et al.* (2005) and Heller *et al.* (2000).

Students with impaired vision

In some countries the term *vision impairment* is replacing the older term *visually impaired* – often at the request of adults who have this disability. When a child is described as vision impaired it does not necessarily mean that he or she is blind; it means that the child has a serious defect of vision that cannot be corrected by wearing spectacles. In the population of children with impaired vision there are those who are totally blind, those who are 'legally' blind, and those with varying degrees of partial sight.

While impaired vision represents the lowest-incidence disability category, it is important to note that it occurs as a secondary handicap present in many cases of severe and multiple disability. For example, many students with cerebral palsy also have serious problems with vision, as do many individuals with traumatic brain injury.

Impaired vision has multiple causes, including structural defects or damage to the retina, lens, or optic nerve, inefficiency in the way the brain interprets and stores visual information, or an inability of the retina to transmit images to the brain. Some vision problems are inherited, including those associated with albinism, congenital cataracts and degeneration of the retina, while others may be due to disease or to medical conditions such as diabetes or tumours. Prematurity and very low birth weight can contribute to vision problems, with 'retinopathy of prematurity' (ROP) being reported as one of the most common causes of impaired vision in the very young child.

It is not necessary to describe in detail the various conditions that lead to impaired vision. Teachers are referred to relevant chapters in Batshaw (2002) or Silverstone *et al.* (2000). The books by Catellano (2005) and Bishop (2004) contain excellent information on the learning characteristics of children with impaired vision.

The special educational needs of children with impaired vision

There are at least three areas in which blind children and those with seriously impaired vision may need to be taught additional skills. These areas are mobility, orientation, and the use of Braille.

Mobility

Blind students and those with very limited sight need to be taught mobility skills to enable them to move safely and purposefully in their environment. The skills include:

- self-protection techniques: for example, in unfamiliar environments holding the hand and forearm in front of the face for protection while trailing the other hand along the wall or rail;
- checking for doorways, steps, stairs and obstacles;
- using auditory information to locate objects: for example, the air-conditioner, an open doorway; traffic noise;
- long-cane skills: moving about the environment with the aid of a long cane swept lightly on the ground ahead to locate hazards and to check surface textures;
- using electronic travel aids such as 'sonic spectacles' with a sound warning built into the frame;
- using a sighted guide.

The person with severely impaired vision needs sufficient mobility skills and confidence to negotiate the outside environment, including crossing the road, catching buses or trains, and locating shops. Increased mobility adds significantly to the quality of life for persons with impaired vision. Mobility training is usually regarded as a specialist area of instruction. While the classroom teacher and parents can certainly assist with the development of mobility skills, a mobility-training expert usually carries out the planning and implementation of the programme.

Orientation

Orientation is the term used to indicate that a person with impaired vision is familiar with a particular environment and at any time knows his or her own position in relation to objects such as furniture, barriers, open doors or steps. Teachers should realise that for the safety and convenience of students with vision impairment the physical classroom environment should remain fairly constant and predictable. If furniture has to be moved or some new object is introduced into the room, the blind student needs to be informed of that fact and given the opportunity to locate it in relation to other objects. In classrooms it is necessary to avoid placing overhanging obstacles at head height, and to make sure that equipment such as boxes and books are not left on the floor. Doors should not be left half open, with a hard edge projecting into the room.

Mobility and orientation together are two of the primary goals in helping the blind student towards increased independence. Without these skills the quality of life of the blind person is seriously restricted.

Braille

Braille is of tremendous value as an alternative communication medium for those students who are blind or whose remaining vision does not enable them to perceive enlarged print. Braille is a complex code so its use with students who are below average in intelligence is not always successful. Obviously if an individual's cognitive level is such that he or she would experience difficulties in learning to read and write with conventional print, Braille is not going to be an easier code to master. The notion that all legally blind and totally blind students use Braille is false. However if a child's intelligence is adequate, the younger he or she begins to develop some Braille skills the better, as this will prepare the child to benefit from later schooling.

Blind children learning to read Braille are observed go through similar stages to those noted in readers of print – beginning at a pre-reading level of tactile awareness, moving through bottom-up 'decoding' of characters, to eventual fluency through contextual supports (Steinman et al. 2006). Braille 'readiness' activities are stressed during the pre-reading stage and include tactile sensitivity training.

stive technology

e same way that students with physical disabilities can be helped to access urriculum and participate more effectively in daily life through the use of ive technology, so too children with partial sight impairment can be assisted. Many devices have been designed to enable the student to cope with the medium of print. The devices include magnification aids, closed-circuit television and microfiche readers (both used to enlarge an image), talking calculators, speaking clocks, dictionaries with speech outputs, 'compressed speech' recordings, and thermoform duplicators used to reproduce Braille pages or embossed pictures, diagrams and maps. *Low vision aids* are magnification devices or instruments that help the individual with some residual sight to work with maximum visual efficiency. Some students with impaired vision benefit from modified furniture such as desks with bookstands or angled tops to bring materials closer to the child's eyes without the need to lean over, or with lamp attachments for increased illumination of the page.

Instructing students with low vision

Teachers in the mainstream with no prior experience of vision-impaired children may tend to have fairly low expectations of what these children can accomplish. Inexperienced teachers may not expect enough of the children and may assume that they cannot participate in certain activities. It is essential, however, to provide many new challenges for these students and encourage them to do as much as possible (Lieberman and Wilson 2005). Having a problem with vision should not exclude the children from access to the normal curriculum, although modifications may need to be made (Jones 2004).

The following suggestions for teaching are adapted from many sources. Useful advice can also be found in Catellano (2005) and Bishop (2004).

- Allow the partially sighted students when writing to use a fibre-tip black ink pen that will produce clear, bold writing.
- Prepare exercise paper with dark ruled lines.
- Enlarge all text, notes and handouts to 24, 36, or even 48 point size.
- Allow much more time for students with impaired vision to complete their work.
- Read written instructions to students with impaired vision to reduce the amount of time required to begin a task and to ensure that the work is understood.
- Use very clear descriptions and explanations; verbal explanation will have to compensate for what the student cannot see.

- Train other students, and any classroom aide or assistant you may have, to support the student with impaired vision (e.g. for note taking, repeating explanations).
- Speak to blind students frequently by name during lessons to engage them fully in the group-learning processes. Make sure they contribute. Value their contributions.
- Call upon other students clearly by name so that the blind student knows who is responding.
- Get all the advice you can from the visiting support teacher and other advisory personnel.
- Make sure that any specialised assistive equipment is always at hand and in good order.
- Note that almost all students with impaired vision in mainstream classes will have partial sight rather than total or legal blindness. It is essential to encourage them to use their residual vision effectively. Using the remaining vision is helpful, not harmful to these students.
- If the student with impaired vision uses assistive equipment such as magnification aids, lamps, or adjustable bookstands, make sure that (a) you know when and how the equipment needs to be used; (b) you ensure that the student does not avoid using the equipment.
- Use a photocopier when necessary to make enlarged versions of notes, diagrams and other handouts for the student. Use large type size when preparing materials on the word processor or for Powerpoint presentations.
- Seat the student in the most advantageous position to be able to see the blackboard or screen.
- Ensure that your own material on the blackboard or screen is neat and clear, using larger script than usual. Keep the blackboard surface clean to ensure clarity of words against background.
- Avoid overloading worksheets with too much information and heavy density of print.
- Some forms of vision impairment respond well to brighter illumination, but in some other conditions very bright light is undesirable. Obtain advice on illumination from the visiting teacher or other support personnel who are aware of the student's characteristics.
- If the student has extremely limited vision, make sure that any changes to the physical arrangement of the room are explained and experienced by the student to avoid accidents. The student needs to develop fresh orientation each time an environment is changed.
- Try to ensure that the student establishes a network of friends within the class. Social interaction is often not easily achieved without assistance. Blind students need accurate feedback on their social behaviour because they cannot observe the behaviour of sighted persons; in particular, they can't see the reaction of others to their own behaviours. Blind students may not develop natural non-verbal communication skills, such as positive facial

expression and stance, and this can impede their easy acceptance into social groups (Jindal-Snape 2005).

Students with impaired hearing

Hearing impairment is a general term used to describe all degrees and types of hearing loss and deafness. Individuals are usually referred to as *deaf* if they are unable to detect speech sounds and if their own language development is disordered. In some countries, those who can hear some sounds and can make reasonable use of their residual hearing are either termed *hard of hearing* or *partially hearing.*

Most hearing loss can be classified as either *conductive* or *sensori-neural.* The key features of each type are summarised below.

Conductive hearing loss

Conductive hearing loss indicates that the individual's hearing problem is due to the fact that sounds are not reaching the middle ear or the inner ear (the cochlear) because of some physical malformation, blockage or damage to the ear canal or middle ear. Common causes are excessive build-up of wax in the outer ear canal, a ruptured eardrum, abnormality of the ear canal, infections in the middle ear (e.g. otitis media), or dislocation or damage to the tiny bones of the middle ear. Hearing loss due to middle-ear infection is usually temporary and will improve when the infection is treated successfully. If infections are allowed to continue untreated, damage may be done to the middle ear resulting in permanent hearing loss. The use of a hearing aid may significantly help an individual with conductive hearing loss.

Sensori-neural loss

Sensori-neural loss is related to the inner ear and the auditory nerve. The most serious hearing losses are often of this type. As well as being unable to hear many sounds, even those that are heard may be distorted. This problem of distortion means that the wearing of a hearing aid may not always help because amplifying a distorted sound does not make it any clearer. It is reported that in some cases individuals with sensori-neural loss are particularly sensitive to loud noises, perceiving them to be painfully loud (Roeser and Downs 2004).

Many students with impaired hearing have no other disability, but hearing impairment is often present as a secondary disability in children with intellectual disability, cerebral palsy, or language disorders.

Degrees of hearing loss

Acuity of hearing is measured in units called decibels (dB). Zero dB is the point from which people with normal hearing can begin to detect the faintest sounds. Normal conversation is usually carried out at an overall sound level of between 40 and 50 dB. Loss of hearing is expressed in terms of the amplification required before the individual can hear each sound. The greater the degree of impairment the less likely it is that the child will develop normal speech and language, and the more likely it is that they will need special education services. Individuals with a hearing loss above 95 dB are usually categorised as 'deaf' or 'profoundly deaf'. Other categories are:

- *slight loss*: 15–25 dB*. Vowel sounds still heard clearly. Some consonants may be missed.
- *mild loss*: 25–40 dB*. Can hear only loud speech sounds. Usually requires hearing aid. May need speech therapy. Some difficulty with normal conversation.
- *moderate loss*: 40–65 dB*. Misses almost all speech at normal conversational level. Requires hearing aid. Serious impact on language development. Speech therapy and special education often required.
- *severe loss*: 65–95 dB*. Unable to hear normal speech. Major problems with language development. Hearing aid required (but may not help in some cases). Language training and other special services required.
- *profound loss*: Above 95 dB*. Cannot hear speech or other environmental sounds. Severe problems in language acquisition. Normal conversation impossible. Alternative forms of communication usually required (e.g. sign language). Special class placement often indicated.

* Note: The specific dB range varies slightly from country to country.

The impact of deafness on development

An inability to hear places a young child at risk of delay in many areas, including the acquisition of spoken language, literacy skills and social development. For example, the speech of children with impaired hearing often has very poor rhythm and phrasing, together with a flat and monotonous tone of voice. Many factors, including time of onset, severity, type of hearing loss, and different instructional approaches used, all interact to produce large variations in the spoken language performance of children with hearing loss (Monreal and Hernandez 2005). A priority goal in the education of all children with impaired hearing is to advance their language skills as much as possible. Any improvement in language will allow each child to make better use of his or her intellectual potential, understand much more of the curriculum, and develop socially.

Helping a deaf child acquire intelligible speech can be a long and difficult process. Early intervention and active parental involvement are essential elements in language stimulation. In some cases speech training and auditory training are advocated for hearing-impaired students. Speech therapists or language teachers may, for example, use speech and articulation coaching, based mainly on behavioural principles of modelling, imitation, rewarding, and shaping. In recent years, however, speech therapists and teachers have placed even more importance on trying to stimulate language development through the use of naturally occurring activities in the classroom ('milieu teaching': Kaiser and Grim 2006). Such teaching is thought to result in better transfer and generalisation of vocabulary, language patterns and skills to the child's everyday life.

The inability to hear language from an early age not only creates a major problem in developing speech but can also have a negative impact on some aspects of intellectual development. It is often said that deaf students' lack of vocabulary slows down development of cognitive skills necessary for learning in school. In recent years there has been some criticism of this viewpoint and it is now suggested that although deaf children may lack depth in *spoken* language they still encode and store information and experience in other ways (Hardman *et al.* 2005). They often have some other more visual representations of language such as signing or gesture that enable them to express their ideas.

Over the past two decades the movement towards integration of children with disabilities into ordinary schools has stressed the value of including hearing-impaired children in mainstream classes. It is argued that these children will experience the maximum social interaction and communication by mixing with other students using normal spoken language. They will be exposed to more accurate language models than they might hear in a class for deaf students. It is believed that regular class placement increases the need and motivation for deaf children to communicate. It is also hoped that students with normal hearing will develop improved understanding and tolerance for individuals who are slightly different from others in the peer group.

Basic academic skills

Careful attention must be given to the explicit teaching of reading and spelling skills to students with impaired hearing. It is typical of these students that as they progress through primary school they fall three to four years behind the peer group in terms of reading ability (Hardman *et al.* 2005). This reading lag has a detrimental impact on their performance in all subjects across the curriculum.

Many of their difficulties in reading and spelling are thought to stem from their problem in accurately perceiving speech sounds (phonemic awareness). Limited phonemic awareness results in serious difficulty in learning decoding and encoding skills. At one time, it was believed that deaf and hard-of-hearing students would need to learn to read by visual memory methods alone, because they lacked the underlying capacity to master decoding. That is no longer the popular view among educators, and instructional methods now aim to help these students acquire an understanding of orthographic units (letters and letter groups) and their relation to speech sounds (Trezek and Malmgren 2005). While the beginning stages of reading instruction can focus on building a basic sight vocabulary by visual methods, later the teaching of word-analysis skills must also be stressed for students with hearing loss. Without the phonic concept their ability to read and spell unfamiliar words will remain seriously deficient. It is also essential when providing reading instruction for hearing-impaired children that due attention be given to developing comprehension strategies (Wurst *et al*. 2005). Their restricted vocabulary and limited awareness of complex sentence structures can cause major problems in fluency and comprehension. In the beginning stages there is a strong case for using graded reading books with careful control of vocabulary and syntax (Hardman *et al*. 2005).

The written expression of deaf children is often reported to be problematic (Antia *et al*. 2005), with syntax and vocabulary the major weaknesses. Their difficulties often include inaccurate sentence structure, incorrect verb tenses, difficulties representing plurals correctly, and inconsistencies in using correct pronouns. The written work of older deaf students has many of the characteristics of the writing of younger children, and may also contain *deafisms* involving incorrect word order (e.g. 'She got black hair long', instead of 'She has long black hair'). In a later chapter reference is made to activities involving sentence building and sentence transformations; such activities are particularly valuable for students with impaired hearing.

Spelling instruction needs to be systematic rather than incidental. For deaf children, it is likely that more than usual attention will need to be given to the development of visual memory processes to enable them to spell and check by eye rather than ear. The 'look-say-cover-write-check' strategy is particularly helpful and needs to be taught thoroughly (see Chapter 11). The book by Stewart and Kluwin (2001) contains much valuable advice on teaching different school subjects to students with impaired hearing.

Modes of communication

While listening and speaking remain the preferred methods of communication for students with mild and moderate degrees of impairment, for those who are severely to profoundly deaf, alternative manual methods may be needed. These methods include gesture, sign language, cued speech, and finger-spelling.

Sign language

There are different forms of sign language (e.g. Signed English, Auslan, American Sign Language), sharing obvious characteristics in common but also having some unique features. Deaf children from deaf families will almost certainly have been exposed to, and become competent in, manual communication even before entering formal education. There is no strong evidence that early exposure to sign language has a detrimental effect on oral communication skills, such as speech and lip reading (Meadow 2005), but sign language remains a controversial issue in the field of deaf education.

Often the use of sign language is the only thing that attracts the attention of others to the fact that the person is deaf. Many parents and some teachers feel that to encourage manual forms of communication will cause the child to be accepted only in the deaf community rather than in the wider community of hearing persons. They also believe that the use of signs will retard the development of speech, thus isolating the child even further. Experts suggest however that sign language should be respected as a language in its own right, with its own vocabulary, grammar and semantics, and it should be valued and encouraged as an effective mode of communication.

Oral–aural approach (oralism)

The belief underpinning *oralism* is that to be accepted and to succeed in a hearing world you need to be able to communicate through oral–verbal methods (Steinberg and Knightly 1997). The approach virtually places a ban on manual communication and stresses instead the use of residual hearing, supplemented by lip reading and speech training. The feasibility of lip reading for many hearing-impaired individuals is often greatly overestimated; it is an extremely difficult and inaccurate method of interpreting the communication of others.

Total communication approach

The relative popularity of signing versus oralism ebbs and flows from decade to decade. In response, *total communication* (TC) or simultaneous communication (SC) deliberately combines signing and gesture with oral–aural methods to help deaf children comprehend and express ideas and opinions to others. A combination of oral and manual training at an early age appears to foster optimum communicative ability (Meadow 2005).

Assistive technology

Hearing aids

Hearing aids are of various types, including the typical 'behind the ear' or 'in the ear' aids, and radio frequency (FM) aids. An audiologist assesses the specific needs of the child and a hearing aid is prescribed to suit the individual's sound-loss profile. The aid is adjusted as far as possible to give amplification of the specific frequency of sounds needed by the child. No hearing aid fully compensates for hearing loss, even when carefully tailored to the user's characteristics.

The great limitation of the conventional type of hearing aid is that it amplifies all sound, including noise in the environment. The advantage of the radio frequency (FM) aid is that it allows the teacher's voice to be received with minimum interference from environmental noise. The teacher wears a small microphone and the child's hearing aid receives the sounds in the same way that a radio receives a broadcast transmission. The child can be anywhere in the classroom, and does not need to be close to or facing the teacher, as with the conventional aid.

A valuable chapter on integrating technology into teaching of students with impaired hearing appears in the text by Stewart and Kluwin (2001).

Cochlear implants

A cochlear implant is a device used to produce the sensation of sound by electrically stimulating the auditory nerve. The device has two main parts, the internal component (electrodes implanted into or on the cochlear) and an external receiver embedded in the temporal bone. Many developed countries are now carrying out the surgery required to implant this form of assistive device at a very young age. Some of the dilemmas and issues surrounding cochlear implantation are discussed by Hyde and Power (2006).

Cochlear implants are normally recommended only for children who are profoundly deaf and cannot benefit at all from other forms of hearing aid. However, there are signs that the procedure is now extending to some individuals with severe hearing loss (Stewart and Ritter 2001). While the child can begin to perceive the electrical stimulation soon after surgery it normally takes at least a year for gains in the child's language skills to become evident. The child's effective adaptation to the cochlear implant needs support and encouragement from the parents. Many children with cochlear implants still need ongoing support from sign language to understand fully what is said.

It must be noted that not all experts are convinced that implants are a good innovation. For example, Moores (2005) expresses a view that there is no clear evidence that a cochlear implant is more effective than the present generation of powerful hearing aids. Moores also raises the issue of possible long-term effects on health of having an implanted device in the head.

General strategies for the teacher

Using some of the following basic strategies will also often be helpful to students with other types of learning difficulty in the classroom. It is recommended that teachers:

- Make greater use of visual methods of presenting information whenever possible.
- Use clear and simple language when explaining new concepts. Don't be afraid to introduce new terminology but teach the new words thoroughly.

- Write new vocabulary on the blackboard. Ensure the student with hearing impairment hears the word, sees the word, and says the word. Revise new vocabulary regularly. Revise new language patterns (e.g. 'Twice the size of ...'; 'Mix the ingredients ...'; 'Invert and multiply ...').
- Repeat instructions clearly while facing the student with impaired hearing.
- Don't give instructions while there is noise in the classroom.
- Where possible, write instructions in short statements on the blackboard.
- Attract the student's attention when you are about to ask a question or give out information.
- Check frequently that the student is on task and has understood what he or she is required to do.
- Where possible, provide the student with printed notes to ensure that key lesson content is available (it may not have been heard during the lesson).
- When group discussion is taking place, make sure the deaf student can see the other students who are speaking or answering questions.
- Repeat the answer that another student has given if you think the deaf student may not have heard it.
- Make sure you involve the deaf student in the lesson as much as possible.
- Ensure that the student has a partner for group or pair activities and assignments.
- Encourage other students when necessary to assist the deaf student to complete any work that is set – without doing the work for the student!
- Don't talk while facing the blackboard; the deaf student needs to see your mouth and facial expression. When explaining while using an overhead projector, face the class and not the screen.
- Don't walk to the back of the room while talking and giving out important information.
- Try to reduce background noise when listening activities are conducted.
- Don't seat the student with impaired hearing near to sources of noise (e.g. fan, open window, generator).
- Do seat the student where he or she can see you easily, can see the blackboard, and can observe the other students.
- Make sure that you know how to check the student's hearing aid, and check it on a regular basis. The student won't always tell you when a battery needs replacing or a connection is broken.
- Seek advice from the visiting teacher of the deaf and from the support teacher. Use such advice in your programme.

Further reading

Best, S.J., Heller, K.W. and Bigge, J.L. (2005) *Teaching Individuals with Physical or Multiple Disabilities* (5th edn), Upper Saddle River, NJ: Pearson-Merrill-Prentice Hall.

Beukelman, D.R. and Mirenda, P. (2005) *Augmentative and Alternative Communication: Supporting Children and Adults with Complex Communication Needs* (3rd edn), Baltimore, MD: Brookes.

Bishop, V.E. (2004) *Teaching Visually Impaired Children* (3rd edn), Springfield, IL: Thomas.

Haynes, W.O., Moran, M.J. and Pindzola, R.H. (2006) *Communication Disorders in the Classroom* (4th edn), Sudbury, MA: Jones and Bartlett.

Mahshie, J.J. (2006) *Enhancing Communication Skills of Deaf and Hard-of-hearing Children in the Mainstream*, Clifton Park, NY: Thomson-Delmar.

McLinden, M. and McCall, S. (2002) *Learning Through Touch: Supporting Children with Visual Impairment and Additional Difficulties*, London: Fulton.

Orelove, F.P., Sobsey, D. and Silberman, R.K. (eds) (2005) *Educating Children with Multiple Disabilities: A Collaborative Approach* (4th edn), Baltimore, MD: Brookes.

Pickles, P.A. (2004) *Inclusive Teaching, Inclusive Learning: Managing the Curriculum for Children with Severe Motor Learning Difficulties* (2nd edn), London: Fulton.

Spencer, P.E. and Marschark, M. (eds) (2006) *Advances in the Spoken Language Development of Deaf and Hard-of-hearing Children*, Oxford: Oxford University Press.

Chapter 4

Teaching children self-management and self-regulation

> Efficient learners use metacognitive strategies, but students with learning disabilities tend to lack the skills to direct their own learning. However, once they learn the metacognitive strategies that efficient learners use, students with learning disabilities can apply them in many situations.
>
> (Lerner and Kline 2006: 184)

Self-regulation and self-management are essential capacities that children need to develop if they are to become autonomous learners. In the case of students with intellectual disability, emotional disturbance or learning disability, the skills and strategies involved in self-management and self-regulation may need to be taught. When children acquire adequate self-management skills and independent learning strategies it is much easier for them to be accommodated effectively in inclusive classrooms (Deshler 2005).

Definition of terms

The terms self-regulation and self-management are often used interchangeably in educational discourse, but in the field of psychology each has its own precise meaning.

Self-regulation is a term commonly used in relation to an individual's ability to monitor his or her own approach to learning tasks and to modify thinking processes or strategies as necessary (Eggen and Kauchak 2004). Self-regulation in learning involves a significant amount of *metacognition* – the ability to monitor and control one's own cognitive processes such as attention, rehearsal, recall, checking for understanding, self-correction and strategy application. Self-regulation in learning is discussed fully later in the chapter.

Self-management refers to an individual's ability to function independently in any given learning environment, without the need for constant supervision, prompting or direction (Mooney *et al.* 2005). In the classroom, for example, it relates to such behaviours as knowing how to organise one's materials, knowing what to do when work is completed, recognising when to seek help from the teacher or a peer, understanding how to check one's own work for careless errors, how to maintain attention to task, how to observe the well-established routines such as ordering lunch, having sports equipment or books ready for a specific lesson, knowing when a change of lesson or room is to occur, and so on.

Self-management in children

The specific self-management skills required by a child in school will tend to differ slightly from classroom to classroom according to a particular teacher's management style, routines and expectations. For example, in some classrooms a premium is placed upon passive listening, note-taking and sustained on-task behaviour, while in other classrooms initiative, group-working skills and cooperation with other children are essential prerequisites for success. The self-management skills required in an informal classroom setting tend to be different from those needed in a more formal or highly structured setting. Knowing how to respond to the demands and constraints of different lessons or settings is an important aspect of a student's growth towards independence (Good and Brophy 2003).

The type of classroom learning environment created by the teacher, and the teacher's instructional approach, can both markedly influence the development of self-management and independence in children. Some teachers seem to operate with students in ways that foster their *dependence* rather than encourage their independence. For example, they may offer too much help and guidance for children with special needs in an attempt to prevent possible difficulties and failures. They may virtually spoon-feed the children using individualised support programmes that offer few challenges and call for no initiative on the child's part. Too much of this support restricts the opportunities for a child to become autonomous and may operate in such a way as to segregate the child from the mainstream curriculum or from the peer group for too much of the day.

Why are self-management skills important? The answer to this question is simple: the possession of self-management skills by a child with a disability or a learning problem seems to be one of the most important factors contributing to the successful inclusion of that child in a regular classroom (Salend 2005). It is essential that students with special needs, whether placed in special settings or in the regular classroom, be helped to develop adequate levels of independence in their work habits, self-control, social skills and readiness for basic academic learning. Self-management shares much in common with what some psychologists term 'self-determination' (Browder *et al.* 2001), which in turn is related to feelings of 'self-efficacy'.

Some students, for example those with intellectual disability, or with social, emotional or psychological disorders, frequently exhibit poor self-management (Lerner and Kline 2006). One of the major goals of intervention with such students is to increase their independence by improving their self-regulation. Even students with milder forms of disability or learning difficulty often display ineffective self-management and need positive help to become more independent learners (Deshler 2005).

Self-management can be taught

Evidence is accumulating to support the view that training in self-management and self-regulation can be effective in promoting students' independence (Meese 2001; O'Brien 2005). An overall effect size (ES) of 1.80 has been reported from intervention studies involving self-management and strategy training, suggesting there are very strong positive effects (Mooney *et al.* 2005). Cole (2000: 1616) concludes, 'Although total self-management is not possible for many special education students, most can be taught to be more self-reliant.' When students are able to manage the routines in the classroom and look after their own needs during a lesson, the teacher is able to devote much more time to teaching rather than managing the group.

What can be done to teach self-management? First, teachers must believe that such teaching is important. Second, teachers need to consider precisely which skills or behaviours are lacking in the students but are required in order to function independently in their particular classrooms – for example, staying on task without close supervision, self-monitoring, using resource materials appropriately, or seeking help from a peer.

For students with special needs, a five-step procedure can be used to teach self-management. The steps are:

- *Explanation*: Discuss with the student why a specific self-managing behaviour is important. Help the student recognise when other students are exhibiting the target behaviour.
- *Demonstration*: The teacher or a peer can model the behaviour.
- *Role play*: The student practises the behaviour, with descriptive feedback.
- *Cueing*: Prompt the student when necessary to carry out the behaviour in the classroom. Praise examples of the student displaying the behaviour without prompting.
- *Maintenance*: Check at regular intervals to ensure that the student has maintained the behaviour over time.

In some situations a teacher might employ a 'star chart' or other visual recording system to reward at regular intervals all those students who demonstrate the specific self-management skills expected of them. Rewarding would be most frequent immediately after the teaching of the behaviour, and would be phased out after several weeks once the behaviour is established and maintained.

It is important to develop the idea of maintaining the appropriate behaviour *without prompting*. When teachers are constantly reminding the class of what to do (e.g. 'I've told you before, if you have finished your work, please put it on my desk and start on your activity book') they are maintaining the students' dependence. Teachers may need to remind children with special needs rather more frequently than other students, and may have to reward them more frequently for their correct responses, but the long-term aim is to help these children function independently. When they do display improved self-management they have become more like other children in the class. Teaching self-management skills as part of an inclusive programme should have a high priority in all classrooms, particularly with young children and those with developmental delay.

Locus of control

Self-management, and the notion of learned helplessness (Chapter 1), link quite closely with the personality construct known as *locus of control* (Ormrod 2006). To explain locus of control one needs to understand that individuals attribute what happens to them in a particular situation either to internal factors (e.g. their own ability, efforts or actions) or to external factors (e.g. luck, chance, things outside their control). Children with an internal locus of control recognise that they can influence events by their own actions and believe that they do to some extent control their own destiny. Appreciating the fact that outcomes are under one's personal control is also a key component of one's feelings of 'self-efficacy' (Pajares and Urdan 2006). At classroom level, an example of internality might be when students recognise that if they concentrate and work carefully they get much better results.

The internalisation of locus of control usually increases steadily with age if a child experiences normal satisfaction and reinforcement from his or her efforts and responses in school and in daily life outside school. However, it has been found that many children with learning problems and with negative school experiences remain markedly external in their locus of control in relation to school learning, believing that their efforts have little impact on their progress, that they lack ability, and that what happens to them in learning tasks is unrelated to their own actions (Bender 2004; Marrone and Schutz 2000). Young children enter school with highly positive views of their own capabilities, but this confidence rapidly wanes if they experience early failures and frustrations.

The child who remains largely external in locus is likely to be the child who fails to assume normal self-management in class and is prepared to be managed or controlled by powerful others such as the teacher, parent, teacher's aide or more confident peers. There exists a vicious circle wherein the child feels inadequate, is not prepared to take a risk, seems to require support, gets it, and develops even more dependence upon others. The teacher's task is one of breaking into this circle and causing the child to recognise the extent to which he or she has control over events and can influence outcomes (Galbraith and Alexander 2005). It is natural for a teacher or aide to wish to help and support a child with special needs, but it should not be done to the extent that all challenge and possibility of failure are eliminated (Fox 2003). Failure must be possible and children must be helped to see the causal relationship between their own efforts and the outcomes. Children will become more internal in their locus of control, and much more involved in learning tasks, when they recognise that effort and persistence can overcome failure (Bender 2004).

It is important that teachers and parents publicly acknowledge and praise children's positive efforts, rather than emphasising lack of effort or difficulties. Teachers' use of praise has been well researched. Good and Brophy (2003) reviewed studies in this area and concluded that praise does seem particularly important for low-ability, anxious, dependent students, provided that it is genuine and deserved, and that praiseworthy aspects of the performance are specified. A child should know precisely why he or she is being praised if appropriate connections are to be made in the child's mind between effort and outcome. Trivial or redundant praise is very quickly detected by children and serves no useful purpose. *Descriptive* praise, however, can be extremely helpful (Doveston and Keenaghan 2006):

> 'That's beautiful handwriting, Leanne. I really like the way you have taken care to keep your letters all the same size.'

> 'Good, David! You used your own words instead of simply copying from the reference book.'

In general, teachers' use of praise has a strong positive influence on children's beliefs about their own ability and the importance of effort. When descriptive praise is perceived by children to be genuine and credible it appears to enhance the children's motivation and feelings of self-efficacy.

Attribution retraining

An external locus of control can have a negative impact upon a student's willingness to persist in the face of a difficult task. It is easier for the child to give up and develop avoidance strategies rather than persist if the expectation of failure is high. In the instructional approach known as *attribution retraining* (McInerney and McInerney 2006) students are taught to appraise carefully the results of their own efforts when a task is completed. They are taught to verbalise their conclusions aloud: 'I did that well because I took my time and read the question twice'; 'I listened carefully and I asked myself questions'; or 'I didn't get that problem correct because I didn't check the example in the book. Now I can do it. It's easy!' The main purpose in getting students to verbalise such attribution statements is to change their perception of the cause of their successes or failures in schoolwork. Verbalising helps to focus their attention on the real relationship between their efforts and the observed outcomes.

Grainger and Frazer (1999) have discussed the negative attributional styles of students with reading disabilities, many of whom have developed learned helplessness in relation to their own ability to improve. They suggest that these children may not respond to remedial teaching if the intervention focuses only on skill development. They recommend first helping the child explore his or her feelings, beliefs and attitudes linked to their reading difficulty, and then teaching the child to use positive self-talk to overcome personal reluctance and to restore some feeling of self-efficacy.

In most cases, attributional retraining seems to have maximum value when it is combined with the direct teaching of effective task-approach strategies necessary for accomplishing particular tasks. Evidence suggests that strategy training does produce definite improvement in learning for students with special needs (Ellis 2005; Graham and Bellert 2005).

Teaching task-approach strategies

Some teachers add to students' learning problems by failing to demonstrate the most effective ways of approaching each new task. Often, task-approach strategies are not taught explicitly and they may therefore remain obscure to many students. A teacher needs to provide clear modelling of an appropriate strategy to maximise the chances of early success. A teacher who says, 'Watch and listen. This is how I do it – and this is what I say to myself as I do it', is providing the learner with a secure starting point. The teacher who simply says, 'Get on with it', is often providing an invitation to failure and frustration.

It was noted in Chapter 1 that many students with learning difficulties appear to lack appropriate task-approach strategies. They seem not to understand that school tasks can be carried out effectively if approached with a suitable plan of action in mind. For example, attempting to solve a routine word problem in mathematics usually requires careful reading of the problem, identification of what one is required to find out, recognition of the relevant data to use, selection of the appropriate process, completion of the calculation, and a final checking of the reasonableness of the answer. This approach to solving the mathematical problem involves application of a *strategy* (an overall plan of action) and utilisation of *procedural knowledge* (knowing how to carry out the specific calculation and record the result) and *declarative knowledge* (an understanding of the factual information presented in the problem).

Cognitive strategies (or 'learning strategies') are mental plans that help students solve problems, complete tasks, and self-regulate (Lerner and Kline, 2006). A typical strategy includes both cognitive (thinking) and behavioural (action) elements that guide and monitor the individual's engagement in the task. Strategy training involves teaching students to apply effective step-by-step procedures when approaching and completing a particular task or problem (O'Brien 2005). The teaching involves explicit instruction through teacher demonstration, imitation by the students, feedback, practice and application. The initial stages of teaching and learning will often involve the teacher 'thinking aloud' and directing actions through verbal self-instruction. The students may also need to be taught a method for remembering the steps for implementation (e.g. a mnemonic).

Maintenance and generalisation of strategy training have always been problematic, particularly for students with learning difficulties. Students may learn successfully how to apply a given strategy to a specific task but not recognise how the same approach could be used more widely in other contexts. To help students overcome this problem, teachers might:

- provide strategy training that makes use of a variety of different authentic tasks from across the curriculum;
- discuss situations in which a particular strategy could be applied; and
- involve students as much as possible in creating or adapting strategies to the demands of particular tasks.

It is important to ensure that the specific strategies taught to students are actually needed in the daily curriculum to facilitate their immediate application. O'Brien (2005) suggests that strategies should be taught that focus on tasks the students usually find difficult. Students will find most relevance in strategies they can use to complete classroom assignments and homework more successfully. Hay *et al.* (2005) remark that students with learning difficulties take very much longer than other students to adopt new learning strategies and they suggest that the process can take as long as six months.

Effective strategy training incorporates elements of cognitive and metacognitive instruction. It is essential that students not only complete tasks independently but also monitor and control their own performance. It is this attention to *metacognition* that brings strategy training and strategy use clearly into the realm of self-regulated learning.

One of the common observations concerning many students with learning problems is that they have become passive learners (or even non-learners). They show little confidence in their own ability to control learning events, or to bring about improvement through their own efforts or initiative (Westwood 2004a). Teaching a student how to learn and how to regulate and monitor his or her own performance in the classroom must be a major focus in any intervention programme. Studies over many years have yielded data indicating that self-regulated students tend to do well in school. They are more confident, diligent and resourceful, and they tend to have a stable internal locus of control (Gettinger and Stoiber 1999). One of the goals of education should be to help all students to achieve a similar level of self-efficacy.

The development of self-regulation in learning

There is a difference between task-approach strategy training and metacognitive instruction. Task-approach training involves teaching the student mainly procedural knowledge – the specific steps to follow and skills to use when working on a particular task, for example, the exchanging rule in subtraction, the 'look-say-cover-write-check' method of learning to spell an irregular word, or the appropriate way to read a six-figure grid reference to locate a point on a map. Metacognitive instruction goes far beyond this, focusing on tactics that require the learner to monitor the appropriateness of his or her responses and to weigh up whether or not a particular strategy needs to be applied in full, in part, or not at all in a given situation.

Reading comprehension and mathematics problem solving are often cited as examples of academic areas that can be improved by task-approach and metacognitive strategy training. Students can be taught how to approach printed information and mathematical problems strategically, and then given abundant opportunity to practise the application of the strategies on a wide variety of texts and problems (Deshler 2005). Several practical examples of strategies are provided in later chapters.

Self-regulation in learning requires that students play an active role in monitoring closely the effects of various actions they take and decisions they make while engaging in learning activities. This involves the capacity to think about their thought processes (*metacognition*) and to modify a learning strategy if necessary while tackling a particular problem. This self-management of thinking includes mental activities such as pre-planning, monitoring, regulating, evaluating, and modifying a response. It is considered that metacognition helps a learner recognise that he or she is either doing well or is having difficulty learning or understanding something. A learner who is monitoring his or her own on-going performance will detect the need to pause, to double-check, perhaps to begin again before moving on, to weigh up possible alternatives, or to seek outside help.

Metacognition often involves inner verbal self-instruction and self-questioning – talking to one's self in order to focus, reflect, control or review. Training in self-regulation involves teaching students to tell themselves specifically what they need to do and how they need to monitor and self-correct. Part of the scaffolding that teachers provide is the modelling of 'thinking aloud' that later influences the student's own use of inner language. The teaching of verbal self-instruction is considered very important in helping all students become better self-regulated in terms of both learning and behaviour (see *cognitive behaviour modification* below).

The view is widely held that many learning problems that students exhibit are related to inefficient use of metacognition, that is, the learners lack the ability to monitor or regulate their responses appropriately. Some students undoubtedly develop their own efficient strategies without assistance; others do not. For self-regulated learning to develop, teachers need to demonstrate convincingly how to use appropriate strategies, explain in ways that students can understand, and make frequent and consistent use of metacognition and strategy training in all parts of the school curriculum. It is essential that teachers realise the need to devote time and effort to encourage students to think about their own thinking in a variety of learning situations. Paris *et al.* (2001) recommend that strategy use can be fostered by scaffolded support, discussions about strategies and how to apply them, and making visible the tactics used by effective learners. Once the basics of strategic learning have been established, Gettinger and Stoiber (1999) suggest that cooperative learning activities, peer tutoring, sharing views on how problems can be solved or tasks accomplished, may help to foster, generalise, and maintain self-regulation.

Cognitive behaviour modification (CBM)

Cognitive behaviour modification is closely related to metacognitive training. It involves the application of a set of procedures designed to help students gain better personal control over a learning situation (or of their own behaviour) by use of self-talk that guides their thoughts and actions (Lerner and Kline 2006). The students are taught an action plan or mental 'script' in which they talk themselves through a task or a problem situation in order to control their performance, modify their responses and monitor their results. Cognitive behaviour modification is different from other forms of behaviour management in that the students themselves, rather than teachers or powerful others, are the agents for change.

The training procedure for a typical cognitive behaviour modification programme usually follows this sequence:

- *Modelling*: The teacher performs the task or carries out the new procedure while thinking aloud. This modelling involves the teacher self-questioning, giving self-directions, making overt decisions, and evaluating the results.
- *Overt external guidance*: The student copies the teacher's model and completes the task, with the teacher still providing verbal directions and exercising control.
- *Overt self-guidance*: The learner repeats the performance while using self-talk as modelled by the teacher.
- *Faded self-guidance*: The learner repeats the performance while whispering the instructions.
- *Covert self-instruction*: The learner performs the task while guiding his or her responses and decisions using inner speech.

Typical self-questions and directions a student might use at steps 3, 4 and 5 would include: *What do I have to do? Where do I start? I will have to think carefully about this. I must look at only one problem at a time. Don't rush. That's good. I know that answer is correct. I'll need to come back and check this part. Does this make sense? I think I made a mistake here, but I can come back and work it again. I can correct it.* These self-questions and directions cover problem definition, focusing attention, planning, checking, self-reinforcement, self-appraisal, error detection and self-correction. They are applicable across a fairly wide range of academic tasks.

Sometimes the instructions, cue words or symbols to represent each step in the procedure may be printed on a prompt card displayed on the student's desk while the lesson is in progress. Training in self-instruction techniques of this type is considered to be particularly useful for students with mild intellectual disability or with Asperger Syndrome to improve their self-management (Meese 2001). The application of cognitive behaviour modification to cases of chronic behaviour disorder is discussed in the next chapter.

Further reading

Agran, M. (2003) *Student-directed Learning*, Baltimore, MD: Brookes.

Baumeister, R.F. and Vohs, K.D. (eds) (2004) *Handbook of Self-regulation: Research, Theory and Applications*, New York: Guilford.

Benevento, J.A. (2004) *A Self-regulated Learning Approach for Children with Learning/ Behavior Disorders*, Springfield, IL: Thomas.

Brophy, J.E. (2004) *Motivating Students to Learn* (2nd edn), Mahwah, NJ: Erlbaum.

Dawson, P. and Guare, R. (2004) *Executive Skills in Children and Adolescents*, New York: Guilford.

Lerner, J. and Kline, F. (2006) *Learning Disabilities and Related Disorders* (10th edn), Boston, MA: Houghton Mifflin.

Olson, J.L. and Platt, J.C. (2004) *Teaching Children and Adolescents with Special Needs* (4th edn), Upper Saddle River, NJ: Pearson-Merrill-Prentice Hall.

Pajares, F. and Urdan, T. (eds) (2006) *Self-efficacy Beliefs of Adolescents*, Greenwich, CT: Information Age Publishing.

Reid, R and Lienemann, T. (2006) *Strategy Training for Students with Learning Disabilities*, New York: Guilford.

Sabornie, E.J. and deBettencourt, L.U. (2004) *Teaching Students with Mild and High-incidence Disabilities at Secondary Level* (2nd edn), Upper Saddle River, NJ: Merrill-Prentice Hall.

Chapter 5

The management
of behaviour

On a daily basis, educators face the challenge of remediating problematic student behaviors. These behaviors may range from noncompliance and off-task [behaviour] to more severe behavioral concerns such as aggression and assault.

(Barton-Arwood *et al.* 2005: 430)

Teachers in both primary and secondary schools place great importance on students' ability to control their own behaviour and to work cooperatively with others (Lane *et al.* 2006). Many teachers report that one of their main concerns in the regular classroom is the child who disrupts lessons, seeks too much attention from the teacher or peers, and who fails to cooperate when attempts are made to provide extra help. The teachers feel that although they may know what the child needs in terms of basic instruction it proves impossible to deliver appropriate teaching because the child is unreceptive.

Teachers with emotionally disturbed children, or children with behaviour disorders, in their classes need the moral and professional support of their colleagues. In particular they need acknowledgement and understanding from colleagues that the student's behaviour is not due to their own inability to exercise effective classroom control. There is a tendency in some schools to see the management of a student's problem behaviour as being the responsibility only of the teacher in whose class the child is enrolled, rather than accepting it as a whole-school matter. Unless a school adopts a collaborative approach to the management of difficult and disruptive behaviour, certain problems tend to arise. These problems include:

- individual teachers feeling that they are isolated and unsupported by their colleagues;
- teachers feeling increasingly stressed by the daily conflict with some students;
- the problem becoming worse over time.

This chapter presents an overview of some of the approaches for reducing behaviour problems in school through effective use of proactive strategies.

Preventing behaviour problems

It is generally agreed that the first step in prevention of problem behaviour is to have a clear school policy on behaviour management issues. This leads to consistent implementation and practice by all staff. The school policy will describe ways in which individual teachers and the whole school staff should approach general matters of discipline and classroom control. The policy may also make specific reference to the management of students with significant emotional or behavioural disorders, and to students with disabilities (Taylor and Baker 2002).

A school-level policy document must be much more than a set of rules and consequences. A good policy will make clear to students, teachers, parents and administrators that schools should be safe, friendly, and supportive environments in which to work. In many ways, a school policy on student behaviour should be seen as dealing more with matters of welfare, safety and social harmony rather than procedures for punishment and enforcing discipline. The heart of any behaviour management policy should be the stated aim of teaching all students responsible and effective ways of managing their own behaviour and making appropriate choices. A good policy in action will not only protect teachers' rights to teach and students' rights to feel safe and to learn, but will also help students recognise the personal and group benefits that self-control and responsible behaviour can bring.

Positive Behaviour Support (PBS)

The typical approach to behaviour problems in schools tends to be reactive and aversive rather than preventive. The Positive Behaviour Support (PBS) model attempts instead to be proactive and reduce the likelihood that serious problems will arise (Allen *et al.* 2005; Barton-Arwood *et al.* 2005). For example, a student who frequently gets into fights with other students while waiting for the bus to arrive at the end of each day is given an important job to do in the classroom instead of waiting in line. When the bus arrives he quickly joins the other students.

PBS intervention strategies include:

- modifying or eliminating classroom conditions that increase the probability of challenging behaviour arising (for example, reducing group size; changing teaching method; introducing alternative materials; arranging seating differently; eliminating interruptions and distractions);
- teaching students self-control strategies;
- using positive reinforcement, rather than reprimands;
- providing active and supportive supervision;

- discussing behaviour codes and personal rights and responsibilities with students;
- explicitly teaching students the behaviours they need to display to meet the teachers' expectations.

To facilitate this pro-active approach at the whole-school level it is recommended that teams of teachers and assistants in the school be established. Such teams have the role of developing and implementing behaviour policy, helping to solve specific problems related to behaviour and learning, and assisting with staff development (Oswald *et al.* 2005). In Britain, as part of the government's *Behaviour Improvement Programme* (BIP), multi-agency 'Behaviour and Education Support Teams' (BESTs) have been established to work closely with defined groups of schools and families to address the needs of children and young people with emotional, behavioural and school attendance problems (DfES 2004b; Halsey *et al.* 2005). Schools using BESTs include those with high proportions of students with, or at risk of developing, behavioural problems as demonstrated in levels of exclusions and poor attendance. Services offered to such schools by BESTs range from individual work with students, family therapy, case conferences, parent support groups, and whole-school behaviour improvement interventions. Similar support teams operate in most states in Australia and the US.

Classroom behaviour

While it is true that some students exhibit behavioural problems in school that are a reflection of stresses or difficulties outside school, it is also evident that disruptive behaviour can result from factors within the learning environment. For example, an unsuitable curriculum quickly leads to poor behaviour because students who are bored may well become troublesome. In addition, research has shown that class size, grouping, and seating arrangements are factors influencing behaviour (Biddle and Berliner 2002).

One of the factors adding to a student's problems in secondary school is the frequent change of teachers for different subjects. Within the course of one day a student may encounter quite different and inconsistent management styles, ranging from authoritarian to permissive. This lack of consistency can have an unsettling effect on students who have emotional or behavioural difficulties. When cases of disruptive or challenging behaviour are reported, it is important to consult with other teachers to discover whether the student is also a problem when in their classes. All teachers who have contact with the student will need to get together to agree upon a consistent approach to be used when dealing with the problem behaviour. There has to be a whole-school recognition that behaviour problems are best dealt with from a shared perspective and tackled with a team approach.

Occasionally of course it is necessary to seek expert advice when a child's behaviour does not respond to standard forms of effective management; but in many cases behaviour can be modified successfully within the school setting.

When possible, teachers need to adopt a proactive rather than a reactive approach to classroom control. A sound starting point is the establishment of positive classroom rules (Rogers 2004), building upon sound principles set out in the school policy.

Classroom rules

Classroom rules are essential for the smooth running of any lesson and should be negotiated jointly by the children and the teacher early in the school year. Students should appreciate why rules are necessary, and must agree on appropriate consequences if a rule is broken. For example, the first time a rule is broken the teacher will give a warning in the form of a rule reminder. The second time a student violates the rule he or she should be given time out for five minutes.

Rules should be clear, consistent, few in number, expressed in positive terms (what the students *will do*, rather than *must not do*), displayed where all students can see them, and based on personal rights and responsibilities, and on the rights of others. While the actual rights and the rules that protect them are important, the process by which they are developed is just as important. Students should feel ownership of rules through contributing to their formulation. Rules might include matters like movement in the room, noise level, safety, personal property, sharing of equipment, and respect for others' ideas.

Classroom-based research on the management style of teachers has yielded an indication that the most effective teachers establish rules and procedures as a top priority at the beginning of the year. They discuss the rules with the students and apply them systematically and fairly. Such teachers are also more vigilant in the classroom, use more eye contact, are more proactive to prevent behaviour problems arising, set appropriate and achievable tasks for students to attempt, avoid 'dead spots' in lessons, keep track of student progress, check work regularly and provide feedback to the whole class and to individuals (Lovitt 2000).

Classroom procedures

Rogers (2004) suggests that all teachers should develop their own *discipline plan* to enable them to know in advance what to do when classroom behaviour is disruptive. The plan gives a teacher confidence when the pressure is on. Corrective actions a teacher might decide to use include:

- tactical ignoring of the student and the behaviour (low-level disruptions);
- simple directions ('Ann, get back to your work please');
- positive reinforcement ('Good, Ann');
- question and feedback ('What are you doing, Mark? OK, I'll come and help you');
- rule reminders ('David, you know our rule about noise. Please work quietly');

- simple choices ('Excuse me, Joanne. You can either work quietly here, or I'll have to ask you to work at the carrel – OK?');
- isolation from peers (take the student aside and discuss the problem, then place him or her in a quiet area to do the work);
- removal from class (time out under supervision in a different room may sometimes be needed).

Teachers may also use strategies such as deflection and diffusion to take the heat out of a potential confrontation. Teacher: 'Sally, I can see you're upset. Cool off now and we'll talk about it later; but I want you to start work please.' The judicious use of humour can also help to defuse a situation, without putting the student down. Sometimes it is appropriate to ask senior students to write a self-reflection about an incident of inappropriate behaviour in which they have been involved. They must say what they did, what they should have done, and what they are going to do to remedy the situation. This written paper might then become the basis of a discussion with the teacher or school counsellor, and might be used as a starting point from which to formulate a plan of action for behaviour change.

Identifying the problem

According to Levin and Nolan (2004), a discipline problem exists whenever an incident interrupts the teaching process, interferes with the rights of others to learn, and results in lost instructional time. Children who are constantly seeking attention, interrupting the flow of a lesson and distracting other children are often very troubling to teachers. Naturally, teachers may feel professionally threatened by children who constantly challenge their discipline. The feeling of threat can cause the situation to get out of hand, and a teacher can get trapped into confrontations with a child, rather than looking for possible solutions that will provide responsible choices and save face for the child and the teacher (Lindberg et al. 2005).

All too often teachers react overtly to undesirable behaviour, thus reinforcing it. Many behaviour problems in the classroom, particularly disruptive and attention-seeking behaviours, are rewarded by the adult's constant reaction to them. For example, the teacher who spends a lot of time reprimanding children is in fact giving them a lot of individual attention at a time when they are behaving in a deviant manner. This amounts to a misapplication of social reinforcement, and the teacher unintentionally encourages what he or she is trying to prevent. Some control techniques used by teachers (e.g. public rebuke) can have the effect of strengthening a child's tough image and status in the peer group.

If a teacher has a student who presents a problem in terms of behaviour in the classroom it is useful to analyse possible reasons for this behaviour in the context in which it is occurring. The following questions may be helpful when teachers attempt to analyse a case of disruptive behaviour.

- How frequently is the behaviour occurring?
- In which lesson is the behaviour less frequent (e.g. the more highly structured sessions, or the freer activities)?
- At what time of day does the behaviour tend to occur (a.m. or p.m.)?
- How is the class organised at the time (groups, individual assignments, etc.)?
- What am I (the teacher) doing at the time?
- How is the child in question occupied at the time?
- What is my immediate response to the behaviour?
- What is the child's initial reaction to my response?
- How do other children respond to the situation?
- What strategies have I used in the past to deal successfully with a similar problem?

The analysis deals with issues that are immediately observable in the classroom. Behaviour analysis does not need to examine the child's past history or search for deep-seated psychological problems as causal explanations for the child's behaviour. A simple plan for setting up a behaviour-change intervention might follow this sequence (Sparzo and Walker 2004):

- identify precisely the target behaviour to be changed;
- observe and record the current frequency and duration of this behaviour;
- set attainable objectives, involving the student in this process if possible;
- select teaching procedures such as modelling, prompting, role play;
- identify potential reinforcers by observing what this student finds rewarding;
- have the child rehearse the target behaviour;
- implement and monitor the programme, providing reinforcement and feedback to the child;
- ensure the new behaviour is maintained over time, and help the child generalise the behaviour to different settings and contexts.

It should be understood that changing a student's behaviour is often difficult. Sometimes the behaviour we regard as inappropriate has proved to be quite effective for the child in attaining certain personal goals. It has been practised frequently and has become very well established. In order for a positive behaviour change to occur the child must first *desire* to change. The responsibility of the teacher is then to help the child understand exactly *how* to bring about and maintain the change.

Behaviour modification

One approach that is commonly used is the behavioural approach, more often referred to as *behaviour modification*. It is based on principles of applied behaviour analysis (ABA) (Alberto and Troutman 2006). In this approach three assumptions are made:

- all behaviour is learned;
- behaviour can be changed by altering its consequences;
- factors in the environment (in this case the classroom) can be engineered to reward specific behaviours.

Typically, a problematic behaviour is observed and analysed. The factors that are possibly causing the behaviour, and the factors maintaining it, are identified. A programme is devised to reshape this behaviour into something more acceptable and more productive through a consistent system of reward (reinforcement), ignoring, or punishment.

It is always important in behaviour modification plans to select reinforcers that are effective for the individual (Ardoin et al. 2004). However, in cases of very persistent negative behaviour such as aggression or severe disruptiveness, positive reinforcement procedures may not be sufficient alone to bring about change. In such cases it may be necessary to introduce negative consequences and reductive procedures, such as loss of privileges, loss of points, or time out. Attention must also be given to improving the student's own self-monitoring and decision-making in order to increase self-control over the problem behaviour.

Criticism is sometimes levelled at behaviour modification approaches on the basis that the control is exercised by powerful others from outside the individual. It is suggested that the manipulation of the individual's behaviour is somehow out of keeping with humanistic views on the value of interpersonal relationships, the social nature of learning, and the need for personal autonomy. However, the very precise planning and management of a behaviour modification programme requires careful observation of how the child, the teacher and other children are interacting socially with one another and influencing each other's behaviour. Far from being impersonal, the techniques used to bring about and maintain change are usually highly interpersonal.

Regardless of criticisms that have been made, the behavioural approach has proved its value in an impressive number of research studies over a long period of time, and there can be no doubting the power of behaviour modification techniques in changing students' behaviour and enhancing learning. In particular, ABA techniques are of great practical value to parents, carers, and teachers working with students who have severe disabilities, autism, or challenging behaviour.

Additional information on behaviour modification techniques can be found in Alberto and Troutman (2006) and Zirpoli (2005).

Strategies for reducing disruptive behaviour

Levin and Nolan (2004) define disruptive behaviour as the upsetting of orderly conduct of teaching. Disruptions often prevent a teacher from achieving the objectives for a particular lesson and may also impair the quality of personal and social interaction within the group. Frequent disruptions have a ripple effect and can cause major reduction in the overall quality of learning and teaching occurring in that classroom, as well as destroying a positive classroom atmosphere. It is reported that teachers can lose about half of their teaching time in some classrooms due to students' disruptive behaviour (Charles and Senter 2005).

Sometimes simple changes such as modifying the seating arrangements, restructuring the working groups, reducing noise level, and monitoring more closely the work in progress will significantly reduce the occurrence of disruptive behaviour. The following strategies are also recommended.

Deliberate ignoring

If a child begins some form of disruptive behaviour (e.g. shouting to gain attention) the teacher ignores that child's response, and instead turns away and gives attention to another student who is responding appropriately. When the first student is acting appropriately the teacher will ensure that he or she is noticed and called upon. If the peer group can also be taught to ignore a disruptive student and not reinforce the behaviour by acknowledging it and reacting to it, the planned ignoring technique will be even more successful.

Clearly it is not sufficient merely to ignore disruptive behaviour. It is essential that planned ignoring be combined with a deliberate effort to praise descriptively and reinforce the child for appropriate behaviours at other times in the lesson – 'catch the child being good'. While it is common to view the frequency of undesirable behaviour in a child as something to reduce, it is more positive to regard the non-disruptive (appropriate) behaviours as something to reward and thus increase. It is a golden rule to be much more positive and encouraging than to be critical and negative in interactions with students.

Obviously, a teacher cannot ignore extremely disruptive behaviour when there is a danger that someone will be hurt or damage will be done. Nor can a teacher go on ignoring disruptive behaviour if it is putting other children at risk through lost learning time. The teacher must intervene to prevent physical danger but should do so quickly, quietly and privately. Private reprimands coupled if necessary with 'time out' are less likely to bring the inappropriate behaviour to the attention and approval of other children.

Reinforcement and rewards

In order to modify behaviour according to ABA principles, particularly in young or immature children, it may be necessary to introduce a reward system (Lindberg *et al.* 2005). If social reinforcers like praise, smiles and overt approval are not effective it will be necessary to apply more tangible rewards, selected according to students' personal preferences (Ardoin *et al.* 2004). Children are different in their preferences for rewards – what one child may find rewarding another may not. It may be that one child likes a stamp or coloured star, another child will work hard or behave well for a chance to play a particular game on the computer or watch a DVD.

Some teachers use tokens to reinforce behaviour or academic work in class. Tokens are simply a means of providing an immediate concrete reward. Tokens are usually effective because of their immediacy and students can see them accumulating on the desk as visible evidence of achievement. Tokens can be traded later for back-up reinforcers such as time on a preferred activity, being dismissed early, or receiving a positive report to take home to parents. While not themselves sensitive to individual preferences for particular types of reinforcement, tokens can be exchanged for what is personally reinforcing.

Most textbooks on educational psychology provide some general rules for using reinforcement (e.g. Eggen and Kauchak 2004). It is worth repeating them here:

- Reinforcement must be given immediately after the desired behaviour is shown and must be given first at very frequent intervals.
- Once the desired behaviours are established, reinforcement should be given only at carefully spaced intervals after several correct responses have been made.
- The teacher must gradually shift to unpredictable reinforcement so that the newly acquired behaviour can be sustained for longer and longer periods of time without reward.

Time out

Time out refers to the removal of a student completely from the social group situation to some other part of the room or even to a separate but safe setting for short periods of isolation. While time out may appear to be directly punishing, it is really an extreme form of ignoring. The procedure ensures that the child is not being socially reinforced for misbehaviour.

If the time out technique is being used, it is important that every instance of the child's disruptive behaviour be followed by social isolation. The appropriate behaviour will not be established if sometimes the inappropriate behaviour is tolerated, sometimes responded to by punishment, and at other times the child is removed from the group. It is essential to be consistent.

Avoid placing a student outside the classroom for time out if in that situation he or she gets other interesting rewards – being able to peer through the window and attract the attention of other students in the room, making contact with other students in the corridor, watching more interesting events in other parts of the school. Bartlett *et al.* (2002) warn that removing a student frequently from a lesson or activity that he or she does not like becomes negatively reinforcing rather than punitive, and the student is likely to continue to misbehave in order to be removed.

Cooling off

Explosive situations may develop with some disturbed children and a cooling-off period will be necessary. A set place should be nominated for this (e.g. a corner of the school library where worksheets may be stored for use by the student). The student should be under supervision for all of the time spent out of the classroom. The student will not return to that particular lesson until he or she is in a fit emotional state to be reasoned with and some form of behaviour contract can be entered into between teacher and student. Following a period of time out it is usually beneficial to have the child participate in a debriefing session in which he or she is encouraged to discuss the incident, reflect upon the behaviour, identify behaviour that might have been more effective, and set a goal for improvement.

Behavioural contracts

A behavioural contract is a written agreement signed by all parties involved in a behaviour-change programme (Bartlett *et al.* 2002). After rational discussion and negotiation the student agrees to behave in certain ways and carry out certain obligations. The staff and parents agree to do certain things in return. For example, a student may agree to arrive on time for lessons and not disrupt the class. In return the teacher will sign the student's contract sheet indicating that he or she has met the requirement in that particular lesson, and adding positive comments. The contract sheet accompanies the student to each lesson throughout the day. At the end of each day and the end of each week, progress is monitored and any necessary changes are made to the agreement. If possible, the school negotiates parental involvement in the implementation of the contract, and the parents agree to provide some specific privileges if the goals are met for two consecutive weeks, or loss of privileges if it is broken. When behavioural contracts are to be set up it is essential that all teachers (and school support staff) are kept fully informed of the details.

The daily report card can specify precisely which features of behaviour are to be appraised each lesson by the teacher. A simple yes/no response column makes the recording task quick and easy for a teacher to complete at change of lesson. For example:

Arrived on time	Y	N
Remembered to bring correct books	Y	N
Followed instructions	Y	N
Stayed on task	Y	N
Did not disturb others	Y	N
Completed all class work	Y	N
Completed homework	Y	N

A copy of the report can be sent home to parents, if appropriate, to ensure they are also monitoring their child's behaviour at school.

Punishment

Punishment represents yet another way of eliminating undesirable behaviours – but the use of punishment in schools is a contentious issue. The principal objection to punishment or *aversive control* is that while it may temporarily suppress certain behaviours, it may also evoke a variety of undesirable outcomes (fear, a feeling of alienation, resentment, an association between punishment and schooling, a breakdown in the relationship between teacher and student). Punishment may also suppress a child's general responsiveness in a classroom situation as well as eliminating the negative behaviour.

If it is absolutely necessary to punish a child the punishment should be administered immediately after the unacceptable behaviour is exhibited. Delayed punishment is virtually useless. Punishment also needs always to be combined with positive reinforcement and other tactics to rebuild the child's self-esteem. The goal of intervention should be to help students gain control over their own emotions and behaviour, but this goal will not be achieved if aversive control is the only method implemented.

Aggressive behaviour

Teachers are bothered most by aggressive behaviour in children. Increases in work-related stress among teachers are related in part to increases in acting-out and aggressive behaviour among students. Blum (2001) suggests that teachers should be trained in simple strategies for dealing with students' anger.

There is evidence that a *cognitive behavioural approach* can be effective in helping students understand and control their own anger – although the students must genuinely want to change their own behaviour if the approach is to work. Humphrey and Brooks (2006) report positive outcomes (effect size 0.5) from the use of six one-hour intervention sessions over a period of four weeks. During the sessions participants explored the following issues:

- what anger is, and why we need it;
- when anger becomes a problem;
- things that trigger our anger;
- how we can take control by recognising that we are becoming angry;
- how to use self-instruction and relaxation strategies.

Similarly, Cullen-Powell *et al.* (2005) report some benefits for students in upper primary and secondary school from a 16-session 'self-discovery programme' (three modules over one school year) to teach relaxation and self-control strategies that students can implement when feeling anxious or stressed.

It is reported that less aggression is found in schools where a caring and supportive environment has been nurtured and where curricular demands are realistic. Schools where there is constant frustration and discouragement seem to breed disaffection and stimulate more aggressive and anti-social behaviour in students (Hart 2002; Levin and Nolan 2004). Effective schools honour their responsibility of meeting students' emotional needs.

Bullying

While bullying may have been evident for as long as schools have existed, this fact does not make it any less serious. It is crucial not to ignore bullying in schools, as this problem will not cease of its own accord. The lives of too many children are made miserable when they become the victims of bullying. Some estimates put the prevalence of bullying at about one child in every ten, but self-report studies reveal many more students who later indicate that they were bullied when they were at school but did not report the problem. For the victim, bullying is known to cause absenteeism, psychosomatic illnesses, low self-esteem, impaired social skills, feelings of isolation, learning problems and depression. From the number of adults who report the impact that bullying had on them, it is clear that the experience frequently has long-lasting effects.

Bullying may take several different forms – direct physical attacks, verbal attacks, or indirect attacks such as spreading hurtful rumours or by excluding someone from a social group. Boys are more likely to be physically violent, while girls tend to use more indirect ways to make life unpleasant for their victims (although reports suggest that there has been an increase in aggression and violence among girls). There is some evidence that students with intellectual disability are sometimes subjected to teasing and bullying in both mainstream and special school settings (Norwich and Kelly 2004). Children with behaviour disorders and with poor personal and social skills are more likely than others to be victimised (Hardman *et al.* 2005).

Bullying is different from generally aggressive behaviour because bullies pick their targets very selectively. Olweus (1993) suggests that there are often characteristics of victims that make them targets for bullies; for example, they may appear to be vulnerable, weaker, shy, nervous, overweight, of different ethnic background, or 'teacher's pet'. Bullies are typically needing to feel powerful, sometimes to cover their own feelings of inadequacy. They are generally older or more physically advanced than their victims. Four out of five bullies come from homes where physical and emotional abuse are used frequently, and are therefore victims themselves to some degree (Hazler 1996). They appear to have less empathy than non-bullies. When bullying is carried out by gangs of students, factors come into play such as the importance of roles and status within the group. Some individuals feel that they are demonstrating their power by repressing the victim. Even those who are not themselves bullies get carried along with the behaviour and do not object to it or report it. Few would ever intervene to help the victim.

/ithin a school's behaviour management policy there should be agreed
:dures for handling incidents of bullying so that all staff approach the problem
similar strategies. Much bullying occurs in the schoolyard, particularly if
vision is poor. Increased supervision is one intervention that schools can
uce to reduce bullying. Obviously the behaviour of the bully or the gang
members needs to be addressed with direct intervention; but in addition, the issues
of consideration and respect for others and the right of every student to feel safe
also need to be discussed. It is suggested that issues of bullying and aggressive
behaviour should become the focus of attention within the school curriculum
– perhaps under the general heading 'human relationships'.

Cognitive approaches to self-control

The main goal of any type of behaviour-change intervention should be the
eventual handing-over of control to the individual concerned, so that he or she is
responsible for managing the behaviour. One way of achieving this is to employ
the cognitive behaviour modification (CBM) approach described in Chapter
4. The teacher or trainer provides coaching in the use of 'self-talk' to help the
student monitor his or her own reactions to challenging situations. The self-talk
enables the student to process aspects of the situation rationally, and enables him
or her to control and manage responses more effectively. A key ingredient in the
approach is teaching the student to use self-talk statements that serve to inhibit
impulsive and inappropriate thoughts or responses, allowing time for substitution
of more acceptable responses – for example, to be assertive but not aggressive; to
approach another student in a friendly rather than confrontational manner.

The intervention must help the student analyse the inappropriate behaviour
and understand that that response is not helping them in any way (e.g. lashing
out at others, arguing with staff). Next the student is helped to establish both the
desire to change and the *goals* to be aimed for over the following week (to stop
doing the negative behaviour and to start doing the more positive behaviour).
Over a number of sessions the student is helped to change negative thoughts and
beliefs to more appropriate positive perspectives.

Social stories

Another cognitive approach to behaviour change is the use of 'social stories'.
The use of stories with autistic children was discussed in Chapter 2. Social
stories can also be used with young or intellectually disabled students to help
them discriminate between appropriate and inappropriate patterns of behaviour.
Haggerty *et al.* (2005) explain that social stories, with pictures of the children
engaging in desirable and undesirable behaviour, can be used to help the children
observe and reflect upon their own behaviour and the reaction it gets from others.
For example, a first picture might show the children lining up in front of a cake
stall at the school Open Day. One child is pushing another out of the line in order

to take his place. The children on each side are looking very unhappy. In the next picture two of the other children are beginning to push the naughty child away from the line and a fight starts. In the third picture the lady in charge of the cake stall is telling the children that she will stop selling the cakes unless children line up in a neat queue. The final picture shows a neat queue of children with happy faces, each paying in turn for a cake. The sentences associated with the pictures might say:

> Today is Open Day at school, and there are many stalls for children and parents to buy food and drink.
>
> Some children in Kate's class have seen the beautiful cakes at the cake stall and want to buy some.
>
> At first the children line up very nicely and wait their turn to pay the money and get their cakes.
>
> The lady selling cakes smiles at them very happily.
>
> 'You are a very polite and friendly group', she says. 'You are lining up so smartly.'
>
> But Kate does not want to wait in the line and tries to push her friend Martin out of the line so that she can be first.
>
> Then the other children look very unhappy and try to push Kate away, so Kate pushes them too.
>
> The lady suddenly looks very unhappy.
>
> 'Oh dear. I am sorry, but I will not sell any cakes to anyone unless you line up nicely as before.'
>
> What should the children do now?
>
> How does Kate feel?
>
> What do the other children think of Kate?
>
> What does the lady think of Kate?

The story can be prepared, read, and discussed with several children in a small group using 'Big Book" format (see Chapter 7). However, social stories are most frequently used to target the negative behaviour of one particular child, in which case the story is personalised with the child's own name and the activity conducted individually. The story approach can also be used to help children who are shy or lacking in social skills.

Additional information on social stories as a teaching strategy can be found in Howley and Arnold (2005) or Crozier and Sileo (2005).

Attention-deficit hyperactivity disorder (ADHD)

Some students display severe problems in maintaining attention to any task, both in and out of school. These children have been classified as having Attention Deficit Disorder (ADD). Often these students also exhibit hyperactive behaviour so the term Attention-Deficit Hyperactivity Disorder (ADHD) has been coined to describe this form of learning difficulty. Children with ADD and ADHD display diminished persistence of effort, have difficulty sustaining attention to task, are overactive, and do not seem able to inhibit impulsive actions or responses. To be diagnosed as ADHD the child must exhibit six or more of the nine symptoms described under 'inattention' and 'hyperactivity' sections in the *Diagnostic and Statistical Manual of Mental Disorder, DSM IV-TR* (APA 2000). Of course, no single test or checklist exists that can lead to certain identification; usually information from several sources is combined to help the doctor or psychologist reach a conclusion.

It is considered by experts that approximately 3 to 5 per cent of school-age children present symptoms of ADD or ADHD (Rappley 2005), but in the past ten years there has been an increase in the number of students diagnosed (correctly or incorrectly) as having ADHD, resulting in suggestions that as many as 12 children in every 100 might have the disorder. This is unlikely to be the case, and estimates of 12 per cent prevalence rate are probably too high. The labels ADD and ADHD are often misused and applied to children who are merely bored and restless, or who are placed in a class where the teacher lacks good management skills. However, there are genuine cases of attention deficit and hyperactivity where the children do experience great difficulty in controlling their motor responses and exhibit high levels of inappropriate activity throughout the day. Hyperactivity is also sometimes present as an additional problem in certain disabilities (e.g. cerebral palsy, acquired brain injury, specific learning disability, and emotional disturbance).

No single cause for ADHD has been identified, although the following have all been put forward as possible explanations: central nervous system dysfunction (perhaps due to slow maturation of the motor cortex of the brain), subtle forms of brain damage too slight to be confirmed by neurological testing, allergy to specific substances (e.g. food additives), adverse reactions to environmental stimuli (e.g. fluorescent lighting), inappropriate management of the child at home, maternal alcohol consumption during pregnancy causing Foetal Alcohol Syndrome (Clarren 2003). Most investigators now tend to agree that the hyperactivity syndrome encompasses a heterogeneous group of behaviour disorders with multiple causes of possibly neuropsychological origin.

ADHD children, while not necessarily below average in intelligence, usually exhibit poor achievement in most school subjects (Lucangeli and Cabrele 2006). Impaired concentration and restlessness associated with ADHD have seriously impaired the child's learning during the important early years of schooling. These children may also be poorly coordinated and often have problems with peer relationships. The literature indicates that most hyperactivity diminishes with age even without treatment, but in a few cases the problems persist into adult life.

Interventions for ADHD

Owing to the possibility that ADHD is caused by different factors in different individuals, it is not surprising to find that quite different forms of treatment are advocated; and what works for one child may not work for another. Treatments have included diet control, medication, psychotherapy, behaviour modification and cognitive behaviour modification. The conclusion must be that any approach to the treatment of ADHD needs to attend to *all* factors that may be maintaining the behaviour. According to Lerner and Kline (2006) the most effective treatment for ADHD requires the integrated use of effective teaching strategies, a behaviour management plan, parent counselling, home management programme, and medication.

There is strong agreement among experts that children with ADHD need structure and predictability in the learning environment. Effective teaching strategies must be used to arouse and hold the child's interest. Children with ADHD need to be engaged as much as possible in interesting work, at an appropriate level, in a stable environment. Enhancing the learning of children with ADHD will also involve:

- providing strong visual input to hold attention;
- using computer-assisted learning (CAL);
- teaching the student better self-management and organisational skills;
- monitoring the children closely during lessons and finding many opportunities to praise them descriptively when they are on task and productive.

Additional advice on teaching modifications for children with ADHD can be found in Zentall (2006) and Kewley (2005).

Further reading

Alberto, P.A. and Troutman, A.C. (2006) *Applied Behavior Analysis for Teachers* (7th edn), Upper Saddle River, NJ: Pearson-Merrill-Prentice Hall.

Bambara, L.M. and Kern, L. (eds) (2005) *Individualized Supports for Students with Problem Behaviors: Designing Positive Behavior Plans*, New York: Guilford Press.

Bear, G.G., Cavalier, A.R. and Manning, M.A. (2005) *Developing Self-discipline and Preventing and Correcting Misbehavior*, Boston, MA: Pearson-Allyn and Bacon.

Chandler, L.K and Dahlquist, C.M. (2006) *Functional Assessment: Strategies to Prevent and Remediate Challenging Behavior in School Settings* (2nd edn), Upper Saddle River, NJ: Merrill-Prentice Hall.

Emmer, E.T., Evertson, C.M. and Worsham, M.E. (2006) *Classroom Management for Middle and High School Teachers* (7th edn), Boston, MA: Pearson-Allyn and Bacon.

Henley, M. (2006) *Classroom Management: A Proactive Approach*, Upper Saddle River, NJ: Pearson-Merrill-Prentice Hall.

Kauffman, J.M. (2006) *Managing Classroom Behavior: A Reflective Case-based Approach* (4th edn), Boston, MA: Pearson-Allyn and Bacon.

Kerr, M.M. and Nelson, C.M. (2006) *Strategies for Addressing Behavior Problems in the Classroom* (5th edn), Upper Saddle River, NJ: Pearson-Merrill-Prentice Hall.

Mackay, J. (2006) *Coat of Many Pockets: Managing Classroom Interactions*, Melbourne: Australian Council for Educational Research.

Mennuti, R.B., Freeman, A. and Christner, R.W. (eds) (2006) *Cognitive-behavioral Interventions in Educational Settings: A Handbook for Practice*, London: Routledge.

Orpinas, P. and Horne, A.M. (2006) *Bullying Prevention: Creating a Positive School Climate and Developing Social Competence*, Washington, DC: American Psychological Association.

Scarpaci, R.T. (2007) *A Case Study Approach to Classroom Management*, Boston, MA: Pearson-Allyn and Bacon.

Zirpoli, T.J. (2005) *Behavior Management: Applications for Teachers* (4th edn), Upper Saddle River, NJ: Merrill-Prentice Hall.

Chapter 6

Improving social skills and peer group acceptance

Many students with mild disabilities demonstrate difficulties in developing social relationships with adults and peers in their environment. These students often evidence reduced social perceptiveness, finding it challenging to read verbal and nonverbal social cues and appropriately interpret these cues within a social and cultural context.

(Pavri and Monda-Amaya 2001: 392)

The quotation above reminds us of the need to consider how best to enhance the social acceptance of children with special needs when they are placed in a regular classroom. Inclusive educational settings create an opportunity for these children to engage in more positive social interaction with their peers – but social acceptance of students with special needs does not always occur spontaneously (Brodkin 2005; Canney and Byrne 2006). The results of most studies of inclusion give no support at all to the belief that merely placing a child with a disability in the mainstream will automatically lead to his or her social integration into the peer group (Frederickson *et al.* 2005). The situation is most problematic for children who have an emotional or behavioural disorder; and there is a danger that such children become marginalised, ignored or even openly rejected by classmates.

Even students without disabilities are at risk in school if they lack social skills and are rejected or victimised by others (Fox and Boulton 2005). It is for this reason that establishing good social relationships with other children has been described as one of the most important goals of education. It is evident that poor peer relationships during the school years can have a lasting detrimental impact on social and personal competence in later years. The risk of problems is reduced however when children with special needs are able to establish healthy social relationships (Wiener 2004).

Opportunities for social interaction

At least three conditions must be present for positive social interaction and the development of friendships among children with and without disabilities. These conditions include:

- *Opportunity*: Being within proximity of other children frequently enough for meaningful contacts to be made.
- *Continuity*: Being involved with the same group of children over a reasonable period of time; and also seeing some of the same children in your own neighbourhood out of school hours.
- *Support*: Being helped to make contact with other children in order to work and play with them; and if possible being directly supported in maintaining friendships out of school hours.

Inclusive schooling provides the opportunity for friendships to develop in terms of proximity and frequency of contact, and also has potential for continuity. It creates the best possible chances for children with disabilities to observe and imitate the social behaviours of others. What inclusive classrooms must provide is the necessary support for positive social interactions to occur (Sparzo and Walker 2004). This is particularly important for students who are low in self-esteem or confidence and lacking in basic social skills.

When students with disabilities are placed in regular settings without adequate preparation or on-going support, three problems may become evident:

- The children without disabilities do not readily demonstrate easy acceptance of those with disabilities.
- The children with disabilities, contrary to popular belief, do not automatically observe and copy the positive social models that are around them.
- Some teachers do not intervene to promote social interaction on the disabled child's behalf.

There is an urgent need for teachers to identify as soon as possible any children in their classes who appear to be without friends at recess and lunch breaks and who seem unable to relate closely with classmates during lessons.

Identification of children with peer relationship problems

There are several appropriate ways to identify children with social acceptance problems. Each approach will be described briefly, but they can be used in combination.

Naturalistic observation

The most obvious strategy for identifying children with problems is the informal observation of social interactions within and outside the classroom. Naturalistic observation is probably the most valuable method of identification for the teacher to use because it focuses on the child within the dynamics of peer-group situations. A teacher who takes the trouble to note ways in which children play and work together will quickly identify children who are neglected by their peers or who are openly rejected or become the target of ridicule and teasing. It is very important also to try to identify the factors that give rise to this situation. For example, is the child in question openly obnoxious to others through aggression, hurtful comments, spoiling games or interfering with work? Or at the other extreme, does the child seem to lack confidence and skills to initiate contact with others, instead remaining very much on the outside of any action?

Sociometric survey

Naturalistic observation tends to identify the most obvious cases of popularity or rejection. It may not pick up some of the less obvious social relationships in the class. For this reason some teachers find it useful to carry out a whole-class survey in which all the children indicate, in confidence, their main friendship choices. The teacher may interview each child privately or, if the children can write, may give out slips of paper with the numerals 1 to 3 printed on them. The teacher then requests that each child write down first the name of the person he or she would most like to play with or work with as a partner in a classroom activity or at lunchtime. The teacher may then say, 'If that person was away from school, who would you choose next?' and that name is listed second. The procedure is then repeated for a third choice. When the papers are collected the teacher calculates a score for each child on the basis of three points for the first choice, two points for second choice, and one point for third. For example, Susan obtains a total score of ten points if two other children choose her as first preference and two others choose her as second preference. The results will identify children who are popular, those who are reasonably accepted in the group, and those who are not chosen at all by their classmates. Sociometric data of this type can sometimes guide the teacher when establishing working groups.

Peer ratings

This procedure ensures that some children are not overlooked if absent, as may happen with a traditional sociometric survey described above. Each child is provided with a list of the names of all children in the class. They are required, in confidence, to place a score from 1 (not liked very much) to 5 (liked very much indeed) against each name. Summation of the completed scores will reveal the children who are not well liked by class members as well as showing the general level of acceptance of all children. The result may sometimes correlate highly with naturalistic observation, but occasionally quite subtle positive or negative relationships appear that are not immediately obvious to casual observation.

Teacher ratings

The use of checklists that specify important indicators of social adjustment can be helpful in providing a clear focus for teachers' observations. The items in the checklist would normally be those responses and behaviours considered to comprise 'social skills', such as greeting, interacting with others, sharing, and avoiding conflict.

Creating a supportive environment

A positive and supportive school environment is, of course, important for the social development of all children (Bremer and Smith 2004). To facilitate social interaction for children with special needs in regular classrooms three conditions are necessary:

- The general attitude of the teacher and the peer group towards students with special needs must be as positive and accepting as possible.
- The environment should be arranged so that the child with a disability has the maximum opportunity to spend time socially involved in group or pair activities, during recess and during academic work in the classroom.
- The child needs to be taught the specific skills that may enhance social contact with peers.

To enhance social development, teachers must first create classroom environments where competition is not a dominant element. They must then use group activities frequently enough to encourage cooperation among students (Johnson and Johnson 2003).

Influencing attitudes

It has long been acknowledged that one of the key factors influencing the effectiveness of inclusive education is the *attitude* of those involved in the process – teachers, children, and parents. Teachers and classmates tend to become more accepting of children with disabilities when they gain experience in working with them and acquire a better understanding of the nature of disabilities. Children's attitudes are likely to be influenced most when teachers work to build a climate of concern for others and a respect for individual differences. Facilitating and encouraging peer assistance in the classroom can be useful in increasing non-disabled students' closer contact with others who have difficulties in learning. Studies have shown that a combination of information about, and direct contact with, disabled children provides the most powerful positive influence for attitude change in both teachers and in the peer group. It is also evident that attitude change tends to be a gradual process.

The following activities, particularly when used in combination, have proved beneficial in improving children's attitudes towards those with disabilities.

- Viewing videos depicting children and adults with disabilities coping well and doing everyday things. Many videos and VCDs are available showing inclusive classroom environments and the accommodations made for students with special needs.
- Reading and discussing stories about disabled persons and their achievements.
- Conducting factual lessons and discussion about particular disabilities.
- Having persons with disabilities as visitors to the classroom or as guest speakers.
- Using simulation activities, e.g. simulating deafness or vision impairment or being confined to a wheelchair. (But note that two conditions that cannot be simulated are intellectual disability and emotional disturbance. These are also the two disabilities producing the greatest problems in terms of social isolation and rejection in the peer group.)
- Organising regular visits as helpers to a local special school or centre.

Throughout these awareness-raising activities attention should be drawn to the various strengths possessed by every person with a disability or learning difficulty, as well as to any problems or special needs they may have. The theme of discussion should focus on: 'How will we respond positively and supportively to someone with this difficulty in our class?' 'How will we help to make these students feel happy and productive?'

The class activity called 'Circle Time' can be used to great advantage as an opportunity for children to discuss aspects of behaviour such as helping one another, preventing bullying or teasing, building self-esteem, looking for strengths in other people, and showing interest in the ideas of others. Circle Time is often associated with kindergarten and early primary years, but the value of having students coming together in a relaxed situation in which they can voice their opinions can extend easily into secondary schools (Taylor 2003). Circle Time can also be used as an opportunity for social skills development with intellectually disabled students (taking turns; listening to others; sharing; praising) (Canney and Byrne 2006).

Circle of Friends

Circle of Friends is a peer-group support strategy to help children (particularly those with special educational needs) who have difficulty finding a friend and coping in class (Barrett and Randall 2004). The approach originated in Canada but is now used in the US, the UK and Australia as one way to foster social inclusion for students with SEN. Circle of Friends operates by involving some of a child's classmates as natural supporters to help the child acquire more positive behaviours and self-management. Improvements in these areas will make him or her more socially acceptable and successful.

The teacher first discusses with the whole class in a positive manner the particular needs of the child with a social or behavioural problem, and invites up to five or six students to volunteer to form a collaborative support group for this child. They must greet the child each day, be friendly and helpful at all times, assist with routines at lunch and break times, make sure the child is counted in for all activities, and help the child solve any problems that may arise. The members of the group meet frequently to set goals and devise possible strategies. The role of the teacher is to facilitate and encourage this process. Each week a debriefing meeting is held for the volunteers and they report back on any positive progress in the week and discuss any problems that have occurred.

Additional information on *Circle of Friends* can be obtained from these online sources:

http ://www.inclusive-solutions.com/circlesoffriendsarticle.asp
http://www.cesa5.k12.wi.us/SKIP/circleofriends.htm
http://www.ualberta.ca/~jpdasddc/inclusion/raymond/ch4.html

Facilitating social interaction

The following strategies can be used to increase the chances of positive social interaction for students with disabilities:

- Make more frequent use of non-academic tasks (e.g. games; model-making; painting) because these place the child with special needs in a situation where he or she can more easily fit in and contribute.
- 'Peer tutoring' and 'buddy systems' have been found effective. Several versions of these exist, including Classwide Peer Tutoring (CWPT). Research over two decades has confirmed the effectiveness of peer tutoring for improving learning outcomes for students at all age and ability levels (McMaster *et al.* 2006).
- Make a particular topic – for example, 'friends' or 'working together' – the basis for class discussion. 'If you want someone to play with you at lunchtime, how would you make that happen?' 'If you saw two children in the schoolyard who had just started at the school today, how would you make them feel welcome?' Sometimes teachers prepare follow-up material in the form of worksheets with simple cartoon-type drawings and speech balloons into which the children write the appropriate greetings or comments for the various characters.
- Peer-group members can be encouraged to maintain and reinforce social interactions with less-able or less-popular children. Often they are unaware

of the ways in which they can help. They, too, may need to be shown how to initiate contact, how to invite the child with special needs to join in an activity, or how to help that classmate with particular school assignments.

Organisation for group work

The regular use of group work in the classroom is one of the main ways of providing children with opportunities to develop social skills through collaborating with others. Careful planning is required if group work is to achieve the desired educational and social outcomes. The success of collaborative group work depends on the composition of the working groups and the nature of the tasks set for the students.

When utilising group work as an organisational strategy it is important to consider the following basic principles:

- Initially there is some merit in having groups of children working cooperatively on the same task at the same time. This procedure makes it much easier to prepare resources and to manage time effectively. When each of several groups are undertaking quite different tasks it can become a major management problem for the teacher, unless the students concerned are already very competent and experienced in group work.
- Choice of tasks for group work is very important. Tasks have to be selected which *require* collaboration and teamwork. Children are sometimes seated in groups in the classroom but are expected to work on individual assignments. Not only does this negate the opportunities for collaboration, it also creates difficulties for individuals in terms of interruptions and distractions.
- It is not enough merely to establish groups and to set them to work. Group members may have to be taught how to work together. They may need to be shown behaviours that encourage or enable cooperation – listening to the views of others, sharing, praising each other, and offering help to others. If the task involves the learning of specific curriculum content, teach the children how to rehearse and test one another on the material.
- The way in which individual tasks are allotted needs to be carefully planned (division of labour); the way in which each child can assist another must also be made explicit, e.g. 'John, you can help Craig with his writing then he can help you with the lettering for your title board.' Contingent praise for interacting with others should be descriptive. 'Well done, Sue. That's nice of you to help Sharon with that recording.'
- Teachers should monitor closely what is going on during group activities and must intervene when necessary to provide suggestions, encourage the sharing of a task, praise examples of cooperation and teamwork and model cooperative behaviour themselves. Many groups can be helped to function efficiently if the teacher (or classroom assistant or a parent helper) works as a group member without dominating or controlling the activity.

- The size of the group is important. Often children working in pairs is a good starting point. Select the composition of the group carefully to avoid obvious incompatibility among students' personalities. Information from a sociometric survey may help to determine appropriate partners.
- When groups contain students with special needs it is vital that the specific tasks and duties to be undertaken by these students are clearly delineated. It can be useful to establish a system whereby the results of the group's efforts are rewarded not merely by what individuals produce, but also by the way in which they have worked together positively and supportively. Under this structure, group members have a vested interest in ensuring that all members learn, because the group's success depends on the achievement of all. Helping each other, sharing, and tutoring within the group are behaviours that must be modelled and supported.
- Talking should be encouraged during group activities. It is interesting to note that sub-grouping in the class has the effect of increasing transactional talk (talk specifically directed to another person and requiring a reply) by almost three times the level present under whole-class conditions.
- Seating and work arrangements are important. Group members should be in close proximity but still have space to work on materials without getting in each other's way.
- Group work must be used frequently enough for the children to learn the skills and routines. Infrequent group work results in children taking too long to settle down.

Group work can become chaotic if the group tasks are poorly defined or too complex. Other problems arise if the students are not well versed in group-working skills, or if the room is not set up to facilitate easy access to resources. It is essential that all tasks have a very clear structure and purposes that are understood by all. Doveston and Keenaghan (2006) suggest that there is great value in discussing openly with a class the best ways of making group work effective, and identifying the skills necessary to cooperate productively with others.

At times a teacher needs to intervene to help a child gain entry to group activity or to work with a carefully chosen partner. The teacher must also praise and reinforce both the target child and the peer group for all instances of cooperative, helpful and friendly behaviour. In the case of children displaying extreme withdrawal or rejection, simply relying on milieu intervention is not always sufficient. Sometimes it is necessary for a child to be removed from the classroom situation and coached intensively in a particular social skill before that skill can be applied in the peer group setting.

What are social skills?

Social skills are the specific behaviours an individual uses to maintain effective interpersonal communication and interaction. Social skills comprise a set of competencies that allow children or adolescents to initiate positive social interactions with others, establish peer acceptance, and cope effectively and adaptively within the social environment.

Some children with disabilities or with emotional and behavioural difficulties are particularly at risk of social isolation (Gresham *et al.* 2001), although it is important to stress that some students with disabilities are popular with classmates in the mainstream, particularly if they have a pleasant personality. One of the main reasons why certain children are unpopular is that they lack appropriate social skills that might make them more acceptable. They are in a Catch-22 situation since friendless students have fewer opportunities to practise social skills, and those who don't develop adequate social skills are unable to form friendships. It is argued that these children need social skills training (Siperstein and Rickards 2004).

Cartledge (2005) recommends that social skill instruction should begin in the preschool years or the primary grades, when children are most receptive to behaviour change. Early training in social skills can be instrumental in reducing or preventing problem behaviour in later years. Cartledge also advises that social skill instruction should be embedded in the context of events that occur naturally within the children's own classroom setting. Research shows that there is very limited transfer or maintenance of skills when they are taught in contrived exercises unrelated to the real classroom.

Social skills training

Many lists of important pro-social behaviours have been created (e.g. Cohen and Jaderberg 2005), as have many checklists allowing teachers, parents and psychologists to assess a child's social skill level (e.g. Elksnin and Elksnin 1995). Guidelines have also been published to give teachers suggestions for what to teach and how to teach it in the domain of social skill development.

Social skills training usually includes the teaching of some or all of the following behaviours:

- making eye contact;
- greeting others by name;
- gaining attention in appropriate ways;
- talking in a tone of voice that is acceptable;
- knowing when to talk, what to talk about, and when to hold back;
- initiating a conversation;
- maintaining conversations;
- answering questions;
- listening to others and showing interest;
- sharing with others;
- saying please and thank you;
- helping someone;

- making apologies when necessary;
- being able to join in a group activity;
- taking one's turn;
- smiling;
- accepting praise;
- giving praise;
- accepting correction without anger;
- coping with frustration;
- managing conflict.

The basic list above is similar to that found in most texts on social skills training. Each skill can be broken down into smaller sub-skills if necessary, and each skill or behaviour needs to be considered relative to the particular child's age and specific deficits. For example, the conversational skills needed to function adequately in an adolescent peer group are obviously far more complex and subtle than those required by the young child just starting school. Similarly, skills needed to deal with conflict situations become more complex as a child gets older.

There is no shortage of training programmes and curricula available to schools, as reviewed for example by Kavale and Mostert (2004). The designers of these programmes believe that teaching social skills can have lasting positive benefits, particularly for those students with only mild degrees of social difficulty. Studies suggest that programmes for students with special needs can be effective if (a) they target the precise skills and knowledge an individual lacks; (b) they are intensive and long term in nature; (c) they promote maintenance, generalisation and transfer of new skills outside the training context into the individual's daily life (Gresham 2002). The most meaningful settings in which to enhance the child's skills are usually the classroom and schoolyard. It is pointless to teach skills that are not immediately useful in the child's regular environment.

Most programmes for training social skills are based on a combination of modelling, coaching, role-playing, rehearsing, feedback and counselling. At times, video recordings are also used to provide examples of social behaviours to discuss and imitate, or to provide the trainee with feedback on his or her own performance or role-play. In each individual case the first step is to decide what the priorities are for this child in terms of specific skills and behaviours to be taught. The skills to be targeted need to be of immediate functional value to the child in the social environment in which he or she operates.

Typical steps in coaching social skills include:

- *Definition*: Describe the skill to be taught. Discuss why the particular skill is important and how its use helps social interactions to occur. The skill may be illustrated in action in a video, a picture or cartoon, a simulation using puppets, or pointed out to the child by reference to activities going on in the peer group. The teacher may say 'Watch how she helps him build the wall with the blocks.' 'Look at the two girls sharing the puzzle. Tell me what they might be saying to each other.'

- *Model the skill*: Break the skill down into simple components and demonstrate these clearly yourself, or get a selected child to do this.
- *Imitation and rehearsal*: The child tries out the same skill in a structured situation. For this to occur successfully the child must be motivated to perform the skill and must attend carefully and retain what has been demonstrated.
- *Feedback*: This should be informative. 'You've not quite got it yet. You need to look at her while you speak to her. Try it again.' 'That's better! You looked and smiled. Well done.' Feedback via a video recording may be appropriate in some situations.
- *Provide opportunity for the skill to be used*: Depending upon the skill taught, use small group work or pair work activities to allow the skill to be applied and generalised to the classroom or other natural setting.
- *Intermittent reinforcement*: Watch for instances of the child applying the skill without prompting at other times in the day and later in the week. Provide descriptive praise and reward. Aim for maintenance of the skill once it is acquired.

To a large extent, these behaviours once established are likely to be maintained by natural consequences – that is, by a more satisfying interaction with peers. Individuals with acceptable social skills are less likely to engage in problem behaviour, are better at making friends, are able to resolve conflicts peacefully, and have effective ways of dealing with persons in authority (Poulou 2005).

As well as having appropriate positive pro-social skills, a socially competent individual must also *avoid* having negative behavioural characteristics that prevent easy acceptance by others – for example, high levels of irritating behaviour (interrupting, poking, shouting), impulsive and unpredictable reactions, temper tantrums, abusive language, or cheating at games. In many cases these undesirable behaviours may need to be eliminated by behaviour modification or through cognitive self-management.

Is social skills training effective?

Some researchers warn against over-optimism in regard to the long-term efficacy of social skills training (e.g. Frederickson and Furnham 2004; Kavale and Mostert 2004; Maag 2005). While most social skills training produces positive short-term effects, there are usually major problems with maintenance and generalisation of the trained skills over time (Barton-Arwood *et al.* 2005; Cartledge 2005). In particular, it is suggested that social skills training appears to have limited effect when applied to seriously behaviourally-disordered children and others with chronic relationship difficulties (Gresham *et al.* 2001). It must also be noted that even when children with disabilities are specifically trained in social skills, some may still not find it any easier to make friends. For example, Margalit (1995) found that students with intellectual disability reported on-going loneliness even after successfully participating in a social skills programme. Unexpected outcomes may also occur, for example, Elliott *et al.* (2002) found that some students with intellectual disability may feel *less* socially competent after training because the training has made them more aware of their own deficiencies.

The failure of many social skills programmes to bring about lasting change in students may be due to:

- a mismatch between the exact social deficits a child displays and the activities provided in the training programme (with some programmes reportedly being much too generic and not based on an accurate assessment of the student's specific needs) (Cartledge 2005);
- poor or inconsistent quality of the training provided in some programmes (Gresham *et al.* 2001);
- training sessions too infrequent and too lacking in intensity to have any lasting impact (Bullis *et al.* 2001);
- a failure to plan for and support generalisation from the training or coaching context to natural social environments (Barton-Arwood *et al.* 2005; Gresham *et al.* 2001).

Training in social skills is not a matter simply of teaching a child something that is missing from his or her repertoire of behaviours, but rather it usually involves *replacing* an undesirable behaviour that is already strongly established with a new alternative behaviour. Gresham *et al.* (2001) suggest that the negative behaviours we often take as indicative of lack of social skill in some children (e.g. aggression, non-compliance, verbal abuse) may actually be very rewarding behaviours for the individuals concerned and represent more powerful and effective forces than the new pro-social skills we attempt to teach. This residual influence of pre-existing behaviours is one of the reasons why skills taught during training are often not maintained – they are competing with powerful behaviours that have already proved to work well for the child.

Even given the cautionary comments above it is still a high priority for any students who lack specific social skills to be provided with every opportunity (including specific training) in order to acquire them. There is much still to be discovered about how best to implement social skills training. Bullis *et al.* (2001: 89) are probably accurate in their conclusion:

> Unfortunately we do not know the necessary intensity or duration for the social skills intervention to be effective, and we are uncertain of the precise combination of components that should be added to the treatment to achieve maximum effect.

Poor scholastic achievement seems to be one factor contributing to poor social acceptance, even after social skills have been taught. Unless achievement within the curriculum can also be increased, acceptance may remain a problem for some children. Attention is therefore focused in the following chapters on approaches for teaching basic academic skills to students with special needs.

Further reading

Bliss, T. and Tetley, J. (2006) *Circle Time: A Resource Book for Primary and Secondary Schools* (2nd edn), London: Paul Chapman.

Bloomquist, M.L. (2006) *Skills Training for Children with Behavior Problems*, New York: Guilford Press.

Cornish, U. and Ross, F. (2004) *Social Skills Training for Adolescents with General Moderate Learning Difficulties*, London: Jessica Kingsley.

Kaltman, G.S. (2006) *Help! For Teachers of Young Children: 88 Tips to Develop Children's Social Skills and Create Positive Teacher–Family Relationships*, Thousand Oaks, CA: Corwin Press.

Kostelnik, M.J. (2006) *Guiding Children's Social Development; Theory to Practice* (5th edn), Clifton Park, NY: Thomson-Delmar.

Mathieson, K. (2005) *Social Skills in the Early Years: Supporting Social and Behavioural Learning*, London: Paul Chapman.

Petersen, L. and Lewis, P. (2004) *Stop, Think, Do: Social Skills Training*, Melbourne: Australian Council for Educational Research.

Sandieson, R. and Sharpe, V. (eds) (2004) *Social and Communication Skills in Developmental Disabilities*, Austin, TX: PRO-ED.

Siperstein, G.N. and Rickards, E.P. (2004) *Promoting Social Success: A Curriculum for Children with Special Needs*, Baltimore, MD: Brookes.

Walker, H.W., Ramsey, E. and Gresham, F.M. (2004) *Antisocial Behavior in School: Evidence-based Practices* (2nd edn), Belmont, CA: Thomson-Wadsworth.

Chapter 7

Developing early literacy skills: principles and practices

Instructional approaches have generated much interest and controversy for several decades, especially in relation to 'best practice' in the literacy domain.

(Ellis 2005: 10)

According to the description in *No Child Left Behind Act* (Congress of USA 2002) in the US, skilled reading is a complex act that requires the integrated use of the following:

- an understanding of how phonemes (speech sounds) are represented in print;
- the ability to decode unfamiliar words;
- the ability to read fluently;
- sufficient background information and vocabulary to support reading comprehension;
- the development of appropriate strategies to construct meaning from print;
- the development and maintenance of motivation to read.

Learning to read is a challenging task even for children of average intelligence. It can be a very difficult task indeed for children with disabilities. Yet despite the difficulties, almost all children can be helped to acquire skills in word recognition and comprehension through application of effective teaching.

The most effective methods for teaching reading have been the focus of recent enquiries in several different countries, for example Australia (DEST 2005), the UK (House of Commons Education and Skills Committee 2005; Rose 2005), and the US (National Reading Panel 2000). The main purpose of these enquiries has been to find methods that are supported by research that proves their efficacy, rather than methods that are simply based on teachers' personal whims and idiosyncratic styles. Some of the conclusions from these reports are included in this and the following chapter.

Differing perspectives on reading methodology

In the past 50 years, the teaching of reading has been dominated at various periods either by a 'skills-based approach' or by a 'meaning-emphasis approach' (most recently termed 'whole language'). The former stresses the importance of explicitly teaching children the component skills necessary for decoding and interpreting text; the latter stresses that reading should be a thinking process and must be driven by a 'top down' process of constructing meaning. There continues to be heated argument between advocates of the two approaches concerning the superiority of one over the other. However, the consensus emerging from current research favours a combined or 'balanced' approach (Ellis 2005; House of Commons Education and Skills Committee 2005).

Much has been written recently about 'balance' within the overall methodology used to teach reading – 'balance' implying here an appropriate combination of explicit teaching of word-identification skills and comprehension strategies on the one hand with immersion in real literature on the other. Balance also implies a combination of teacher-directed and student-centred activity within the reading curriculum (Pressley 2006; Tompkins 2006). In the early stages of learning to read, the best curricula offer an amalgam of elements, including reading for meaning, reading for thinking, experience with high-quality literature, systematic instruction in phonics, development of sight vocabulary, and ample opportunities to read and write. Those favouring a balanced approach to instruction recognise that skilled reading involves both a top-down search for meaning and a bottom-up decoding of text (Manset-Williamson and Nelson 2005). As Cunningham *et al.* (2004) indicate, children *need* a balanced literacy programme if they are to develop all necessary skills and strategies for independence in reading and writing.

It is important to consider the contribution that both skills-based and meaning-emphasis approaches can make to the creation of a balanced reading programme.

A skills-based approach to reading

In the earliest stages of learning to read, children have not yet built up a large vocabulary of words they know instantly by sight, so they must use knowledge of letters and groups of letters to help identify unfamiliar words. Children cannot really become independent readers unless they master the code. It is now generally accepted that explicit instruction in phonic principles needs to be part of all early reading programmes. Goswami (2005: 273) remarks:

> To access meaning from print, the first step is to learn the code used by the culture for representing speech in a visual code. The child needs to acquire the system for mapping distinctive visual symbols to units of sound.

A skills-based approach explicitly teaches students decoding skills to aid word identification. It also develops comprehension strategies to facilitate processing of text for different purposes. The approach usually involves a high degree of teacher direction in the early stages, using direct instruction and a carefully sequenced curriculum, rather than unstructured student-centred discovery. Within the skills-based approach to reading there are many ways of ensuring that children acquire an understanding of the alphabetic principle and can also apply appropriate strategies for comprehending what they read. Later chapters provide more detailed coverage of some of these decoding and comprehension strategies.

On the issue of decoding skills (phonics), research evidence very strongly supports direct and systematic instruction in phonic knowledge, soon after the child reaches the age of 5. This early start provides a firm foundation on which to build higher-order literacy skills (DEST 2005; Pullen *et al.* 2005; Rose 2005). The current evidence suggests that the method known as *synthetic phonics* (learning to identify words in print by building them from their component sounds) produces the best results. For example, a longitudinal study involving some 300 children taught by the synthetic phonics method reported that significant gains made in word reading in Primary 1 had increased six-fold by the end of Primary 7 (Johnston and Watson 2005). These researchers point out that this continuing gain long after a training procedure ceases is very unusual; the effects of specific methods usually diminish, not increase, with time. They suggest that perhaps instruction in synthetic phonics helps children acquire a word-analysis technique that they can continue to develop independently for themselves.

In contrast to the synthetic phonics approach, the method called *analytic phonics* works in the opposite direction. Analytic phonics teaches children essential letter-sound relationships by analysing words they already recognise. For example, the sound of letter 't' is taught from words like '*tin; top; tap; tip*'. Or, the consonant blend 'cl' might be taught from the words '*class; clap; clip*', and so forth. Analytic phonics is favoured as a method by some teachers because it moves in the direction from whole to part, rather than part to whole. However, research has not shown it to be more effective than synthetic phonics.

The criticism is sometimes made that phonic knowledge is of little value because of the irregularity of English spelling. This is true only if children's phonic knowledge is limited to single letter-to-sound correspondences. If students become proficient in identifying larger phonic units represented by clusters of letters (*orthographic units*), such as *pre-, str-, -tion, -eat, -ough, -ight, -oon, -oo-, -ea-,* they can decode many more words. When children equate strings of letters with pronounceable units such as syllables in spoken words, many inconsistencies in English spelling patterns are removed. More detailed information on the teaching of phonic skills will be found in Chapter 9.

It must be stressed here that no teacher ever uses a phonic approach *exclusively*; to do so would be to teach early reading and writing in the most unnatural and boring way, working from parts to whole and only engaging in meaningful reading once all the skills were in place. Valid criticisms have been made of some forms of remedial teaching of reading that err on this side and involve nothing but repetitive drilling of isolated skills (Moody *et al.* 2000). The teachers who embed explicit instruction within their total literacy programme represent the most effective use of a skills-based approach (Pullen *et al.* 2005). They give due attention to developing and applying skills for decoding, spelling and comprehending text, but always with an emphasis on *meaningful* reading and writing. When skills-based instruction is integrated fully into children's daily reading and writing it overcomes the criticism that skills drilled and practised in isolation are boring and do not transfer to authentic literacy activities.

The meaning-emphasis approach

The meaning-emphasis approach is based on a belief that readers recognise words and interpret print mainly on the basis of the overall meaning conveyed by the text. It is suggested that readers pay very little attention to lower-level processes such as phonic decoding. Many years ago, Goodman (1967) described reading as a psycholinguistic guessing game in which skilled readers use their knowledge of language (vocabulary and syntax), together with knowledge of the topic, to predict many of the words on the page. Only when the reader cannot predict a word, or when meaning is lost, does he or she have to resort to the use of appropriate phonic cues. This appears to be the way in which skilled readers operate – so the argument from the advocates of the meaning-emphasis 'whole language' approach is that even beginning readers need to be encouraged to develop the same general 'guess-from-meaning' strategy.

Whole-language (meaning-emphasis) theory holds that authentic literacy experiences foster a child's understanding of the true nature and purposes of reading, whereas the teaching of component skills may fail to achieve this goal. A key belief underpinning whole language is that children acquire literacy skills in much the same way as they learned to use speech for purposes of communication – that is without having to be taught. Young learners immersed in a print-rich environment are considered capable of constructing meaning and developing reading skills for themselves by drawing on their experience of spoken language when engaging actively with print (Weaver 2002). The teacher's role is to provide opportunities for children to work with text and to support ('scaffold') their efforts. Through experimenting with written language – recognising some words, guessing others, and self-correcting when necessary – they begin to acquire basic reading skills without direct instruction. The teacher is there as a model and a resource, but also engages in much indirect and incidental teaching. This approach to literacy learning is one that is essentially child-centred and involves providing children with daily experiences in using reading and writing for real purposes, rather than engaging in exercises.

At classroom level, the implementation of the whole-language approach usually embodies at least the following teaching strategies:

- reading good literature to students every day, and having 'real' literature available for students to read for themselves;

- providing time each day for shared reading;
- discussing and reflecting upon stories or other texts;
- encouraging silent reading;
- providing daily opportunities for children to read and write for real purposes;
- encouraging children to invent the spelling for words they do not know;
- adopting a conference-process approach to writing (drafting, sharing, editing and revising with feedback from teacher and peers);
- assisting children with any particular aspect of reading and writing at the time they require such guidance (the 'teachable moment');
- teaching specific skills always within the context of material being read or written;
- integrating language and literacy activities across all areas of the curriculum.

Studies evaluating the effectiveness of the whole-language approach (e.g. Stahl and Miller 1989; Stahl *et al.* 1994) tend to conclude that when whole-language practices are skilfully implemented they can:

- benefit children in the earliest stages of learning to read;
- increase children's awareness of the purposes and processes of reading and writing;
- build positive attitudes towards books and writing;
- help children develop strategies for interpreting text beyond the literal level (e.g. prediction, inference, critical reading, reflection);
- enrich a child's vocabulary and general knowledge;
- encourage risk-taking with invented spelling.

With these positive features in mind it is clear that the whole-language approach makes a major contribution to children's overall progress towards literacy. The question remains, however, whether whole-language practice is comprehensive and *intensive enough* to ensure that all children become knowledgeable and competent in every aspect of reading, writing and spelling. The whole-language approach may not suit the learning characteristics of every student. It was remarked in Chapter 1 that teaching approaches lacking clear direction and structure might cause difficulties for some learners. It is also generally accepted that students with intellectual disability do not make effective progress if taught by immersion methods alone.

The study by Stahl and Miller (1989) suggested that while the whole-language approach produced encouraging results with the most able students, positive effects were much less evident in weaker students and in those students disadvantaged by low socio-economic background. This finding is not surprising, as many studies have shown that readers with learning difficulties, or with socio-cultural disadvantage, tend to need highly systematic, direct, and intensive instruction that matches their developmental level (Ellis 2005). Birsh (2005) and Manset-Williamson and Nelson (2005) observe that informal instruction, if used in isolation, is not helpful for children with learning disabilities because they do not pick up effective decoding skills merely through incidental learning. It seems safe to assume that the best features of the whole-language approach create a necessary *but far from sufficient* condition to ensure that all children become proficient readers.

The beginning-reading approaches described below encourage a combined application of skills-based and meaning-emphasis principles. Shared-book experience, language-experience approach, and guided reading are teaching approaches entirely compatible with modern theories of language acquisition and reading skill development. When used for remedial teaching purposes the approaches require a greater degree of structuring than is necessary when applied to children without learning problems. These methods do not preclude the teaching of specific word-attack skills.

Shared-book experience

The shared-book approach is highly appropriate for young children in the first stages of learning to read (Combs 2006); but the basic principles can also be applied to older children with learning difficulties if age-appropriate books are used. As a beginning-reading method, the shared-book approach has proved equal or superior to other methods and produces very positive attitudes towards reading, even in the slower children (Allington 2001).

Shared-book experience aims to:

- develop children's enjoyment and interest in books and stories;
- develop concepts about books and print;
- focus on comprehension;
- build children's awareness of English language patterns (syntax);
- develop word-recognition skills;
- build phonic skills for decoding and spelling;
- provide opportunities for discussion, reflection and writing.

In the shared-book approach children enjoy stories, poems, jingles and rhymes read to them by the teacher using a large-size book with enlarged print and colourful pictures. Sitting in a group close to the teacher, all children can see the 'big book' easily. They can see the pictures and the words, and can follow the left-to-right direction of print as the teacher reads aloud. The book should have the same visual impact from several feet away as a normal book would have in the hands of a child.

The children's attention is gained and maintained by the teacher's enjoyable and enthusiastic presentation of the story and discussion of the pictures. Familiarity with the language patterns in the story is developed and reinforced in a natural way. Stories that children may already know and love are useful in the early stages because they present an opportunity for the children to join in even if they cannot read the words. The first time the story is read, the teacher does not interrupt the reading with too many questions or teaching points. The main aim is to enjoy and understand the story.

The basic steps for implementing the shared-book approach include:

△ BEFORE READING

- read together the story title;
- refer to the cover picture or other pictorial material;
- stimulate discussion about the topic or the title;
- praise children's ideas.

△ DURING READING THE TEACHER

- reads the story aloud;
- maps the direction of print with finger or pointer;
- thinks aloud sometimes: 'I wonder if she is going to ...';
- pauses sometimes at predictable words to allow children to guess;
- sometimes asks children, 'What do you think will happen next?'

△ AFTER FIRST READING

- children and teacher discuss the story;
- recall main information.

△ DURING SECOND READING OF THE STORY THE TEACHER

- aims to develop word-recognition skills;
- covers certain words to encourage prediction from context (cloze procedure);
- increases children's phonic knowledge;
- encourages writing (spelling) of a few of the words.

△ POSSIBLE FOLLOW UP

- writing and drawing activities;
- word families;
- individual and partner reading of small books (same story);
- children can make up some questions about the story.

Shared-book experience embodies all the basic principles of effective teaching, particularly the elements of motivation, demonstration by the teacher, student participation, feedback, and successful practice. It also encourages cooperative learning and sharing of ideas between children and adults in a small-group situation. The method can serve a valuable compensatory role for children with special needs who enter school lacking rich language and literacy experiences from the preschool years. The discussion of each story should not simply focus on low-level questions of fact and information, but rather should encourage children to make personal connections, think, feel, predict and extend ideas. The study of the text should also facilitate vocabulary growth.

Liboiron and Soto (2006) describe the application of shared-book activities with SEN students using alternative and augmentative communication. They recognise that children with disabilities or communication disorders tend to be very passive listeners and do not ask questions or initiate discussion during typical story reading. These writers emphasise the use of scaffolding procedures such as oral cloze, statement expansion, choice of options, pointing or cueing, and questioning to maximise the chances of eliciting responses from the children.

Additional information on strategies for shared-reading activities can be found in Ezell and Justice (2005).

Language-experience approach

The principle of language-experience is summed up in the following statements:

> What I know about, I can talk about.
> What I say can be written down by someone.
> I can read what has been written.

In both mainstream-class and remedial-group situations shared-book experience can operate in parallel with the individualised language-experience approach. The language-experience approach uses the child's own thoughts and language to produce carefully controlled amounts of personalised reading material. It can be described as a form of 'dictated-story' approach. Young children, or older children with literacy problems, are helped to write something that is relevant and personally meaningful to them. With assistance and practice they can read what they have written and can begin to store some of the words in long-term memory (Norton and Land 2004). From the language-experience recordings, and from activities conducted in parallel with the recordings, the children can also be taught important phonic knowledge and skills.

From the viewpoint of the failing reader, the approach combines two major advantages: first, there is the possibility of utilising the child's own interests to generate material for reading and writing; and second, the teacher is able to work within the child's current level of language competence. This is of great value for children who are well below average in general language ability, due perhaps to restricted preschool language experience, hearing impairment or language disorder. The work produced in the child's language-experience book (or language-experience wall chart) is usually relevant and motivating. The language-experience approach forges a clear connection between speech and print (Cramer 2004).

The basic principles of the language-experience approach can also be used within intervention programmes for non-literate adults or those learning English as a second language (Rasinski and Padak 2004). The procedures for using the language-experience approach in a remedial context are described in detail below. It is not necessary to follow quite such highly controlled steps when using language experience with normal learners in whole-class settings.

△ STEP I

The starting point for language experience with young children (or older children of limited ability) can be the labelling of some of the child's drawings.

'This is my cat, Moonbeam.'
'I can ride my BMX bike fast.'
'This is a photo of me and Moonbeam.'

The child and teacher together read the captions and review them regularly. At this stage the reading approach is holistic and attention is not drawn to individual letters or words. A little later, the written recordings can be cut into separate word cards and the child can be encouraged to build the sentences again using the word cards in the correct left-to-right sequence. The word cards can also be used separately to practise word recognition.

During this early stage of the programme the child can contribute a dictated sentence associated with an experience shared by the class – for example, a class excursion to the airport ('I saw a jumbo jet'). These sentences are added, along with others from the class, to the big picture-map produced by the children as part of the follow-up to the excursion. Again, the recordings are not in any way analysed at the phonic level; they merely serve the purpose of establishing in the learner's mind the notion that 'What I say can be written down.'

△ STEP 2

After a week of this introductory work, the child is ready to make his or her first book. A topic is carefully selected related to the child's personal interests, e.g. motorcycle speedway. The teacher produces some visual material that will provide the illustration for the first page, perhaps a picture of the child's favourite speedway rider from a magazine. Teacher and child talk together about the rider and from the discussion they agree upon one brief statement that can be written under the picture: 'This is Chris Copley.' The teacher prints the agreed statement for the child, who then copies it carefully under the teacher's version. If the child cannot copy due to physical disability or coordination problems, he or she can perhaps trace over the words with a wax crayon. Both teacher and child then read the statement together once or twice and the child is left to paste the picture carefully into the book. Older children can be encouraged to type or word-process the same sentence on a sheet of paper and paste that into the book. When the student sees the same sentence in different styles and fonts it is an aid to generalisation from handwritten to printed form of the same words.

△ STEP 3

Next day the child is presented with the same statement written on a strip of card: 'This is Chris Copley.' Without reference to the book, the child is encouraged to read the words. He or she may have forgotten the material so some brief revision may be needed. The child then cuts the strip of card into separate word cards. These are placed at random on the desk and the child has to arrange them in the correct left-to-right sequence. If at first the child cannot do this he or she may spend time matching the word cards against the original version in the book until the sequencing task can be performed correctly. At this point the teacher picks up one of the cards – perhaps the word 'is' – and using it as a small flashcard asks the child to pronounce the word. This procedure is continued until the child can recognise each word out of context as well as in context. The word cards are then placed in an envelope stapled in the back cover of the book, ready to be revised the following day.

△ STEP 4

Over the next week the child continues to produce a page of his or her book with much guidance and encouragement from the adult. Regular revision of the previous day's words ensures repetition and overlearning to the point of mastery. The teacher's control over what is written will ensure that not too much is added to the book each day. If the child is allowed to dictate too much material this will result in failure to learn and loss of satisfaction.

△ STEP 5

Once important sight words have been mastered these can be checked off or coloured in on a vocabulary list in the front cover of the child's book. Such charting of progress within the book gives the child visual evidence of progress, and also indicates to the teacher what core material has been covered so far and what still needs to be taught. If certain words seem to present particular problems for the child, games and activities can be introduced to repeat and overlearn these words. Gradually the amount written each day can be increased, and after some months the child will need less and less direct help in constructing sentences. The use of the language-experience approach in this way is highly structured and is based on mastery principles at each step. The approach may sound slow and tedious but it does result in progress in even the most resistant cases of reading failure. The growth in word recognition skills is cumulative.

△ STEP 6

At some appropriate stage in the programme the teacher will help the child expand his or her word-attack skills. For example, perhaps the child has used the word 'crash' in writing about the speedway interest. In a separate booklet the teacher can help the child to learn the value of the blend /cr/ by collecting other /cr/ words (crab, crook, cross, cry, etc.). Similarly he or she can experiment with the unit /ash/ from the word 'crash' by building the appropriate word family (b-ash, d-ash, c-ash, r-ash, fl-ash, tr-ash, etc.). This incidental word study linked with meaningful material from the child's own book is important but will be inadequate on its own for developing functional decoding skills. It will be necessary to teach word-attack and spelling skills explicitly for certain students (see Chapter 9).

△ STEP 7

Once a child has made a positive start using this language-experience approach he or she can be introduced to a graded reading book. It is wise to prepare the way for this transition by including in the child's language-experience material some of the new words that will be met in the reader.

For additional information on the language-experience approach see Mariotti and Homan (2005), Antonacci and O'Callaghan (2006), or Norton and Land (2004).

Guided reading

In the literature on reading methodology 'guided reading' is most often presented as an approach for use with children after the third year of schooling. It is described as an excellent way to develop a strategic, reflective and critical approach in children who are beyond the beginner stage (Cappellini 2005). Most of the suggestions for providing guidance are, however, merely extensions of what should have been occurring from an early age during shared-book experience and in discussions stemming from students' language-experience material.

Guided reading is an approach in which the teacher supports each child's acquisition of effective reading strategies for unlocking text at increasingly challenging levels. For this reason guided reading is considered an essential part of any balanced approach to literacy. It addresses the need to help students become efficient in comprehending various genres of text. The guidance provided for the students may focus at times on sub-skills such as word identification and decoding, but its main emphasis is the development of a strategic approach to comprehension.

The guided reading sessions are usually conducted by the teacher, but with heavy emphasis placed on students' active participation through discussion, cooperative learning, and sharing of ideas. There are three main stages at which guidance from the teacher is provided: *before* reading the text, *during* the reading, and *after* reading the chosen text.

Δ *Before reading*: Guidance before reading prepares the reader to enter the text with some clear purpose in mind. At the 'before reading' stage the teacher may, for example, focus children's attention on their prior knowledge related to the topic, encourage them to generate questions or make predictions about information that may be presented in the text, remind them of effective ways of reading the material, alert them to look out for certain points, and pre-teach some difficult vocabulary to be encountered later in the text.

Δ *During reading*: The guidance during reading may encourage the student to generate questions, look for cause–effect relationships, compare and contrast information, react critically, check for understanding and highlight main ideas.

Δ *After reading the text*: The guidance provided by the teacher may help the children summarise and retell, check for understanding and recall, and encourage critical reflection and evaluation.

The processes involved in guided reading sessions, while primarily serving a teaching function, also allow the teacher to observe and assess the students' comprehension strategies. This is a very important diagnostic function, enabling a teacher to adapt reading guidance to match students' specific needs.

One of the best sources for additional information on guided reading is the text by Fountas and Pinnell (1996). The texts by Vacca *et al.* (2006), Combs (2006) and Cappellini (2005) all contain useful ideas.

A traditional method revisited

Merttens and Robertson (2005) have reported on a new version of a very old teaching method that is proving effective with children in the age range 4 to 6 years. The method, *Rhyme and Ritual*, is based on the principle that instead of approaching early reading as a process in which a reader must decipher an unknown text to obtain the message, one can work in the reverse direction and teach word recognition from stories and rhymes that are already very familiar to children because they have heard them many times. *Rhyme and Ritual* capitalises on the oral story-telling tradition using repetition and enjoyment, but has supplemented listening with the provision of text-and-picture books, audio-tapes and (finally) texts without pictures. Take-home materials ensure that there is continuity and support outside school hours. Details of the method and materials can be found in the paper by Merttens and Robertson (2005).

A focus on comprehension

Reading comprehension is not something that comes *after* learning the mechanics of reading; reading for meaning must be the focus of any literacy programme from the very beginning. When teachers read stories to children they can discuss the material and encourage children to think about and evaluate the ideas in the story. In guided reading activities, attention should be devoted to seeking and clarifying meaning, explaining, interpreting, and summarising.

Reading comprehension has been defined as an active thinking process through which a reader intentionally constructs meaning and deepens understanding from text (Neufeld 2006). Understanding text involves word identification, activation of prior knowledge, and the application of cognitive strategies. Children who are good comprehenders use a variety of cognitive process as they read. For example, they may visualise as they read narrative material; they may pose questions to themselves; they may reflect upon the relevance of what they are reading; they may challenge the accuracy of stated facts; and they monitor their own level of understanding.

As long ago as 1969, Nila Banton Smith identified four levels of comprehension, each level containing a cluster of component skills and each dependent upon competence at the previous level. The following summary is adapted from Smith's model.

- *Literal comprehension*: This is the most basic level of understanding, involving a grasp of the factual information presented in the text. Literal comprehension is dependent upon sub-skills such as understanding word meanings, recognition of main idea, grasp of sequence and order of detail or events. This level depends greatly upon the learner's own previous knowledge and experience. Even literal comprehension and recall will be difficult if concepts being presented are completely new to the reader.
- *Inferential*: This level of comprehension involves the reader in going beyond what is actually presented in the text, and 'reading between the lines' to predict and draw tentative conclusions. Sub-skills at this level include anticipating outcomes, making generalisations, reasoning cause-and-effect when these are not stated, and discovering real or possible relationships. Some reading experts prefer to call this *interpretive level*, believing that the skills involved cover more than prediction and inference.
- *Critical reading*: This level of comprehension involves judgements of the quality, value, accuracy and truthfulness of what is read, or detecting bias or overstatement. Critical reading requires a personal (and sometimes emotional) response from the reader.
- *Creative reading*: At this level the reader goes beyond the message of the text to generate new ideas or develop new insights triggered by the reading and related to the theme or topic but not explicit in the text.

It is argued that in many classrooms comprehension activities rarely demand responses beyond the literal level (recall of facts). This level is important since it is basic to the other three levels, but a curriculum that sets out to develop comprehension skills in children should include other more challenging questions that demand thinking at the interpretive, critical and creative levels. For example, following a short story about the crash of a passenger aircraft these questions might be posed:

- How many passengers escaped the crash? (literal)
- Why did failure of cabin pressure lead to the crash? (inferential)
- From the way he behaved before the crash, what kind of man do you think the pilot was, and could his judgement be trusted? (inferential)
- A section of the extract contains information from eyewitness accounts summarised in a newspaper report. Why might this information not be entirely trustworthy? (critical)
- Several air crashes similar to this one occur each year. How might flight be made a safer method of transport? (creative)

Difficulties in comprehension

Some readers are reasonably accurate and fluent in their reading performance but still have problems in comprehending above the literal level. They are weak at inferring meaning beyond the words on the page, poor at prediction, and tend not to read critically or attend to detail (Cragg and Nation 2006). In order to improve students' comprehension it is important to consider the possible underlying difficulties.

Sometimes comprehension problems stem from the student's limited vocabulary knowledge or lack of fluency. If a student has difficulty understanding what is read, it is worth considering whether there is a serious mismatch between the student's own oral vocabulary and the words used in the text. A student may be able to read a word correctly on the page but not know its meaning. In this situation there is a need to devote more time to word study and vocabulary building when comprehension activities are used in the classroom. There is also a need sometimes to pre-teach difficult vocabulary before the text is read.

Obviously the readability level of the text is a major factor influencing whether or not material can be read easily with understanding – difficult text, in terms of concepts, vocabulary, sentence complexity and length, is not easy for any reader to process. Difficult text leads to high error rate, thus impairing comprehension and leading to frustration and loss of motivation. Matching the readability level of books to students' current reading ability level can do much to increase students' comprehension (Fountas and Pinnell 2006).

There appears to be an optimum rate of fluency in reading that allows for accurate processing of information. Automaticity in reading, based mainly on smooth and effortless word identification and contextual cueing, allows the reader to use all available cognitive capacity to focus on meaning (Carver 2000). Children who read very slowly – or much too fast – often comprehend poorly. Slow word-by-word reading makes it difficult for the reader to retain information in working memory long enough for meaning to be maintained. Slow reading also tends to restrict cognitive capacity to the low-level processing of letters and words, rather than allowing full attention to higher-order ideas and concepts within the text. Fast reading may result in important detail being overlooked. Sometimes attention to rate of reading needs to be a specific focus in children's intervention programmes (Allington 2001).

Some children have difficulty recalling information after reading. Recall is dependent partly upon such factors as vividness and relevance of the information in the text; but it is also dependent upon a student giving adequate focused attention to the reading task and knowing that it is important to remember details. Recall is best when readers connect passage content to their own previous knowledge and experience, and when they rehearse key points from the text. These factors may provide clues to help identify why a particular child is having problems in remembering what he or she has read. The use of graphic organisers to summarise key points can help to strengthen recall of information (Sabbatino 2004).

Improving comprehension

The reading comprehension skills of all children can be increased when teachers spend time demonstrating effective strategies for processing text (Ellis 2005; Neufeld 2006; Pressley and Hilden 2006). The explicit teaching of such comprehension strategies requires direct explanation, modelling, thinking aloud, and abundant guided practice (Walker 2005). Strategies such as self-questioning, self-monitoring, rehearsing information, constructing story maps or graphic organisers, and creating mnemonics to assist recall, have all proved valuable. Manset-Williamson and Nelson (2005) report that students with reading difficulties seem to benefit greatly from strategy training, and as a result they tend to make significant gains in reading comprehension. However, Hay *et al.* (2005) remark that students with learning difficulties take very much longer than other students to master reading comprehension strategies, so the training must not be abandoned too quickly.

Comprehension strategies must encompass:

- previewing the material before it is read to gain an overview;
- locating the main idea in a paragraph;
- generating questions about the material by thinking aloud;
- predicting what will happen, or suggesting possible cause-and-effect;
- summarising or paraphrasing the main content.

A successful programme for the development of comprehension should include at least these components:

- large amounts of time devoted to reading;
- teacher-directed instruction in comprehension strategies;
- using text as one source from which to obtain new information;
- frequent occasions when students can talk with the teacher and with one another about their response to a particular text.

One example of a simple reading comprehension strategy is *PQRS*, where each letter in the mnemonic signifies a step in the strategy. The four steps are:

P = PREVIEW

First scan the chapter or paragraph, attending to headings, subheadings, diagrams and illustrations. Gain a very general impression of what the text is likely to cover. Ask yourself, 'What do I know already about this subject?'

Q = QUESTION

Next generate some questions in your mind: What do I expect to find out from reading this material? For example, will it tell me how to make the object? Will it tell me how to use it? Will I need to read the text very carefully or can I skip this part?

R = READ

Then read the passage or chapter carefully for information. Read it again if necessary. Do I understand what I am reading? What does this word mean? Do I need to read this section again? Are my questions answered? What else did I learn?

S = SUMMARISE

Finally, identify the main ideas and state briefly in your own words the key points in the text.

The teacher models the application of the PQRS approach several times using different texts, demonstrating how to focus on important points in the chapter or article, how to check one's own understanding, how to back-track or scan ahead to gain contextual cues, and how to select the key points to summarise. This modelling helps students appreciate the value of having a plan of action for gaining meaning from text, and the value of self-questioning and self-monitoring while reading. The students are helped to practise and apply the same approach with corrective feedback from the teacher. To aid generalisation it is important to use different types of reading material used for different purposes and to remind students frequently to apply the strategy when reading texts in different curriculum areas.

Reading and study-skill strategies are best taught through dialogue between teachers and students working together to extract meaning from the text. Dialogue allows students and teachers to share their thoughts about the process of learning and to learn from the successful strategies used by others. Dialogue also serves a diagnostic purpose by allowing the teacher to appraise the students' existing strategies used for comprehending and summarising texts.

Peers can facilitate each other's learning of reading strategies in small groups. An approach known as *reciprocal teaching* has proved extremely useful in a group situation to facilitate dialogue and to teach specific cognitive strategies (Rosenshine and Meister 1994). In this approach teachers and students work together, sharing and elaborating ideas, generating questions that may be answered from a specific text, predicting answers, checking for meaning, and finally collaborating on a summary. The teacher's role initially is to demonstrate effective ways of processing the text, to ask relevant questions, and to instruct the students in strategic reading; the long-term aim is to have students master these strategies for their own independent use across a variety of contexts.

The following general principles may also help to facilitate comprehension skill development for all students, including those with learning difficulties.

- Ensure that the reading material presented is interesting to the student and at an appropriate readability level.
- Always make sure students are aware of the goals in reading a particular text.
- Apply comprehension strategy training to real texts, read for genuine purposes; don't rely on contrived comprehension exercises for strategy training.
- Prepare students for entry into a new text. Ask: What might we find in this chapter? What do the illustrations tell us? What does this word mean? Let's read the subheadings before we begin.
- Read comprehension questions *before* the story or passage is read so that students enter the material knowing what to look for in terms of key information.
- After reading the text, encourage students to set comprehension questions for each other; then use these questions to discuss what is meant by literal level information, critical reading, inferring, predicting. This type of activity lends itself to the reciprocal teaching format described above.
- Devote time regularly to discussing how a particular sample of text can be summarised. Making a summary is an excellent way of ensuring that students have identified main ideas.
- Make frequent use of graphic organisers or story maps as advance organisers, or to summarise the relationships among key points after reading the text

(Sabbatino 2004). These graphics have proved very helpful for students with learning difficulties (Lerner and Kline 2006).

- Use newspapers and magazine articles sometimes as the basis for classroom discussion and comprehension activities. Highlighter pens can be used to focus upon key ideas, important terms, or facts to remember.
- In general, aim to *teach* comprehension skills and strategies, rather than simply *testing* comprehension.

Additional information on improving reading comprehension can be found in Herrell and Jordan (2006), Cooper and Kiger (2006), Jonson (2006) or Paris and Stahl (2005).

Further reading

Antonacci, P.A. and O'Callaghan, C.M. (2006) *A Handbook for Literacy Instructional and Assessment Strategies, K-8*, Boston, MA: Pearson-Allyn and Bacon.

Cooper, J.D. and Kiger, N.D. (2006) *Literacy: Helping Children Construct Meaning* (6th edn), Boston, MA: Houghton Mifflin.

Cunningham, P.M. (2005) *Phonics They Use: Words for Reading and Writing* (4th edn), Boston, MA: Pearson-Allyn and Bacon.

Gentry, J.R. (2006) *Breaking the Code: The New Science of Beginning Reading and Writing*, Portsmouth, NH: Heinemann.

Glenn, A., Cousins, J. and Helps, A. (2006) *Tried and Tested Strategies: Ready to Read and Write in the Early Years*, London: Fulton.

Heilman, A.W. (2006) *Phonics in Proper Perspective* (10th edn), Upper Saddle River, NJ: Pearson-Merrill-Prentice Hall.

Lapp, D., Flood, J., Moore, K. and Nichols, M. (2005) *Teaching Literacy in First Grade*, New York: Guilford Press.

Miyata, C. and Miyata, K. (2005) *The Reading Edge: Using Phonics Strategically to Teach Reading*, Portland, ME: Stenhouse.

Pressley, M. (2006) *Reading Instruction that Works: The Case for Balanced Teaching* (3rd edn), New York: Guilford Press.

Smith, J.A. and Read, S. (2005) *Early Literacy Instruction*, Upper Saddle River, NJ: Merrill-Prentice Hall.

Tompkins, G.E. (2006) *Literacy for the 21st Century* (4th edn), Upper Saddle River, NJ: Pearson-Merrill-Prentice Hall.

Chapter 8

Planning effective intervention for literacy problems

> The purpose of both assessment and diagnosis is to make instructional decisions about how best to help students. Results of assessments and diagnosis help the teacher determine which instructional objectives to teach (or re-teach), what methods and strategies to use, and what materials are appropriate.
>
> (Mariotti and Homan 2005: 1)

The previous chapter described some effective methods for teaching early reading skills to a wide ability range. In this chapter the focus shifts to students who despite exposure to good-quality teaching are still exhibiting difficulty in becoming proficient readers.

The needs of students with learning difficulties

The child who is experiencing difficulty learning to read needs special consideration in his or her literacy programme. In general these students benefit from a more direct teaching approach, tailored to their current ability levels and coupled with strategies designed to restore lost confidence and motivation. Programmes that give adequate attention to teaching of word building and phonic skills, as well as reading for meaning, are considered to have most value for children with learning difficulties (Ellis 2005).

A student with reading difficulties requires:

- an enthusiastic teacher who can model effective reading strategies;
- a teacher who can provide effective guidance and support;
- abundant opportunity to read for pleasure and for information;
- successful practice, often using material that has become familiar to the student;
- a carefully graded programme, with supplementary materials used for additional practice alongside the mainstream curriculum;

- for beginners, more time spent on early reading activities (phonemic-awareness training, flashcards, word-to-picture matching, sentence building, copying, writing);
- more time spent in overlearning and reviewing new material at each stage;
- systematic teaching of phonic knowledge and word-attack skills;
- explicit instruction in reading comprehension strategies;
- daily expressive writing activities with guidance and feedback;
- handwriting skills taught alongside reading and writing activities;
- improved self-esteem through counselling, praise, encouragement, increased success, and recognition of personal progress.

In order to plan instruction to meet these needs it is necessary to tailor the programme to match the student's current strengths and weaknesses. It is therefore important to find out as much as possible about the student's existing attitude, knowledge, skills and strategies.

Planning intervention from assessment data

The starting point for any literacy intervention programme should be the results from an assessment of the child's current abilities, indicating the stage of reading development he or she has reached (Mariotti and Homan 2005). The assessment need not involve the use of detailed or complicated tests, nor should it be a lengthy procedure. The teacher is basically seeking answers to the following five key questions:

- What can the student already do without help?
- What skills and strategies has the child developed?
- What can the child do if given a little prompting and guidance?
- What gaps exist in the child's previous learning?
- What does the child need to be taught next in order to make good progress?

According to Stanford and Reeves (2005), assessment is necessary before, during and after a teaching programme is implemented. Such assessment may involve testing, observation, or analysis of work samples. When feasible, the results from assessment procedures should be shared with the learner.

Figure 8.1 summarises the key steps involved in implementing an informal assessment procedure leading to programme planning for an individual learner. The outcome of such a procedure may be the writing of an individual education plan (IEP); or the data may simply guide the teacher's daily planning without the need for an IEP. The procedure is described here in relation to reading difficulties, but the same steps, and the same five key questions, are applicable to informal assessment and planning for individual support in any area of the curriculum.

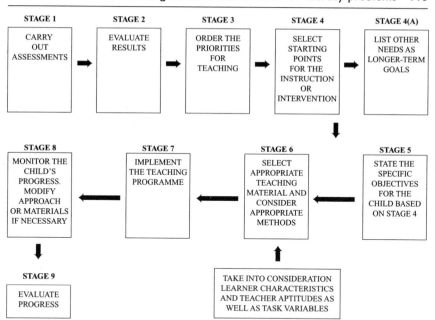

Figure 8.1 Assessment and planning model

The nine stages in Figure 8.1 may be interpreted thus:

Stage 1 involves observation of the student at work, together with possible use of relevant checklists or tests for particular skills (sight vocabulary, phonic knowledge, spelling). The most useful procedure is to listen to the student read from an appropriate text, noting the strategies used and the errors made. A running record of errors, self-corrections, and requests for help can be made if required. Other aspects of reading performance are also informally appraised such as motivation, confidence, fluency, and dependency on adult assistance.

Stage 2 involves analysing the information obtained from Stage 1 and answering the first three diagnostic questions referred to above.

Stage 3 is the identification of the most serious gaps evident in the student's prior learning. For example, gaps may occur in sight vocabulary, knowledge of less-common orthographic units, or use of contextual cues. Teaching to fill these gaps needs to be given high priority in any remedial intervention.

Stage 4 requires the teacher to decide the short-term goals for the intervention, based on data analysed at Stages 2 and 3. What will be the starting points for intervention? Where does the student require most help? Immediate goals would be written in the IEP. Longer-term goals would be recorded for attention at a later date.

Stage 5 involves the design of some specific short-term performance objectives. The advantage of being precise with objectives is that they are to be used as the basis for accurate assessment of learning, and all persons involved in the child's programme are aware of exactly what is to be achieved.

Stage 6 requires the selection of appropriate teaching resources (books, kits, games, computer software, other print materials) to assist in working towards the stated objectives. Careful consideration needs to be given to the most appropriate method of working with this student, based on knowledge of his or her learning characteristics (motivation, interests, concentration span). A decision must be made concerning how the programme will be delivered (e.g. by the teacher; by classroom assistant; through peer tutoring; parent tutoring; computer-assisted learning).

Stage 7 involves implementation of the teaching programme with sufficient intensity and duration to have some impact on the student's learning. The programme may be operated within the whole-class setting if possible, rather than in isolation; and it should be geared as closely as possible to the mainstream curriculum. However, it may be necessary at times to provide individual or small-group tuition in a withdrawal situation, particularly in the case of students with learning disabilities. A combination of in-class and withdrawal may be required.

Stage 8 involves regular and frequent assessment of the student's responses to the programme while it is in operation. It is important to monitor the effectiveness of the teaching methods and materials. This is achieved through on-going (formative) evaluation of the student's performance.

Stage 9 involves assessing how much improvement has occurred in the student's motivation, knowledge, skills, strategies and confidence on completion of the programme. This summative evaluation is carried out at the end of the teaching block and is linked directly with the overall goals and the objectives generated at Stage 5. If appropriate, the programme continues with new objectives and changes to materials.

Lerner and Kline (2006) describe a very similar model for planning, implementing and evaluating a support programme. They refer to it as a 'clinical teaching cycle', having most to offer in the context of individual intensive tutoring.

General principles of assessment

Learning difficulties are rarely due only to factors within the student, so assessment must also involve consideration of the total situation in which the learner operates. It is important to consider the curriculum (level of difficulty, relevance to the child's age and interests). It is also necessary to consider the teaching methods being used, the type of learning involved, the instructional goals, the physical environment in which the child is being taught, and the quality of the relationship between the child, the teacher (or tutor) and the peer group. Learning difficulty usually stems from a complex interaction among all these variables, and effective intervention may require the teacher to manipulate any or all of these variables.

When working with and assessing a student it is important to observe his or her manner of approach to the tasks as well as the responses being given. For example, has the child given a particular answer after careful thought or was it an impulsive guess? Is the child hesitant because he or she is wary of the adult and unwilling to take a risk? Does he or she show genuine interest in the tasks and activities you are presenting? Does he or she self-correct if an error is made?

Diagnostic assessment is referred to as either formal or informal. The 'formal' diagnosis usually implies that published tests (reading attainment tests or reading diagnostic tests) are used to obtain specific information about a learner's current skills or knowledge in certain selected areas, such as comprehension, word recognition, phonic knowledge and spelling. Sometimes particular sub-skills are assessed, such as phonemic awareness, visual discrimination or short-term auditory memory. Formal assessment may be carried out for a whole class simultaneously, for example, by the use of pencil-and-paper group testing. At other times formal assessment involves the careful and detailed testing of one child, using standardised or criterion-referenced tests. Formal assessment can be useful in indicating quickly where current achievement stops and new learning needs begin. The results from formal assessment usually need to be supplemented with information from informal testing, such as observation, classroom records, discussions with parents.

Informal diagnosis involves procedures such as direct observation of learners in action and an examination of what they produce during a lesson. Informal assessment in reading includes, for example, listening to a child read aloud from a class book and detecting the presence or absence of particular strategies for word attack, use of context, prediction, and comprehension. General fluency and expression can also be appraised. The use of teacher-made informal reading inventories is of value for this purpose. The inventory comprises photocopied sample paragraphs, graded from very easy to more complex, selected from books available in the classroom. A child's level of success on the inventory will also help the teacher match him or her to a book at an appropriate readability level. For independent reading the passage should be read with 95 per cent accuracy. For material to be used within an instructional programme the success rate should be at least 90 per cent. Material with an error rate of 15 per cent or more is considered to be too difficult (frustration level). Performance on the reading inventory will also indicate the child's general approach (e.g. slow but accurate; hasty and careless; hesitant and unwilling to guess).

In the following sections, additional suggestions are made for assessing students who are at various levels of reading proficiency. The lists are not prescriptive; it is not expected that a teacher would need to find answers to all the questions. Relevant items can be selected according to the student's characteristics.

Assessing a non-reader

If an individual, regardless of age or degree of disability, appears to be a non-reader it is worth considering some of the following issues:

- Can the student concentrate on a learning task and attend to the teacher for long enough to benefit from instruction; or is he or she too distractible or hyperactive?
- Is the student capable of matching identical letters (visual discrimination)?
- Can the student identify speech sounds (phonemes) at the beginning, middle, and end of spoken words (see also auditory discrimination below)?
- Has the student developed 'word concept' – an understanding that words in print are units separated by spaces?
- Does the student have concepts of 'a sound' and 'a letter'?
- Does the student have an awareness of the left-to-right direction in written language?
- Does the student recognise any words by sight (e.g. own name; environmental signs)?
- Can the student complete picture-to-word matching activities correctly after a brief period of instruction?
- Can the student succeed in a simple learning task involving sight recognition of three words taught from flashcards without picture clues (e.g. 'my', 'key' and 'book')?
- Does the student know the names or sounds associated with any letters?

If the student appears to have very poor phonic knowledge, it is necessary to check in more detail his or her level of phonological awareness. For example, auditory discrimination, auditory analysis (segmentation) and phoneme blending are regarded as key aspects of phonological awareness. It is claimed that these core abilities are essential if children are to learn the alphabetic principle easily. Specific training in abilities such as rhyming, alliteration, segmentation, blending, and identification of sounds within words usually results in improvement in early reading and spelling (Moore *et al.* 2005).

Auditory discrimination

Can the child discriminate between similar but not identical words when these are presented orally as word-pairs (e.g. mouse–mouth; cat–cap; money–monkey)? Do 'dog' and 'doll' begin with the same sound? What is that sound? How about 'dog' and 'fog'? Teachers can devise their own word lists for this purpose.

Auditory analysis

Can the child segment familiar spoken words into their component sounds or syllables? The simplest level at which to begin is at 'onset and rime' division (e.g. st-op; tr-uck; sw-im). Moving on to longer words, can the child say a word like 'remember' as three units, re-mem-ber? It may be necessary first to give some practice in 'stretching' a word in this way so that the child understands what is required.

Sound blending

Can the child synthesise sounds in order to pronounce a given word (e.g. cr-isp, st-o-p, m-i-l-k)? This is a listening activity, not a reading task. The child does not see the word in print. The following simple test is useful for assessment of this blending skill:

Say: 'I am going to say some words very slowly so that you can hear each sound. I want you to tell me what the word is. If I say "i-n" you say "in". If I say "d-o-g" you say ...?' Sound the phonemes at the rate of about one each second. Discontinue after five consecutive failures.

i-f	g-o-t	sh-o-p	c-r-u-s-t
a-t	m-e-n	s-t-e-p	b-l-a-ck
u-p	b-e-d	l-o-s-t	f-l-a-sh
o-n	c-a-t	j-u-m-p	c-l-o-ck
a-m	d-i-g	t-r-u-ck	s-p-i-ll

Assessment for a student above beginner level

For the child who is not a non-reader and has a few functional skills, the following areas may yield useful information to answer the diagnostic questions.

Basic sight vocabulary

What can the child already do in terms of recognising the most commonly occurring words in print? Many vocabulary lists exist for the assessment of sight vocabulary (e.g. Gunning 2001). See also Chapter 9.

Phonic knowledge

The student's knowledge of letter-to-sound correspondences can be checked, either using a test sheet or by presenting each phonic unit on a separate card. Phonic knowledge can also be checked with older students by dictating phonemes and requiring the student to write the appropriate letter or letters representing that sound. Single letters, digraphs and blends should be checked. Examples are provided in Chapter 9.

Word-attack skills

When reading aloud, does the child attempt to build an unfamiliar word without being instructed to do so – for example, by sounding each letter, by identifying component parts of words and sounding out each part, or by 'peeling off' the suffix or prefix (Manset-Williamson and Nelson 2005)? If not, can the child do this when he or she is encouraged to try? Has the child developed any phonic skills? In particular, does the child know all the common single-letter sounds, digraphs, blends, prefixes and suffixes? Can the child divide a phonetically regular word into component syllables?

Miscues and use of context

When the child is reading aloud from age-appropriate material, what errors are made? Do the incorrect words conform to the meaning of the sentence or are they totally out of keeping with the message? Does the child make any use of cues such as initial letter sound? Does the child tend to self-correct when errors are made in order to restore meaning?

Comprehension

Informal questions can be asked after a student has read a passage silently or aloud. The questions should not be restricted to the factual level (literal comprehension) but should also probe for understanding at higher levels of inference and critical interpretation: 'Why did the man in the story act in that way?' 'When the lady suggested they look for the goods in another shop, was she being helpful or rude?' 'What do you think they should do next?'

Exercises using the *cloze procedure* are useful in both testing and developing comprehension and contextual cueing. A passage of some 100 to 150 words is selected and approximately every fifth or sixth word is deleted leaving a gap. Can the child read the passage and provide a word in each case that conforms to the meaning of the passage and the grammatical structure of the sentence? Cloze materials used for teaching can be drawn from any subject area; and cloze exercises can be attempted by individuals or by groups of students (Eells 2000). An example of cloze is provided in Chapter 9.

A useful instrument for evaluating reading rate, accuracy and comprehension in students aged 6 to 13 years is the *Neale Analysis of Reading Ability* (NARA), available in separate editions with norms for British (1997) or Australian (1999) populations. In addition to assessing comprehension, sub-tests in NARA allow for appraisal of a beginner's skills in auditory discrimination, blending and simple spelling. An analysis sheet is provided to facilitate the recording and classification of errors.

Assessing the student who has reached a reading plateau

Some children appear to reach a temporary plateau in reading development at or about a reading age of 8 to 9 years. Possibly the child has not yet recognised that certain letter clusters within words represent pronounceable 'orthographic units', and they will either make random guesses at unfamiliar words or will refuse to attempt words containing these units. Recognising letter clusters quickly is significantly related to speed and accuracy in word recognition, and thus also to comprehension (Neuhaus et al. 2006). The implication is that students who appear to have reached a temporary plateau may need to be taught to use larger letter-groups for decoding, rather than single letters. For details of basic phonic units see Chapter 9.

These students may also need additional practice to build up a more extensive sight vocabulary. Inefficient phonic skills can also result in a failure to add new words to sight vocabulary because of difficulty in decoding the words when first encountered. Poor progress can also be due to lack of regular reading practice.

Many of the assessment techniques covered in the previous section may uncover possible areas of difficulty in these children. The following procedures are also helpful at this level.

Error analysis

With children who have reached a reading plateau, error analysis can be extremely valuable in pinpointing specific weaknesses in the child's current reading skills. When employing error analysis it is usual to listen to the student read aloud on several different occasions, using material that is reasonably challenging but not at frustration level. The performance can be recorded on audiotape for later analysis. Errors can be coded on a *running record* sheet, and classified as: self-correction (SC); appeal for help (A); teacher intervention (TTA if the child is told to 'try that again'; or T for 'told' if the word is supplied by the teacher); substitutions (S – the substituted word is written above the text word); omissions (a cross drawn above the word omitted); repetition (underline word each time the child repeats it). Attempts at decoding a word should also be transcribed phonetically. The procedure also allows for quantitative evaluations to be made leading to the calculation of error rate, self-correction rate and dependency rate. These measures can be used to compare a student's performance before and after an intervention programme. Useful information on the use of running records can be found in Mariotti and Homan (2005).

Affective factors

With a student who has reached a plateau, it is vitally important to consider affective as well as cognitive factors. For example, has the student developed a negative couldn't-care-less attitude towards reading, avoiding the task whenever possible? Does the student experience any enjoyment in reading? Is the material in the book in keeping with the student's real interests? Is the working relationship between the student and the teacher (or tutor) a positive one? Does the student respond positively to extrinsic motivation (rewards)? Where difficulties are detected in these areas it is important to attempt to bring about change if possible. Merely concentrating on the skill aspect of reading will do little to modify the student's attitude or feeling of self-efficacy.

Additional factors to consider when students are not successful

Readability of the text

For the student who has reached a temporary plateau in reading it is important to consider the complexity of the material the child is attempting to read. Has he or she selected books that are at frustration level? Reading skills will not advance if the child is constantly faced with text that is too difficult, and lack of success can reduce motivation and confidence. Sperling (2006) stresses the importance of careful selection of reading material, particularly textbooks and other print resources used in different subject areas such as science, social studies, and environmental education. If students are to learn from these media the text must connect not only with their prior knowledge but also with their vocabulary level and reading skills.

Readability is influenced by much more than the number of difficult words. The ease with which a text is read is also related to the reader's familiarity with the topic, the style of writing, syntax, sentence length, and even the size of print and format of the pages. The most useful index of readability is a student's actual performance on the text. The simplest check for matching book to student is to apply the 'five finger test'. Select a passage of approximately 100 words from the book and ask the child to read aloud. Each time an error is made the teacher folds one finger into the palm of the hand. If the teacher runs out of fingers before the student reaches the end of the passage, the material is too difficult for independent reading (the error rate is more than 5 per cent).

Selecting appropriate reading material

When selecting texts for students to read, teachers should consider the following points:

- Is the topic within the experience of the students?
- Is it meaningful and relevant to the age and interest level of the students?
- Is the book itself attractive and appealing?
- Is the language used in the text natural and easy to predict?
- Are there many unfamiliar words?
- Are the sentences complex?
- Are there many useful contextual and pictorial clues?
- Will this type of text expand the students' experience of different genres?

Intervention programmes

Intervention programmes are based on an underlying belief that reading failure is preventable for nearly all children if intensive additional teaching is provided early for those who need it (Morris and Slavin 2003). Examples of established early intervention programmes are *Reading Recovery* and *Success for All*.

Reading Recovery

Reading Recovery is an early intervention programme first developed in New Zealand and now used in many other parts of the world. Children identified as having reading difficulties after one year in school are placed in the programme to receive intensive tuition tailored to their needs. This is achieved through instruction based on a combination of whole language and skills-based teaching principles. The children receive the 30-minute daily tuition for approximately 15 to 20 weeks.

Evidence has accumulated to indicate that *Reading Recovery* can be effective in raising young children's reading achievement and confidence (e.g. Ng 2006; Reading Recovery Council of North America 2002). It is claimed that the programme is highly successful with the lowest-performing children in Year 1, and at least 80 per cent of children who undergo the full series of lessons can then read at the class average level or better. Evidence also suggests that children who participate in *Reading Recovery* are less likely to be referred later for remedial support (O'Connor and Simic 2002), although data from the Ministry of Education in New Zealand indicate that some 8 per cent of children there still have to be referred for longer-term specialist support (Ng 2006).

A typical *Reading Recovery* lesson includes seven activities:

- re-reading of familiar books;
- independent reading of a book introduced the previous day;
- letter-identification activities, using plastic letters in the early stages;
- writing of a dictated or prepared story;
- sentence building and reconstruction from the story;
- introduction of a new book;
- guided reading of the new book.

The texts selected are designed to give the child a high success rate. Frequent re-reading of the familiar stories boosts confidence and fluency. Optimum use is made of the available time and students are kept fully on-task. Teachers keep 'running records' of children's oral reading performance and use these to target accurately the knowledge or strategies a child still needs to learn. Some attention is given to listening for sounds within words and practising phonic skills in context.

Reading Recovery is not without its critics. Elbaum *et al.* (2000) indicate that up to 30 per cent of children enrolled in the intervention do not complete the programme and do not therefore improve. Other observers question the reported success rate of those who do complete all sessions, and suggest that any gains made in the programme are not always maintained over time. It has also been observed that skills and motivation acquired in the *Reading Recovery* lessons do not necessarily spill over into better classroom performance, possibly because the reading materials provided in the regular setting are not so carefully matched to the child's ability level and the child receives much less individual support. Other criticisms relate to the labour-intense nature of the intervention that places strain on school resources.

Obvious difficulties associated with *Reading Recovery* include the need to organise time in the school day for the child to be taught individually, and the need to provide appropriately trained personnel to give the daily tuition. Cost effectiveness remains an unresolved issue, but Iversen *et al.* (2005) provide evidence to show that children can be taught in pairs without any detrimental effect on their progress. To achieve the same amount of individualised attention under those conditions it takes a little more time, but these researchers report that by increasing instructional time by about a quarter, *Reading Recovery* teachers can double the number of students served without making any sacrifices in outcomes.

Despite the criticisms, a review of research on the effects of *Reading Recovery* concludes:

> A common pattern in several studies using both Reading Recovery and standardized measures is that Reading Recovery students who have successfully completed the program are just within the average band in second grade, but move to within the average band in third and fourth grades, continuing to progress and maintain their gains.
>
> (Smith-Burke 2001: 229)

Several modified versions of *Reading Recovery* have been implemented in various districts in the US, and some schools have attempted to integrate basic principles from the programme into their whole-school approach to early literacy (e.g. Miles *et al.* 2004). It is probable that volunteer helpers used within Learning Assistance Programmes (LAP) in Australian schools would improve the quality and impact of their assistance to individual children if they utilised teaching strategies similar to those in *Reading Recovery* under the teacher's direction.

Details of the *Reading Recovery* programme, including instructional strategies, practical ideas and use of time, are given in Dame Marie Clay's books *The Early Detection of Reading Difficulties* (1985) and *Reading Recovery: A Guidebook for Teachers in Training* (1993). For summaries of research see Reading Recovery Council of North America (2002) or Forbes and Briggs (2003). An Internet search entering 'Reading Recovery' will yield many sources of information.

Success for All

Success for All, an early intervention programme designed in the US by Robert Slavin and his associates, has also been adopted for use in several other countries. It involves intensive one-to-one teaching using teachers or paraprofessionals to help improve the literacy learning rate for at-risk and socially disadvantaged children (Slavin and Madden 2001). Lessons operate daily for 20 minutes. One unique feature of *Success for All* is that junior classes throughout the school usually regroup for reading, with children going to different classrooms based on their own ability level. This arrangement necessitates block timetabling, an organisational pattern that some schools find difficult to adopt.

Chan and Dally (2000: 226) describe the intervention thus:

> The tutoring process in *Success for All* is similar to the *Reading Recovery* program in that its first emphasis is on reading meaningful texts. Initial reading experiences are followed by phonics instruction which provides systematic strategies for cracking the reading code. Emphasis is also given to strategies to assist and monitor comprehension, such as teaching students to stop at the end of a page and ask, 'Did I understand what I just read?'

In an attempt to overcome the reported lack of generalisation and transfer of skills, said to be found with *Reading Recovery*, the *Success for All* teacher also participates in the mainstream reading programme and assists with reading lessons in the regular classroom. This helps to ensure that the one-to-one tutoring is closely linked to the mainstream curriculum, not divorced from it. Slavin and Madden (2001: 9) state that:

> In general the tutors support students' success in the regular reading curriculum rather than teaching different objectives. For example, the tutor generally works with a student on the same story and concepts being read and taught in the regular reading class. However, tutors seek to identify learning problems and use different strategies to teach the same skills. They also teach metacognitive skills beyond those taught in the classroom program.

Research evidence in general has been very supportive of *Success for All* as an effective intervention model (Morrow and Woo 2001), but some observers question its longer-term benefits. A few students with learning disabilities appear to require even more direct and intensive instruction. Allington (2001) remarks that even though students in *Success for All* schools do make progress, they still tend to be well behind national and state averages for reading achievement. For additional information on this programme see Slavin (2004) and Slavin and Madden (2001).

Literacy Hour

In the UK, the Literacy Hour emerged as a component of the *National Literacy Strategy* (DfEE 1998). It should be noted that a similar literacy strategy was introduced to schools by the commonwealth government in Australia (DETYA 1998); and several Australian states are applying the notion of a daily literacy hour. It is believed that a dedicated hour per day for literacy work ensures that all children have adequate opportunities to learn. One hour devoted to literacy ensures that the teaching of reading and writing receives appropriate time and attention. The children are expected to play an active part in each lesson by discussing, asking questions, contributing ideas, and explaining their thinking to the class.

The recommended instructional approach for the Literacy Hour tends to be fairly teacher-directed and embodies many sound principles of effective teaching and time-management. The Literacy Hour, if implemented well, is of great potential value to students with learning difficulties because of the focused teaching, meaningful practice, and frequent reinforcement. The children do not spend time engaging in boring drills and exercises but rather they are exposed each day to a wide range of opportunities to think, read, write, talk and interact with interesting literature. In particular, strategies such as shared-book experience, shared writing and guided reading are strongly recommended for use.

The suggested structure for the hour is:

- shared-text experience with the whole class (approximately 15 minutes);
- activities involving differentiated reading and writing work at sentence and word level – organised as group work or individualised assignments (approximately 35 minutes);
- plenary session with the whole class (reporting and discussion) (approximately 10 minutes).

The National Literacy Strategy and the Literacy Hour have been the focus of a number of research studies since their introduction in 1998 (e.g. Eke and Lee 2004; Wall 2004; Wallace 2005). Evidence seems to suggest that although the National Literacy Strategy has clearly had beneficial effects in terms of student learning in most schools, teachers have not found it easy to adopt the interactive whole-class teaching approach officially recommended for the Literacy Hour. There is an indication that some teachers still lack the pedagogical knowledge and skills required to implement the literacy strategy in the most effective manner

– although they may not fully recognise this weakness in themselves (Earl *et al*. 2003). There is also a tension between the need to operate the session smoothly at whole-class level, and at the same time attempt to address individual needs by differentiating tasks and adjusting the pace of the lesson. In an attempt to overcome some of the problems in gearing the level of work to children' abilities, some schools organise the children into ability groups for the Literacy Hour, instead of having them in mixed-ability groups. Wall (2004) discusses this option, and recommends that additional research be conducted to determine the impact of such regrouping arrangements on children's self-esteem and motivation.

Meeting children's special educational needs in the Literacy Hour remains problematic (Miller *et al*. 2003). It became clear early on that students with learning difficulties still require additional support within and beyond the Literacy Hour if they are to make adequate progress. In 2002, the DfES issued additional guidelines for teachers to attempt to address these concerns.

Excellent practical advice on implementing the Literacy Hour can be found in Berger and Morris (2001) or Smith (2004). For a comprehensive perspective on the National Literacy Strategy in the UK see Earl *et al*. (2003), Hall (2004) and DfES (2002).

Tutoring

In Chapter 6 mention was made of the value of peer tutoring. It is worth reiterating here that the effectiveness of peer tutoring for academic improvement is well documented (e.g. Heron *et al*. 2006). The use of a partner or peer tutor has beneficial effects for students with learning difficulties in terms of increased time-on-task, facilitated practice with feedback, and improved reading performance (Gest and Gest 2005).

It is usually necessary to provide peer tutors with some guidance on how best to support the tutee. In particular they may need help in breaking a learning task down into easier steps, giving positive corrective feedback, listening more and talking less, praising and encouraging the tutee.

Parents can also be of great value as tutors, but they too may need to be taught how to be supportive rather than critical or 'didactic'. In particular, parent volunteers can help in literacy programmes by listening to children read to increase fluency and confidence (Erion and Ronka 2005).

General principles for literacy intervention

In recent years educators have discovered much about the essential ingredients for successful tutoring for learning difficulties in reading (Chandler-Olcott and Hinchman 2005; Morris 2005; Swanson *et al*. 2003). It seems from firsthand observation and from research studies that the following general principles need to be incorporated in any form of intervention:

- At-risk children need to be taught *individually* for part of the time, graduating later to *small groups* and in-class support, before independent progress in the regular class is viable.
- Children experiencing difficulties in learning must spend considerably *more time* receiving help and guidance from teachers and parents.
- *Daily instruction* will achieve much more than twice-weekly intervention.
- *Frequent successful practice* is essential to build skills to a high level of automaticity, and to strengthen children's confidence to learn.
- The instruction provided in intervention programmes must be of a very *high quality* and delivered with *clarity and intensity*.
- As well as attempting to improve basic academic skills, early intervention must also focus on the *correction of any negative behaviours*, such as poor attention to task or task avoidance that are impairing the student's progress.
- Although withdrawing a student for individual or group work can achieve a great deal, it is also essential that the *regular classroom programme be adjusted* to allow at-risk children a greater degree of success in that setting. Failure to adapt the regular class programme frequently results in loss of achievement gains when the student no longer receives assistance.
- Children must perceive a *genuine and realistic reason* for engaging in reading, writing and spelling activities. There is a danger that those with severe reading problems may receive a remedial programme containing too many decontextualised skill-building exercises.
- The *texts* used with at-risk children must be carefully selected to ensure a *very high success rate*. Repetitive and predictable texts are particularly helpful in the early stages.
- Repeated reading of the same text seems to *increase fluency* and *build confidence*.
- For students with reading disability, *training in phonemic awareness, letter knowledge and decoding* is almost always necessary.
- *Multi-sensory and multi-media* approaches often help children with learning disabilities assimilate and remember particular units such as letter–sound correspondences and sight words.
- Children should be *explicitly taught* the knowledge, skills and strategies necessary for identifying words, extracting meaning from text, spelling and writing.
- *Writing* should feature as much as reading in early literacy interventions. Concepts about print can be acquired through writing as well as reading; and a great deal of phonic knowledge can be developed through helping children work out the sounds they need to use when spelling words.
- The use of *other tutors* (aides, volunteers, peers, parents) can be very helpful. These individuals need to be taught how to function in the tutor-supporter role.

- Maximum progress occurs when parents or others can provide *additional support and practice* outside school hours.
- Children should be provided with appropriate *books they can read independently at home*.

Teaching procedures in successful intervention programmes draw on what is known about effective teaching, in particular:

- creation of a supportive learning environment;
- presentation of the learning task in easy steps;
- resource materials provided at an appropriate readability level;
- direct teaching of task-approach strategies;
- clear modelling and demonstrations by the teacher or tutor;
- provision for much guided practice with feedback;
- efficient use of available time;
- close monitoring of the child's progress;
- reteaching particular skills where necessary;
- independent practice and application;
- very frequent revision of previously taught knowledge and skills.

In the following chapter attention will be given to the essential knowledge, skills and strategies that need to be taught to children who are experiencing difficulties in learning to read.

Further reading

Barr, R., Blachowicz, C., Bates, A. and Kaufman, B. (2007) *Reading Diagnosis for Teachers* (5th edn), Boston, MA: Pearson-Allyn and Bacon.

Crawley, S.J. and Merrit, K. (2004) *Remediating Reading Difficulties* (4th edn), Boston, MA: McGraw-Hill.

Daly, E.J., Chafouleas, S. and Skinner, C.H. (2005) *Interventions for Reading Problems: Designing and Evaluating Effective Strategies*, New York: Guilford Press.

DfES (Britain) (2005) *Raising Standards in Reading: Achieving Children's Targets*. Available at: http://www.standards.dfes.gov.uk/primary/publications/literacy/1160815/pns_nls131705stnds_read.pdf (accessed 15 March 2006).

Gaskins, I.W. (2005) *Success with Struggling Readers*, New York: Guilford.

Glynn, T., Wearmouth, J. and Berryman, M. (2006) *Supporting Students with Literacy Difficulties*, Maidenhead: Open University Press.

Gunning, T.G. (2006) *Assessing and Correcting Reading and Writing Difficulties* (3rd edn), Boston, MA: Pearson-Allyn and Bacon.

Jennings, J.H., Caldwell, J.S. and Lerner, J.W. (2006) *Reading Problems: Assessment and Teaching Strategies* (5th edn), Boston, MA: Pearson-Allyn and Bacon.

Mariotti, A.S. and Homan, S.P. (2005) *Linking Reading Assessment to Instruction* (4th edn), Mahwah, NJ: Erlbaum.

McCormick, S. (2007) *Instructing Students who have Literacy Problems* (5th edn), Upper Saddle River, NJ: Pearson-Prentice Hall.

Minskoff, E. (2005) *Teaching Reading to Struggling Learners*, Baltimore, MD: Brookes.

Reutzel, D.R. and Cooter, R.B. (2007) *Strategies for Reading Assessment and Instruction: Helping Every Child Succeed* (3rd edn), Upper Saddle River, NJ: Pearson-Prentice Hall.

Chapter 9

Strategies for overcoming or preventing reading difficulties

If students participate in separate literacy instruction [it] should utilize effective, evidence-based practices, be very focused and prescriptive, and be coordinated with literacy activities in the classroom.

(Janney and Snell 2004: 97)

Following the assessment of a learner's abilities as suggested in the previous chapter, it should be possible to plan appropriate starting points for intervention. This chapter provides some additional strategies and techniques suitable for use at various stages of reading development from beginner to post-secondary school level and with students who may have disabilities. These additional strategies might be included within the general language and reading programme of the regular classroom, or used to match the specific needs of individual students engaged in individual or small-group tutoring sessions.

Pre-reading and early reading experiences

For most children a carefully structured pre-reading programme is unnecessary. Their previous experiences before school and in kindergarten have provided them with an understanding of what reading is all about. In many cases early childhood experiences will have equipped them with the required perceptual, linguistic, and cognitive skills ready to begin reading. For a few children, particularly those with significant intellectual impairment or perceptual difficulties, the situation is rather different; for them it may be necessary to provide specific activities to facilitate their entry into reading. The readiness activities should be clearly and directly linked to the language programme of the classroom, not something that is done out of context. For example, games and activities involving word matching, visual memory and visual discrimination should use words arising from stories the children have just heard, or words that are personally relevant and meaningful to the children.

For a very few children (particularly those with impaired vision or with neurological problems) visual discrimination may need to be the focus of some early reading activities. In order to begin to recognise words by sight a child needs to attend to key features of words, such as initial letters or sequences of letters (Heilman 2006). Undoubtedly, one of the most valuable activities at this level is sentence building. At any age level, a learner who is beginning to read should be given the opportunity to construct and reconstruct meaningful sentences from word cards. This sentence-building procedure is valuable for assessment and as a teaching technique. A child's ability to construct, reconstruct and transform sentences reveals much about his or her language competence, sequencing ability, and memory for words. Sentence building can be incorporated into the language-experience approach described in Chapter 7.

For students with intellectual disability, word-to-picture matching is a useful activity in the beginning stage of word recognition. Colourful pictures can be cut from magazines and catalogues, or the child's own drawings and paintings can be used. Words and captions suggested by the child are printed on slips of card. Teacher and child say the word together. The child places the card on or next to the appropriate picture and reads the word. The activity can be used with groups of children, with the pictorial material and words displayed on an easel. This activity is valuable for holding children's attention, ensuring their active participation, and for establishing word concept and letter concept. It leads naturally and easily to both shared-book experience and language-experience approach.

If very young children or older children with disabilities such as cerebral palsy or traumatic brain injury are experiencing problems with visual perception it may be necessary to begin at an even simpler level. For example, activities can be used involving the fitting of regular and irregular shapes into form-boards, matching and sorting simple shapes, and feeling these shapes hidden within a puzzle box or bag where the child can handle but not see them. Later the activities can be reintroduced using small plastic letters of the alphabet and numerals.

Building sight vocabulary

Children need to acquire, as rapidly as possible, a bank of words they know automatically by sight. Much of a child's learning in this area arises naturally from daily reading and writing experiences. The more frequently a child encounters and uses a word the more likely it is that the word will be retained in the long-term memory. Some students, particularly those with reading difficulties, may need to have sight words practised more systematically. The use of flashcards can be of great value. Playing games or participating in other activities involving the reading of important words on flashcards can help provide the repetition necessary for children to read words with a high degree of automaticity. Immediate recognition of these words contributes significantly to fluent reading and comprehension of text.

Teachers often remark that children with learning difficulties can recognise a word one day but appear to have forgotten it completely by the next day. This problem can be explained in part by what learning theory tells us concerning the acquisition of new knowledge. New information is not necessarily fully assimilated on first exposure. Acquisition of a correct association, say, between the spoken word and the printed word-pattern on the page, involves two distinct stages. The first stage is that of *recognising* the printed word when someone else pronounces the word. For example, with word-cards spread on the table, the teacher might say, 'Kathryn, point to the word "London". Dennis, pick up the word "caravan". Show me the word "castle".' The second stage involves the child's *recall* of the word from long-term memory without prompting. The teacher shows the child a word on a card and asks, 'What is this word, Mary?' Children with learning problems usually need much more practice at the recognition stage before they can easily recall the word from memory.

Many writers have produced lists of words, arranged in frequency of usage, beginning with the most commonly used words (e.g. Gunning 2001; Leech *et al.* 2001). The list below contains the first sixty most commonly occurring words derived from various lists:

a I in is it of the to on and he she was are
had him his her am but we not yes no all said
my they with you for big if so did get boy look
at an come do got girl go us from little when as
that by have this but which or were would what

Some high-frequency sight words are often confused and misread by beginning readers and students with reading difficulties. Sight words often confused include:

were where when went with want which what
here there their they them then than

Teachers of reading and others involved in preparing or assessing reading materials for children will find the book *Word Frequencies in Written and Spoken English* (Leech *et al.* 2001) a valuable reference.

Phonological awareness

Aural and oral language enrichment activities form the basis of beginning reading programmes. Encouraging a liking for stories, establishing familiarity with language patterns, training in listening, and discussions based on the stories are important features of approaches such as shared-book experience. For many children, these experiences, together with their daily exposure to language, will develop the necessary awareness that spoken words are made up from separate sounds (phonemes). Careful listening enables us to identify those sounds, and recognise that some words contain sound units that rhyme.

It has been shown conclusively that auditory skills play a major role in the process of learning to read (Lane *et al.* 2005; Nicholson 2006). Research in recent years has confirmed that difficulties in learning to read are more likely to be related to problems with phonological processing than to problems with visual perception. Students with hearing loss and those with a specific language disorder or dyslexia are most at risk.

Progress in reading beyond the initial stage of building up a basic sight vocabulary using whole-word recognition is totally dependent upon the development of phonic skills. Acquisition of phonic skills is in turn dependent upon a child's phonemic awareness. Understanding the alphabetic principle requires the child to recognise that spoken words are made from separate sounds (Eldredge 2005). Phonemic awareness is thus the foundation for phonics. Phonological processes are involved to a very significant extent also in spelling. The most important phonological skills appear to be auditory discrimination (including the detection of rhyme), auditory analysis and phoneme blending.

Auditory discrimination and rhyme

Auditory discrimination involves the ability to detect similarities and differences among speech sounds – for example, to know that /f/ sound and /th/ sound are different, as in 'finger' and 'thumb'; or that 'church' and 'children' both begin with the same /ch/ sound. To help children who seem to have difficulty with auditory discrimination a teacher might find it useful to collect pictures of objects from catalogues and colour-supplements to use in games requiring careful listening. The pictures may be set out in pairs and the child must quickly touch one picture when the word is called: for example, 'pear' (pictures show 'bear' and 'pear'), 'three' (pictures show '3' and 'tree'). Activities can also use pictures of objects to be identified by the initial sound (bride = /br/; bus = /b/; train = /tr/). It is important to check children's accurate pronunciation of words containing the target sounds.

The ability to detect rhyming words is also considered important for learning to read and spell. It may be that understanding rhyme makes it easier later to recognise and use the letter groups that represent those rhymes (for example, /ent/: bent, sent, tent, rent, went, lent, dent). 'Word families' are often constructed based on common letter groups representing the rhyming units. Attention to rhyme and the use of word families can be incorporated in all beginning reading approaches.

Onset-rime training activities can be devised to help children begin to understand sounds within words: for example, in the word *stick*, /st/ is the onset and /ick/ is the rime. Being able to break single-syllable words into onset and rime units is the starting point for more demanding word analysis and segmentation. Rime units are the basis for many 'word families' such as *stick, lick, sick, trick, kick, pick, wick*. Glass *et al.* (2000) identify the following common rime units that can be used to build more than 650 one-syllable words:

-ay, -ill, -at, -am, -ag, -ack, -ank, -ick, -ell, -ot, -ing, -ap, -unk, -ail, -ain, -eed,
-y, -out, -ug, -op, -in, -an, -est, -ink, -ow, -ew, -ore, -ed, -ab, -ob, -ock, -ake,
-ine, -ight, -im, -uck, -um, -ust

Students with severe reading difficulties appear to have great difficulty in mastering these larger phonic units that represent pronounceable parts of words (sub-word orthographic units). Practice in onset and rime activities may help these students grasp the value of processing letter groups rather than single letters.

Auditory analysis (segmentation)

Some of the activities listed above under auditory discrimination have already included a simple level of auditory analysis. The next level of auditory analysis can be taught by spending a little time taking words apart into their component sounds or syllables, making the learner concentrate and reflect upon the process. For example, 'What's this picture, Jackie? Yes. It's a frog. Let's listen to that word FROG. Let's say it very slowly. Let's stretch the word: FR-O-G. You try it.' The child could be asked to count the number of sounds in the word. Analysing a few target words each day can be used as one of many follow-up activities in shared-book, language-experience and guided reading.

Activities can be extended to listening for final sounds; for example, 'Put a line under the pictures that end like _snake_' (pictures show _rake_, bucket, _cake_, ball). Attention can then be given to middle sounds. Tunmer *et al.* (2002: 18) have observed, 'To discover mappings between spelling patterns and sound patterns children must be able to segment spoken words into subcomponents.' These researchers also report that students with reading disabilities tend to pay too much attention to initial letter and final letter when trying to identify the word; they need to be taught to analyse the whole word more effectively.

Phoneme blending

Phoneme blending is also referred to as 'sound blending' and is the reverse process to auditory analysis. Blending is one of the most important sub-skills required for effective phonic decoding. Teachers or tutors can encourage children to gain more experience in putting speech sounds together to build a word. For example, 'I spy with my little eye a picture of a /CL/ – /O/ – /CK/.' Blending can also be practised in context when the student is reading aloud.

Sound blending is essential even in the earliest stages of learning to decode simple consonant-vowel-consonant words (l-o-t; m-a-n). It is also important much later when dealing with multi-syllabic words (re-mem-ber; cal-cu-la-tor).

Phonological training: general principles

Young children should be exposed to activities that raise their awareness of speech sounds, rhymes and alliteration through daily activities in preschool settings. Listening games and puzzles may require the children to clap out the number of syllables in their names, the number of words in a phrase, and later the number of sounds within a familiar word. Activities can also be introduced which require children to blend sounds or syllables together to make words. Many commercially published phonological training programmes are available – for example, Blachman *et al.* (2000) and Goldsworthy (2001).

In most training programmes, six aspects of phonological awareness are specifically taught alongside reading of authentic texts for enjoyment and information. The six aspects are:

- *Rhyming*: listening to and saying rhymes; finding words that rhyme; generating a new word to rhyme with a given word.
- *Alliteration*: 'the greedy green gremlins are grinning'; 'Hannah's house is high on the hill'.
- *Blending*: combining sounds into syllables and syllables into words.
- *Segmentation*: analysing sentences into words; words into syllables; syllables into separate sounds.
- *Isolation*: identifying the initial, final and medial sounds in a target word.
- *Exchanging*: substituting a new initial sound for another sound to produce a new word: 'met' becomes 'pet'; 'lost' becomes 'cost'.

The use of invented spelling by children almost certainly helps them focus on phonemic aspects of words and at the same time develop an understanding of the alphabetic principle. It is often useful to inspect young children's early attempts at spelling as this can reveal the extent to which they have developed phonemic awareness. The same is true of older students with learning difficulties.

Teaching letter–sound correspondences

Teaching phonics means teaching learners the precise relationships between letters and sounds and how to use this system to identify unfamiliar words. It is now believed that teaching phonics should be done explicitly, systematically, and early (Mesmer and Griffith 2006). Children should not be left to discover phonic principles merely by incidental learning.

Reading experts differ in their views on exactly how phonics should be taught. It was mentioned in Chapter 7 that 'synthetic phonics' and 'analytic phonics' represent two appropriate methods of instruction, with synthetic phonics being strongly supported by research. As a general principle, all agree that phonic knowledge and decoding skills should not be taught and practised totally out of context. Letter knowledge is only useful if it helps with the reading and writing of meaningful text. While students do need specific time devoted to mastering phonic units and working with word families, every effort must be made to ensure that this learning is quickly applied to 'real' reading and writing. Much phonic knowledge can be taught or reinforced from the words children are reading in their books or attempting to write (Pullen *et al.* 2005).

The common associations between letters or letter groups (graphemes) and sounds (phonemes) may be introduced in any order; and in practice the order is often dictated by the nature of the reading materials the children are using, or the writing they are doing each day. However, when working with students who have difficulties mastering phonics, it is useful to consider how the task of learning letter–sound correspondences might be organised into a logical sequence. One systematic approach begins by selecting highly contrastive sounds such as /m/, /k/, /v/, and avoiding confusable sounds such as /m/ and /n/, or /p/ and /b/. It is also helpful to teach first the most consistent letter–sound associations (Heilman 2006). The following consonants represent only one sound, regardless of the letter or letters coming after them in a word: j, k, l, m, n, p, b, h, r, v, w.

Identifying initial consonants can be made the focus within many of the general language activities in the classroom. For example, when children are consolidating their knowledge of single letter-to-sound links they can begin to make picture dictionaries. Each letter is allocated a separate page and the children paste or draw pictures of objects beginning with that letter on the appropriate page. The 'T' page might have pictures of a **T**able, **T**ie, **T**insel, and **T**adpole.

Wall-charts can also be made with pictured items grouped according to initial letter:

Children's names: **M**egan, **M**ichelle, **M**artin, **M**ark, **M**ary, **M**ichael
Animals and birds: **p**arrot, **p**enguin, **p**ig, **p**ython, **p**latypus

Vowel sounds are far less consistent than consonants in their letter-to-sound correspondences. After first establishing the most common vowel sound associations (/a/ as in apple, /e/ as in egg, /i/ as in ink, /o/ as in orange and /u/ as in up) variations are best learned later in combination with other letters when words containing these units are encountered (e.g. -ar-, -aw-, -ie-, -ee-, -ea-, -ai-, etc.).

With the least able children it is likely that even more attention will need to be devoted to mastery of letter–sound correspondences. This can be achieved through games, rhymes and songs rather than 'drills'. Stories can also be used to help establish links between letters and sounds. For example, the *Letterland* system developed in England uses alliteration in the names of the key characters (e.g. Munching Mike, Ticking Tom, Golden Girl, Robber Red) to help the children associate and remember a sound with a symbol and to create a story link in the child's mind (Wendon 2006). The pictograms used in *Letterland* are capital and lower-case letters with features superimposed. The letter h is presented as the Hairy Hatman who walks along in words whispering /hhh/. The /w/ sound is introduced as the Water Witch, with her two pools of water held within the shape of the letter. More complex combinations are also covered in the scheme. For example, when /a/ (for apple) is next to /w/ (for Water Witch) the witch casts a spell which makes the apple taste *awful*, thus introducing the tricky /aw/ phonic unit. Although it is a programme in its own right, *Letterland* could easily be integrated into the shared-book programme. It is a comprehensive scheme covering phonological skills, reading, spelling and writing.

There are many other programmes designed to teach phonic knowledge in a very systematic way. For example, THRASS (*Teaching Handwriting, Reading and Spelling Skills*: Davies and Ritchie 2004) is designed to teach students how specific letters and letter groups represent the 44 phonemes in the English language. Approaches such as THRASS, using direct teaching, are highly appropriate for students with learning difficulties who otherwise remain confused about the fact that the same sound units in English can be represented by different orthographic units (e.g. /-ight/ and /-ite/) and how the same orthographic pattern can represent different sounds (e.g. /ow/ as in flower or /ow/ as in snow).

Another example of a very successful programme is *Jolly Phonics* (Lloyd and Wernham 1995). *Jolly Phonics* sets out to teach 42 basic sound-to-letter correspondences, taught in seven groupings using a multi-sensory approach.

For teachers wishing to have a well-argued rationale for constructing a phonic skills curriculum, this can be found in books such as *Phonics in Proper Perspective* (Heilman 2006) and *Making Sense of Phonics* (Beck 2006).

Simple word-building experience

It is important that word-building and sound-blending activities are included as soon as the common vowel sounds and consonants have been taught. For example, adding the sound /a/ to the /m/ = am; adding /a/ to /t/ = at; adding /o/ to /n/ = on; adding /u/ to /p/ = up, etc. As well as reading these small units in print the children should also learn to write them unaided when the teacher dictates the sounds. As simple as this basic work may appear, for many students with learning problems it is often the first real link they make between spoken and written language. It is vital that children who have not recognised the connection between letters and sounds be given this direction early. The only prerequisite skills required are adequate visual discrimination of letter-shapes and adequate phonemic awareness.

Onset and rime practice: *Example*: 'Add the sound and say the word':

> **t:** -ag, -en, -ub, -op, -ip, -ap
> **s:** -ad, -ix, -un, -it, -ob, -et
> **c:** -up, -ot, -ap, -an, -ub, -ent

Attention may also be given to final sounds: *Example:* 'Add the sound and say the word':

> **d:** da-, ha-, be-, fe-, ki-, ri-, ro-, po-
> **g:** sa-, be-, le-, pi-, di-, ho-, lo-, ru-, tu-, etc.

Experience in attending to the middle vowel in consonant-vowel-consonant (CVC) words should also be provided. Children with learning difficulties frequently pay inadequate attention to medial vowels when trying to identify words. *Example:* 'Add the sound and say the word':

a: r-g, b-t, t-p, b-d, c-n
e: t-n, p-g, n-t, f-d, g-m
i: p-n, b-t, b-d, r-g, etc.

Later, these simple word-building activities will extend to the teaching of digraphs (two letters representing only one speech sound, as in sh, ch, th, wh, ph) and blends (two or three consonants forming a functional sound unit: br, cl, sw, st, str, scr, etc.).

Onset and rime practice: *Example*: 'Add the sound and say the word':

sw: -im, -ing, -ell, -eep
ch: -eer, -in, -op, -urch
ck: ba-, de-, ro-, du-
str: -ong, -ing, -ike, -ap

These letter groups are among the important early orthographic units for children to master. As stated in Chapter 8, some students reach a reading progress plateau at around reading age 8 years because they have not grasped the value of identifying a word from pronounceable groups of letters.

For the highest level of proficiency in recognising and spelling unfamiliar words, children need experience in working with longer and more complex letter-strings (orthographic units) such as: -eed, -ide, -ight, -ound, -own, -ous, -ough, -tion, etc. Bhattacharya (2006) points out that being able to break complex words into pronounceable sub-units of this type is important when reading difficult terminology in subject textbooks.

It must be remembered that all word-building activities are used as a supplement to reading and writing for real purposes, not as a replacement for such authentic literacy experiences. For example, words used to generate lists containing important phonograms for children to learn can be taken from words encountered in their shared-book experience, language-experience books, guided reading activities, or from their daily writing. The aim of word study is to help students recognise important phonic units and to seek out these pronounceable parts of words.

Games and apparatus

The literature on remedial teaching encourages teachers to use games and word-building equipment as adjuncts to their literacy programmes. For example, games and activities can provide fun ways of discovering and reinforcing letter-sound relationships (Morgan and Moni 2005). Games, it is argued, provide an opportunity for learners to practise and overlearn essential material that might otherwise become boring and dull. Such repetition is essential for children who learn at a slow rate or who are poorly motivated. Concrete and visual materials such as flashcards, plastic letters and magnet boards can be very effective in holding the student's attention and ensuring active involvement in the lesson. The use of games and equipment may also be seen as non-threatening, thus serving a therapeutic purpose within a group or individual teaching situation.

There can be little doubt that well-structured games and apparatus perform a very important teaching function. Games and apparatus should contribute to the objectives for the lesson, not detract from them. A game or piece of equipment must have a clearly defined purpose, matched to genuine learning needs in the children who are to use it.

Multi-sensory approaches

For students with severe learning difficulties who cannot easily remember letters or words it is helpful to use methods that engage learners more actively with material to be studied and remembered. The abbreviation VAKT is often used to indicate that multi-sensory methods are visual, auditory, kinaesthetic and tactile. The typical VAKT approach involves the learner in finger-tracing over a letter or word, or tracing it in the air, while at the same time saying the word, hearing the word, and seeing the visual stimulus.

Perhaps the best-known multi-sensory method is the Fernald VAK approach. The following steps are involved in this approach:

- First the learner selects a particular word that he or she wants to learn. The teacher writes the word in blackboard-size writing (cursive) on a card. The child finger-traces the word, saying each syllable as it is traced. This is repeated until the learner feels capable of writing the word from memory. As new words are mastered they are filed away in a card index for later revision. As soon as the learner knows a few words these are used for constructing simple sentences.
- The second stage involves elimination of direct finger-tracing and the child is encouraged to learn the words through studying their visual appearance and then writing them from memory. This stage helps to improve visual imagery and may be used for instruction in correct spelling of irregular words. Words are recorded on cards and stored for later revision.
- The third stage continues to develop visual recognition techniques and encourages more rapid memorisation of the words, followed by swift writing. Word-card drill is usually retained only for specific words that have caused unusual difficulty. At this stage the child is also beginning to read new material prepared by the teacher.
- The final stage involves the child becoming entirely independent in his or her reading and spelling skill, having generalised an understanding of word structure and having been helped to make use of contextual cues.

It can be argued that multi-sensory approaches using several channels of input help a child to integrate, at a neurological level, what is seen with what is heard, whether it be a letter or a word. On the other hand VAKT approaches may succeed where other methods have failed because they cause the learner to focus attention more intently on the learning task. Whatever the reason, this teaching approach, which brings vision, hearing, articulation and movement into play, does appear to result in improved assimilation and retention. It is obviously easier to apply this approach with younger children, but in a one-to-one remedial situation it is still a viable proposition with older students.

Cloze procedure

The cloze procedure was mentioned briefly in Chapter 8. It is a simple technique designed to help a reader become more aware of the value of using contextual cues and meaning as an aid to guessing unfamiliar words. The procedure merely requires that certain words in a sentence or paragraph be deleted and the reader asked to read the paragraph and supply possible words that might fill the gaps.

> It was Monday morning and Leanne should have been going to sch____. She was still in ____. She was hot and her throat was ____. 'I think I must take you to the d____,' said her ____. 'No school for you t____y.'

Variations on the cloze technique involve leaving the initial letter of the deleted word to provide an additional clue; or at the other extreme, deleting several consecutive words, thus requiring the student to provide a phrase that might be appropriate. The use of the cloze procedure can be integrated into shared-book experience and guided reading activities already described.

Cloze activities can involve group work. The prepared paragraphs are duplicated on sheets for the children or displayed on the overhead projector. As a group, the children discuss the best alternative and then present these to the teacher. Reading, vocabulary and comprehension are all being developed by a closer attention to logical sentence structure and meaning.

Repeated Reading and the Impress Method

Repeated Reading is a procedure designed to increase fluency, accuracy, expression and confidence (Lerner and Kline 2006). It simply requires readers to practise reading a short passage aloud until success rate is above 95 per cent and the material can be read aloud fluently (Pullen *et al.* 2005).

The teacher first models the reading while the student follows in the text. The teacher spends a few minutes making sure that the student fully understands the material. The student then practises reading the material aloud with corrective feedback from the teacher. The student continues to practise until nearly perfect, and finally records the reading on tape. When the recording is played back the student hears a fluent performance, equal in standard to the reading of even the most competent student in class. This provides an important boost to the student's self-esteem. Oral reading fluency (ORF) is considered a useful aspect of reading performance, and one that can be measured reasonably accurately over time to provide evidence of improvement (Hasbrouck and Tindal 2006).

Repeated Reading can be particularly useful for secondary school students with reading difficulties and should feature as part of any individual intervention programme (Sample 2005). *Repeated Reading*, if coupled with questioning and discussion after reading, can improve comprehension (Therrien *et al.* 2006).

Allington (2001) reviewed a number of studies evaluating the effectiveness of *Repeated Reading* and concludes:

> The evidence available provides reliable and replicated scientific evidence of the positive impact of repeated readings on a variety of reading tasks and outcome measures. These studies also indicate that engaging children in repeated readings of a text is particularly effective in fostering more fluent reading in children struggling to develop proficient reading strategies.
>
> (Allington 2001: 73)

The *Impress Method* is a unison reading procedure in which the student and teacher read aloud together at a natural rate (Flood *et al.* 2005). The student is permitted to use the index finger to keep place on the page. The *Impress Method* is particularly useful when a child has developed a few word-recognition skills but is very lacking in fluency and expression. It is recommended that sessions should last no more than 5 to 10 minutes, but be provided on a very regular basis for several months. It may be necessary to repeat the same sentence or paragraph several times until the student becomes fluent at reading the material with low error rate.

The *Impress Method* is very appropriate for use in peer tutoring, where one child who is a better reader provides assistance for a less able friend. In such cases the peer tutor usually needs to be shown how to act effectively as a model reader, and how to be supportive and encouraging to the tutee.

Pause, Prompt, Praise (PPP)

A procedure known as *Pause, Prompt, Praise* was developed by Glynn at the University of Auckland. It has been applied very successfully in many reading-intervention contexts. The principles can easily be taught to parents, aides, peer-tutors and volunteer helpers in schools as a strategy to use with children they are assisting.

The procedure involves the following simple steps:

- The child encounters an unfamiliar word.
- Instead of stepping in immediately and saying the word, the teacher/tutor waits approximately 5 seconds for the child to work it out.

- If the child is not successful the teacher/tutor prompts by suggesting perhaps guessing the word from the meaning of the passage, or attending to the initial letter, or reading to the end of the sentence.
- When the child succeeds in identifying the word he or she is praised briefly.
- If the child cannot get the word after prompting, the teacher/tutor quickly supplies the word.
- The child is also praised for self-correcting while reading.

A useful summary of PPP, in the form of advice to parents who are helping their own children, can be located at http://www.schoolparents.canberra.net.au/ reading_help.htm.

Sustained Silent Reading (SSR)

Sustained Silent Reading describes a specific period of classroom time set aside each day for students and teacher to read material of their own personal choice. Often 15 minutes of the afternoon session are devoted to SSR across the whole school. When SSR is implemented efficiently all students engage in much more reading than previously. In doing so they increase their ability to concentrate on reading tasks and develop greater interest in books. In some cases the students are seen to become more discriminating readers, and the range and quality of what they read improves.

If SSR is implemented inefficiently it can result in some students wasting time. A problem emerges when students with reading difficulties select books that are too difficult for them to read independently. Teachers need to guide the choice of books to ensure that all students can read the material successfully during these silent reading periods. Biemiller (1994: 206) warns that poor readers often spend substantial periods of SSR time 'covertly avoiding reading'.

Computers, ICT and reading

The main benefit of computer-assisted learning (CAL) is that the technology makes use of well-established principles of instruction such as clear demonstrations and modelling in easy steps, active participation, and practice to mastery level. Computers are infinitely patient, allow for self-pacing by the student and provide immediate feedback. Students are active throughout the learning session and they have high levels of motivation. Whether used by one student alone, or by students working together, the computer is an excellent tool for learning in the regular classroom.

Information and communication technology has created many new and interesting ways for children to engage in literacy activities for authentic purposes (Polkinghorne 2004). For example, a study by Cooney and Hay (2005) found that a structured use of the Internet as a medium for applying and practising reading skills was very effective in middle school, with improvements in reading achievement, engagement rates, and attitude. Similarly, Minton (2001) described two case studies of students with severe literacy problems who were taught for one hour each week, part of the time on the computer. The greatest value in the computer time was seen to lie in improving the students' self-esteem, giving them independence and control, and making learning enjoyable. The programs themselves provide scaffolding and feedback, while at the same time ensuring practice with high success rate. The students were described as 'enthusiastic' in their approach to the computer sessions.

At the most basic level of CAL, computer programs exist that will help students improve their letter recognition, alphabet knowledge, word recognition, decoding, sentence-completion, cloze, and spelling skills. Spelling and word study may be presented by age-appropriate programmes in which a target word is displayed on the screen and the student is required to copy (retype) the word. The word is then embedded in a sentence for the student to read and again copy. The word is presented again with the initial letter or letters missing and the student is required to complete it. Gradually the cues are removed until the student is reading, writing and using the word correctly in context with a high degree of automaticity.

Children with reading difficulties can gain much from using text-to-speech (TTS) software, with its combined visual and auditory presentation (Fasting and Lyster 2005). Balajthy (2005) reviewed a number of studies showing that TTS programs can significantly improve the comprehension of struggling readers, and can be very effective in gaining and holding children's attention. However, both Balajthy (2005) and Fasting and Lyster (2005) conclude that some students do not find electronic readers helpful.

At higher levels, programs may focus more on comprehension, application, and 'reading to learn' rather than 'learning to read', but as Meyerson and Kulesza (2002) point out, students with reading problems are often limited in their ability to use ICT to research information for classroom projects. Close monitoring by the teacher, and judicious use of peer tutoring, can help to reduce this problem and at the same time help the student acquire computer skills.

In the home situation the computer can also aid literacy development because children can work alone or with a parent on early reading and writing skills. Parents can also help children search for, read and interpret information from the Internet.

Further reading

Allington, R.L. (2006) *What Really Matters for Struggling Readers: Designing Research-based Programs*, Boston, MA: Pearson-Allyn and Bacon.

Antonacci, P.A. and O'Callaghan, C.M. (2006) *A Handbook for Literacy Instructional and Assessment Strategies K-8*, Boston, MA: Pearson-Allyn and Bacon.

Beck, I.L. (2006) *Making Sense of Phonics: The Hows and Whys*, New York: Guilford Press.

Eldredge, J.L. (2005) *Teaching Decoding: Why and How* (2nd edn), Upper Saddle River, NJ: Pearson-Merrill-Prentice Hall.

Fountas, I.C. and Pinnell, G.S. (2006) *Teaching for Comprehending and Fluency*, Portsmouth, NH: Heinemann.

Gunning, T.G. (2006) *Assessing and Correcting Reading and Writing Difficulties* (3rd edn), Boston, MA: Pearson-Allyn and Bacon.

Harp, B. (2006) *Handbook of Literacy Assessment and Evaluation* (3rd edn), Norwood, MA: Christopher-Gordon.

Heilman, A.W. (2006) *Phonics in Proper Perspective* (10th edn), Upper Saddle River, NJ: Merrill-Prentice Hall.

McCormick, R.L. and Paratore, J.R. (2005) *After Early Intervention, Then What? Teaching Struggling Readers in Grades 3 and Beyond*, Upper Saddle River, NJ: Prentice Hall.

Meyerson, M.J. and Kulesza, D.L. (2006) *Strategies for Struggling Readers and Writers* (2nd edn), Upper Saddle River, NJ: Merrill-Prentice Hall.

Moskal, M.K. and Blachowicz, C. (2006) *Partnering for Fluency*, New York: Guilford.

Rasinski, T., Blachowicz, C. and Lems, K. (eds) (2006) *Fluency Instruction: Research-based Best Practices*, New York: Guilford Press.

Chapter 10

Helping students improve their writing

> Students who struggle to develop written language often construct a negative perception of the writing process as well as a negative image of their own capabilities to communicate ideas through writing.
>
> (Gregg and Mather 2002: 7)

In order to help students improve their writing skills, it is necessary first to consider the different stages of development reached by individuals in the class. In the same way that interventions for reading improvement need to be developmentally appropriate, so too do the teaching strategies used to improve children's writing.

Sequential development of writing

The acquisition of skills in writing is generally believed to follow a predictable sequence. Several researchers have described the different stages through which students pass as they move from the 'emergent writing' stage at approximately 5 to 6 years of age to the skilled writing stage in late adolescence and adulthood (e.g. Bissex 1980; Fitzgerald and Shanahan 2000; Søvik 2003). Although much of the work on developmental aspects of writing has focused on children's spelling ability (see Chapter 11), some indicators have also been suggested for observing increases in clarity, vocabulary, style and audience (Gregg and Mather 2002).

Fitzgerald and Shanahan (2000) identified six stages of development in writing, closely linked to parallel developmental stages in reading acquisition, and influenced to some degree by reading experience. While reading and writing are separate processes, and in some respects draw upon different areas of knowledge and skill, there is also considerable overlap between reading and writing. For example, automaticity in recognition of key words is fairly closely linked with automaticity in writing those words, knowledge of phonics helps both reading and spelling, familiarity with grammar and sentence structure is important in writing and is also one of the cueing systems used in fluent reading. In addition, there seems to be a connection between weak reading comprehension and weak ability in producing well-structured and detailed written language (Cragg and Nation 2006). Several authorities have discussed the reading–writing connection in great detail (e.g. Cramer 1998; Nelson and Calfee 1998) and teachers are referred to these sources for additional information. It is generally agreed that reading and writing should be taught together from the earliest stages.

Difficulties in writing

Perhaps more than any other area of the curriculum, writing can present major problems for students with learning difficulties. Written expression is the most difficult of the language skills for children to acquire because its development involves much more than adding discrete skills in a linear sequence. Competence in writing relies heavily on competence in listening, speaking and reading, as well as on possession of necessary strategies for planning, encoding, reviewing, and revising written language.

According to Chalk *et al.* (2005), students with learning difficulties often lack a basic knowledge of how best to approach the writing process. They often display the following weaknesses:

- limited ability in planning, executing, and revising written work;
- difficulties in formulating goals and generating ideas;
- inability to organise an appropriate structure for a composition;
- a tendency to spend no time in thinking before writing;
- slowness and inefficiency in executing the mechanical aspects of writing;
- limited output of written work in the available time.

In addition, weak writers often use either very simple sentence structures, or produce long and rambling sentences with repetitive use of conjunctions. They favour simple words with known spellings over more interesting and expressive words – but still make many spelling errors. Above all else, they do not enjoy writing and would prefer to avoid it.

It seems that boys often have more difficulty than girls in achieving a satisfactory standard in written work (Hansen 2002; UKLA/PNS 2004). However, the results from a project in the UK suggest that boys can improve their skills significantly if writing activities are linked more closely with visual stimuli or ICT, drama or role play. If the writing sessions are carefully structured with adequate discussion, preparation and modelling by the teacher, the boys have a clearer understanding of the demands of the task and gain better control over the process. Among positive outcomes from the project was the observation that both quantity and quality of writing improved, and the boys' willingness to write increased (UKLA/PNS 2004).

Losing confidence and motivation

The child who has problems writing will experience no satisfaction in pursuing the task and will try to avoid writing whenever possible. Avoidance then reduces the opportunities to practise, and lack of practice results in no improvement. The student loses confidence and self-esteem in relation to writing, as well as developing an even more negative attitude. The problem for the teacher is to motivate these students to write and to provide them with enough support to ensure increased success. It is clear that these students need to be taught effective strategies for approaching writing tasks.

It is fortunate that contemporary approaches to the teaching of writing have done much to alleviate the anxiety and frustration that many lower-ability students experienced in years gone by whenever 'composition' appeared on the timetable. To them it meant a silent period of sustained writing, with little or no opportunity to discuss work with others or ask for assistance. Great importance was placed on accuracy and neatness at the first attempt and many children felt extremely inhibited. Even when the teacher wasn't a severe judge of the product, the children themselves sometimes carried out self-assessment and decided that they couldn't write because their product was not perfect. An attitude quickly developed in the child, 'I can't write' or 'I hate writing', and a failure cycle was established. It is therefore important to consider approaches to teaching that may prevent loss of confidence and motivation, and instead make students feel successful as writers.

Teaching approaches

Pollington *et al.* (2001) suggest that there are two main approaches to teaching writing: the 'traditional approach' with a focus on instruction in basic skills of writing, and the 'process approach'. Chan and Dally (2000) also refer to the process approach as the dominant method, but indicate that 'strategy training' has also influenced instruction in writing in recent years.

Skills-based, teacher-centred approach to writing

The skills-based or 'traditional approach' usually involves fairly tight control imposed by the teacher. Writing skills are developed mainly through structured exercises, practice materials, and set topics. When more extensive writing is required, the teacher usually selects a common essay topic about which all students will be expected to write. The audience for the writing is thus the teacher. Pollington *et al.* (2001) point out that often a teacher simply sets a writing topic for the children but provides no instruction in how best to attempt the task. Without support and guidance the writing activity becomes more of an *assessment* procedure rather than a teaching and learning experience.

This traditional skills-based approach is believed to be potentially less motivating for students than having them working on topics and genres they have chosen for themselves. There is also some doubt that skills taught in routine exercises ever transfer to children's free writing, and it is argued that these component skills of writing and editing should be taught in an integrated way as part of the feedback given to children as they write on their own chosen topics. Tompkins (2004) reminds teachers that rather than teaching isolated skills in the hope of improving writing, they should scaffold and support students' own developing strategies as they write for authentic purposes of communication. Unfortunately, the evidence suggests that teachers usually devote significantly more time to the mechanics of transcription than they do to the teaching of strategies necessary for thoughtful drafting and revising (Graham and Harris 2005a).

Chan and Dally (2000) suggest that teacher-centred instruction in writing appears to suit those students who do not learn effectively simply by immersion in opportunities to write. Some students make better gains in writing through explicit instruction, just as some students make optimum progress in reading if more time is spent in direct teaching and practice.

The process approach to writing

A change that occurred in the 1980s was a shift of emphasis from teacher-directed skills-based instruction to child-centred exploration of the processes involved in composing, editing and revising. The new method was termed the *process approach* to writing (Graves 1983). In recent years the approach has become popular in primary and secondary schools around the world, and strategies for using the process approach or its variants (for example, 'writing workshop', 'shared writing' and 'guided writing') have been published in many books and journals. Detailed strategies for process writing can be found in the books *Writing Through Childhood* (Harwayne 2001) and *Readers and Writers in the Primary Grades: A Balanced and Integrated Approach* (Combs 2006).

The process approach helps young children understand that a first attempt at writing rarely constitutes a finished product. Writing usually has to pass through a number of separate stages, from the initial hazy formulation of ideas to the first written draft, through subsequent revisions and editing to a final product (although not *all* writing should be forced to pass through all stages). Teachers themselves should model writing in the classroom and thus demonstrate the planning, composing, editing and publishing stages in action.

In the process approach, children confer with the teacher and with peers to obtain opinions and feedback on their written work as it progresses. Although process writing is very much a child-centred approach, it still provides abundant opportunities for the teacher to give as much individualised direct instruction as necessary to advance children's writing abilities. Students' responses are deliberately shaped and refined through a natural process of feedback and reinforcement (Gilbert 2004). In addition, children are taught specific aspects of drafting, editing, grammar and style through the provision of appropriate 'mini-lessons' from time to time (Feng and Powers 2005).

Since the process approach depends so much upon student-writers having someone with whom to confer, it is important to consider possible sources of assistance in the classroom beyond the teacher and classmates. Teacher aides, older students (cross-age tutoring), college and university students on field placements, and parent volunteers can all provide help within the classroom programme. In all cases these helpers must understand their role and they require some informal training by the teacher if they are to adopt an approach that is supportive rather than critical or didactic.

Writing workshop

A writing workshop is a whole-class process writing session where all children are engaged in various forms of writing activity, and are supported in their endeavours by classmates and the teacher. Children in a writing workshop are helped to go through the complete pre-writing, drafting, revising and publishing cycle, and their products become part of the reading material available in the classroom.

The motivation for a writing workshop comes mainly through the freedom of choice children are offered in terms of topics and genre. Choice of topic on which to write is usually made by the writer, rather than the teacher. Personal narrative is likely to result in the most lively and relevant communications. It is also believed that selecting a personal topic reduces the problem of generating ideas for a teacher-chosen topic because knowledge of a familiar topic is better organised in memory and this reduces the cognitive load in the initial planning and drafting stages.

Typically, a writing workshop session begins with a teacher presentation or sharing time (5–10 minutes), followed by a mini-lesson on some aspect of writing (for example, the use of adjectives) (10 minutes). Students then work independently on their own writing or work in small groups with the teacher (30–40 minutes). During this time, word-processing and access to other forms of information technology may be appropriate and beneficial. Finally, children share their writings with their peers.

The teaching of specific skills takes place in three ways:

• at the beginning of the lesson in the form of a mini-lesson;
• in writing conferences with individual children throughout the lesson;
• through whole-class sharing time at the end of the lesson.

During the session the teacher should confer with almost every student about the writing being produced. This conference with the student involves far more than dispensation of general praise and encouragement. The conference between teacher and student should represent the 'scaffolding' principle in teaching and learning whereby the teacher supplies the necessary support, encouragement and specific guidance to help novice writers gain increasing control over their own writing strategies. Differences in abilities among the students will determine the amount of time the teacher spends with individuals.

Advice and feedback in writing workshops come not only from the teacher but also from peers. A friend or partner can be used as a sounding board for ideas and can read, discuss and make suggestions for written drafts. Group sharing and peer editing are essential elements in the sessions. The underlying principle is 'writers working together', sharing and providing feedback, with peers acting as the audience for the children's writing. By middle primary school, children are capable of evaluating the quality of their own writing but they still need guidance from the teacher or peers on how best to revise their work (Dix 2006).

Peer critiquing is often written about and talked about as if it is a simple strategy to employ in the classroom; but in reality it needs to be done with great sensitivity. Teachers need to spend time modelling the critiquing process before expecting students to implement it proficiently – how to give descriptive praise, how to highlight good points, how to detect what is not clear, how to help with the generation of new ideas, and how to assist with polishing the final product. It must be noted that children are not always skilled in the art of critiquing and providing helpful comments to others, and they may need guidance with this aspect of process writing. Children with learning difficulties or with low social status within the class may not cope well with negative and critical feedback from their peers because it may seem to draw public attention to their weaknesses.

Shared writing

Shared writing is a component within the process approach, and may be an aspect of any writing workshop where the focus is on collaboration. At the simplest level, or in remedial situations, the teacher may do some of the actual writing while incorporating students' ideas. Through questioning and discussion the teacher activates the students' prior knowledge, encourages critical thinking and reflection, and ensures student participation.

Worthy *et al.* (2001: 227) state:

> Shared writing is an effective technique to guide a group of students through a new form of writing. It is also an excellent method to use to support an individual student who will not attempt an assignment. The teacher serves as the recorder, brainstorming with the student and taking a dictation to begin the piece of writing, then handing the paper over for the student to complete.

Guided writing

Guided writing is also an element within the process approach. Guided writing involves modelling by the teacher of specific writing strategies, styles or genres, followed by guided and independent application of the same techniques by the students. Using a whiteboard, a teacher might begin by demonstrating, for example, how to generate ideas for a given topic, how to create and structure an opening paragraph, and how to develop the remaining ideas in logical sequence. Later, students take it in turns to present their own material to the group, receiving constructive feedback from peers.

Fountas and Pinnell (2001) recommend providing writers with guidelines or checklists to help with evaluating and revising their written work. For example, the checklist might ask:

- Did you begin with an interesting sentence?
- Are your ideas easy to understand?
- Are your ideas presented in the best sequence?
- Did you give examples to help readers understand your points?
- Is your writing interesting?
- Have you used paragraphs?
- Have you checked spelling and punctuation?

The guided approach is more effective than either the traditional teacher-direct method, or the unstructured use of process method, in fostering writing skills.

Strategy training

The weaknesses in writing skills described earlier indicate that students need to be taught effective plans of action for tackling writing tasks. In the same way that strategy training can improve reading comprehension, it can also be effective in improving writing, particularly the aspects of planning, drafting, revising and self-correcting. Much of the recent research in this domain has been conducted by Graham and Harris (2005a; 2005b).

An appropriate starting point for strategy training is for the teacher to demonstrate, step by step, an effective plan of action for tackling a particular writing topic. The teacher uses 'thinking aloud' to reveal the way he or she goes about planning, generating ideas, drafting, revising and editing the piece of writing. This can be demonstrated on the whiteboard, overhead projector, or computer screen. The students then apply the steps within the strategy to a similar topic, and receive support and feedback from the teacher.

During strategy training students are typically taught to use self-questioning or self-instruction to assist with the process of planning, writing, evaluating, and improving a written assignment. Questions similar to those listed above under *Guided writing* can be used as prompts within the strategy. Emphasis is placed on metacognitive or self-regulating aspects of the writing process (self-checking for clarity in what is written, self-monitoring, self-correction) (Graham and Harris 2005a). In the early stages, the students may be required to verbalise the steps or questions as they work through the plan of action; later, verbalisation is faded as the student becomes more confident in using the strategy independently. The strategy may also embody the use of graphic organisers such as story planners or cues – described later in the chapter.

A simple example of a task-approach strategy for writing uses the mnemonic LESSER. The strategy helps some students to organise their thoughts for writing and then write a longer assignment than they would otherwise produce ('LESSER helps me write MORE').

L = List your ideas.
E = Examine your list.
S = Select your starting point.
S = Sentence one tells us about this first idea.
E = Expand on this first idea with another sentence.
R = Read what you have written. Revise if necessary. Repeat for the next paragraph.

Many lower-achieving students have, in the past, written very little during times set aside for writing. This is part of the vicious circle which might be described thus: 'I don't like writing so I don't write much, so I don't get much practice, so I don't improve …' Use of strategies such as LESSER can help reduce this problem. A modified form of *precision teaching* can also be used to increase the output of some students, with the number of words or sentences written in a set time counted and charted each day.

It is always necessary to maximise the possibility that a strategy will generalise beyond the training sessions into students' everyday writing. Graham and Harris (2005a) suggest that this may be achieved by:

- continuing with instruction (overlearning) until students have thoroughly mastered the strategy;
- helping students understand how the strategy works, and how it helps them to produce better results;
- leading students to consider when and where a particular strategy can be used;
- discussing how to modify a strategy for different situations;
- teaching students to use self-statements as a means to reinforce strategy use and to cope with any difficulties.

Chalk *et al.* (2005) report that students begin to exhibit more sophisticated writing once they develop effective strategies for planning or revising text, and as they learn to self-regulate.

Intervention for individuals and groups

Students who exhibit difficulties in written expression fall into one of two groups. The groups are not mutually exclusive so there is overlap in terms of instructional needs. The first group comprises those students of any age level who have learning difficulties or who have a learning disability. For these students, the teacher needs to structure every writing task very carefully and then provide appropriate support to ensure the students' successful participation.

The second group comprises those students of any age who can write but don't like to do so – the reluctant and unmotivated students. These students appear not to see the relevance of writing, or have not experienced the excitement of written communication and get no satisfaction from it. Some of these students may have encountered negative or unrewarding experiences during the early stages of becoming writers. They may have acquired what has been termed 'writing apprehension' which now causes them to avoid the task whenever possible. Their problem is one of poor motivation leading to habitually low levels of practice and productivity. Here the teacher must try to regain lost interest and build confidence.

Ideally, a student receiving extra assistance will choose his or her own topics for writing; if not, it is essential to give the student an appropriately stimulating subject. The topic must be interesting and relevant, and the student must see a purpose in transferring ideas to paper. Regardless of whether the activity involves writing a letter or email to a friend or composing a science-fiction fantasy story, the student should perceive the task as enjoyable and worthwhile.

The first important step in improving a student's writing skills is to allocate sufficient time for writing within the school day. It seems that writing is often treated as an adjunct to other subjects rather than something needing to have specific time allocated to it. If writing occurs daily there is much greater likelihood that motivation, confidence and writing skills will improve.

In general, students with difficulties need help in two basic stages of the writing process: (i) planning to write, and (ii) revising or polishing the final product. The teaching of each of these stages should embody the basic principles of effective instruction, namely modelling by the teacher, guided practice with feedback (mainly via the conference between teacher and student) and independent practice through application.

Paving the way to success

A classroom atmosphere that encourages students to experiment with their writing without fear of criticism or ridicule is a very necessary condition for the least able students. In many cases, particularly with the upper primary or secondary student with a history of bad experiences in writing, simply creating the atmosphere is not enough. Much more than the ordinary amount of guidance and encouragement from the teacher will also be needed.

Students with writing difficulties need to be given a framework they can use whenever they write (see *Strategy training* and *Guided writing* above). In particular, novice writers appear to benefit if they are taught a plan of action for generating ideas, composing and editing. They need to be given guidance in how to begin, how to continue and how to complete the writing task. In this context, students could be taught a set of questions to ask themselves which will facilitate the generation of ideas and will assist with the organisation and presentation of the material across different writing genres.

Students with difficulties need to be helped *daily*, during the first 10 minutes of the lesson. With low-achieving students or those lacking in confidence, the teacher will structure the task very carefully at each stage – for example by writing down key vocabulary and possible sentence beginnings for the student to use, then reading these together twice before the child begins to work unaided. During discussion and feedback stages the teacher should not over correct, but rather encourage the student to talk and think. The main aim is to help the student generate ideas and then to sort these into a logical sequence.

In the early stages it is important not to place undue stress upon accuracy of spelling since this can stifle the student's attempts at communicating ideas freely. Invented spelling gives students the freedom to write with attention to content and sequence. As the student becomes more confident and productive, the teacher, while still remaining supportive, will make the conferring stage rather less structured. Open-ended questions are still used to extend the student's thinking and to build upon the writing so far produced.

Paired writing

In the same way that working with a partner can improve reading skills, having a partner for writing is also beneficial. The system can be used with cross-age tutoring, peer tutoring, parent–child tutorial groupings, and in adult literacy classes (Cameron *et al.* 2002). The pairing comprises a helper and a writer. The helper's role is to stimulate ideas from the writer that the helper notes down on a pad. In Topping's method there are set questions for the helper to ask (e.g. Who? Do what? Where? When? What next? etc.) (Topping *et al.* 2000). When sufficient ideas have been suggested, the helper and writer review the notes on the pad and discuss the best sequence for presenting these. A story-planner format could be used (see below). The writer then begins first-draft writing, based mainly on the notes. In the case of students with severe learning difficulties, the helper may act as scribe as the 'writer' dictates. The helper then reads aloud the draft that has been written. The writer then reads the draft. Working together, the pair edit the draft for clarity, meaning, sequence, spelling and punctuation – with the writer taking the lead if possible. The writer then revises the material by writing or word-processing a 'final copy'. Helper and writer discuss and evaluate the finished product.

Suggestions for reluctant writers

Small booklets are usually better than exercise books for students who are unskilled and reluctant writers. The opportunity to make a fresh start almost every week is far better than being faced with the accumulation of evidence of past failures which accrue in an exercise book. For students of all ages, a loose-leaf folder may be a useful replacement for the traditional exercise book. There is a place for the daily diary, journal or news book, but teachers should avoid such writing becoming merely habitual and trite.

The skeleton story

Getting started is the first obstacle faced by many students who find writing difficult. One simple way of helping them complete a story is by giving them the framework first, with sentence beginnings to be completed using their own ideas. For example:

> Something woke me in the middle of the night.
> I heard ....
> I climbed out of bed quietly and ....
> To my surprise I saw ....
> At first I...
> I was lucky because ....
> In the end ....

With groups of low-achieving students it is useful, through collaborative effort, to complete one version of the skeleton story on the blackboard. This completed story is read to the group. Each student is then given a sheet with the same sentence beginnings, but he or she must write a different story from the one on the blackboard. The stories are later shared in the group. Students of limited ability find it very much easier to complete a story when the demands for writing are reduced in this way, and when a beginning has been provided.

Patterned writing

For students with limited writing ability, Lerner and Kline (2006) recommend using the framework of a familiar, repetitive, and predictable story as a basis for writing a new variation on the same theme. The plot remains basically the same but the characters and the details are changed. For example, the children write a new story involving a 'Big Grey Elephant' instead of a 'Little Red Hen'; and the Big Grey Elephant tries to get other animals to help him move a log from the path: 'Who will help me move the log?' 'Not I', said the rat. 'Not I', said the monkey, 'Not I', said the snake'... and so on.

Cues and prompts

Cues and prompts are similar to the questions posed by the helper in paired writing (see above). Graham and Harris (2005a) suggest that students be taught mnemonics representing a framework of questions which they ask themselves during the initial stages of planning – for example, the mnemonic 'WWW, What = 2, How = 2' represents: **Who** are the main characters? **When** does the story take place? **Where** does the story take place? **What** do the main characters want to do? **What** happens when the main characters try to do it? **How** does the story end? **How** do the main characters feel? Questions may also prompt students to become more descriptive in their writing – e.g. What does it look like?' (size, colour, shape, etc.). What does it feel like? How fast would you be travelling? The set of questions needs to be tailored to match the particular theme, topic, or type of writing, but some generic prompts can also be recorded on a wall-chart and displayed in the classroom. These temporary props are useful for students who have difficulty at the planning stage of writing; but the students must not become too dependent upon such starting points. After a suitable period of time, cues and prompts should be withdrawn.

Sentence combining

Activities involving the reconstruction of simple sentences into longer and more interesting sentences have proved valuable for weaker writers (Andrews et al. 2006; Saddler 2005). The activities create an opportunity for writers to construct more interesting, meaningful and varied sentences within their stories or reports. For example:

> The giant was hungry.
> The giant ate the meat pie.
> The meat pie was huge.
> = The hungry giant ate the huge meat pie.

The main benefit from the experience of sentence combining is that the process can be revisited every time a student is asked to read, edit and improve a piece of writing.

Story planner

A story planner is a form of graphic organiser that provides students with learning difficulties with a starting point for generating ideas for writing. A 'story web' is created by writing the main idea in the centre of a sheet of paper, then branching off from the main idea into different categories of information. These ideas and categories might include: the setting for the story, the type of action to take place, the characters involved, the outcome, etc.

Prompts and cues could be used to stimulate the students' thinking as the web is constructed. Students brainstorm for ideas that might go into the story. In random order, each idea is briefly noted against a spoke in the wheel. The class then reviews the ideas and decides upon an appropriate starting point for the story. Number '1' is written against that idea. How will the story develop? The children determine the order in which the other ideas will be used, and the appropriate numbers are written against each spoke. Some of the ideas may not be used at all and can be erased. Other ideas may need to be added at this stage, and numbered accordingly. The students now use the bank of ideas recorded on the story planner to start writing their own stories. The brief notes can be elaborated into sentences and the sentences gradually extended into paragraphs.

By preparing the draft ideas and then discussing the best order in which to write them, the students have tackled two of the most difficult problems they face when composing, namely planning and sequencing.

Expanding an idea

Begin by writing a short, declarative sentence that makes one statement.

> We have too many cars coming into our school parking area.

Next, write two or three sentences that add information to, or are connected with, the first sentence. Leave two lines below each new sentence.

> We have too many cars coming into our school parking area.
> The noise they make often disturbs our lessons.
> The cars travel fast and could knock someone down.
> What can we do about this problem?

Now write two more sentences in each space.

> We have too many cars coming into our school parking area.
> The noise they make often disturbs our lessons. The drivers sound their horns and rev the engines. Sometimes I can't even hear the teacher speak.
> The cars travel fast and could knock someone down. I saw a girl step out behind one yesterday. She screamed when it reversed suddenly.
> What can we do about this problem? Perhaps there should be a sign saying 'NO CARS ALLOWED'. They might build some speed humps or set a speed limit.

Edit the sentences into appropriate paragraphs. Combine some short statements into longer, complex sentences. Edit for style. Use of a word processor makes each of these steps much faster and makes the process of editing and checking spelling easier. The teacher demonstrates this procedure, incorporating ideas from the class. Students are then given guided practice and further modelling over a series of lessons, each time using a different theme.

Writing a summary

Students with learning difficulties often have problems when required to write a summary of something they have just read. Specific help is needed in this area and one or more of the following procedures can be helpful to such students.

- The teacher provides a set of 'true/false' statements based on the text just read. The statements are presented on the sheet in random order. The student must read each statement and place a tick against those that are true. The student then decides the most logical sequence in which to arrange the true statements. When copied into the student's exercise book these statements provide a brief summary of the text.
- The teacher provides some sentence 'starters' in a sequence that will provide a framework for the summary. For example: 'The first thing most travellers notice when they arrive at the airport is …'; 'When they travel by taxi to the city they notice …'. The student completes the unfinished sentences and in doing so writes the summary.
- The teacher provides a summary with key words or phrases omitted (cloze passage). The words may be presented below the passage in random order, or clues may be given in terms of initial letters of word required, or dashes to represent each letter of the word. The student completes the passage by supplying the missing words.
- Simple multiple-choice questions can be presented. The questions may deal with the main ideas from the text with supporting detail. By selecting appropriate responses and writing these down the student creates a brief summary.

All the suggestions above are designed to simplify the task demands for writing, and at the same time motivate the reluctant student to complete the work successfully. In most cases the use of a word processor will also add interest and an important element of control by the learner.

Word processors

Research evidence supporting the benefits of using word processors with learning-disabled students is growing all the time. Undoubtedly, the arrival of word processors in the classroom heralded a new opportunity for students of all levels of ability to enter the realm of writing and composing with enthusiasm and enjoyment. Using a word processor makes the task of writing far less arduous. Word-processing seems to be of great benefit to students who don't usually write very much, and to those with the most severe spelling problems. In particular, students with learning difficulties gain confidence in creating, editing, erasing and publishing their own unique material through a medium that holds the attention and is infinitely patient (Hetzroni and Shrieber 2004).

For students with learning difficulties, word-processing de-emphasises the mechanical aspects, such as handwriting and letter formation, and allows more mental effort to be devoted to generating ideas (Lerner and Kline 2006; Phillips 2004). When using word processors for writing, students tend to work harder and produce longer essays, which are of better quality. Polkinghorne (2004: 26) states:

> Computers can change the whole writing process [making] it easier to plan and record ideas. It is much easier to edit, change and work with those ideas and publish and share the final product. Computer access helps alleviate hesitancy caused by poor spelling, lack of grammar skills, poor handwriting, and inability to proofread and edit hand written work easily.

In a tutorial situation, the use of a computer allows the tutor to observe the writing process more directly and gain better insights into the student's existing strategies for composing, editing and proofreading. Support can then be given to the student with greater precision.

Students with learning difficulties need first to develop some basic keyboard skills if the word-processing is to be achieved without frustration. It is usually necessary to teach only the most essential skills to enable the student to access the program, type the work and save the material at regular intervals. Even this simple level of operation can give some students a tremendous boost to confidence and can encourage risk-taking in writing and composing. Van der Kaay *et al.* (2000) used a word processor with students aged 9 to 11 who were mildly intellectually disabled. They found that the students' written work improved significantly in terms of organisation and control over the writing process.

Further reading

Anderson, J. (2005) *Mechanically Inclined: Building Grammar, Usage and Style into Writer's Workshop*, Portland, ME: Stenhouse.

Barone, D.M. and Taylor, J. (2006) *Improving Students' Writing, K-8*, Thousand Oaks, CA: Corwin Press.

Calkins, L., Martinelli, M., Kesler, T., Gillette, C., McEvoy, M., Chiarella, M. and Cruz, M.C. (2006) *Units of Study for Teaching Writing, Grades 3–5*, Portsmouth, NH: Heinemann.

DfES (Department of Education and Skills) (2005) *Raising Standards in Writing: Achieving Children's Targets*. Available at: http://www.standards.dfes.gov.uk/primary/publications/literacy/1160811/ (accessed 15 March 2006).

Graham, S. and Harris, K.R. (2005) *Writing Better: Effective Strategies for Teaching Students with Learning Difficulties*, Baltimore, MD: Brookes.

Kendall, J. and Khuon, O. (2006) *Writing Sense*, Portland, ME: Stenhouse.

MacArthur, C.A., Graham, S. and Fitzgerald, J. (2005) *Handbook of Writing Research*, New York: Guilford Press.

McKenna, M.C. and Robinson, R.D. (2006) *Teaching Through Text: Reading and Writing in the Content Areas* (4th edn), Boston, MA: Pearson-Allyn and Bacon.

Nagin, C. (2006) *Because Writing Matters: Improving Student Writing in Our Schools*, San Francisco, CA: Jossey-Bass.

Rijlaarsdam, G., Van den Bergh, H. and Couzijn, M. (2005) *Effective Learning and Teaching of Writing* (2nd edn), New York: Kluwer.

Tompkins, G.E. and Blanchfield, C.L. (2005) *50 Ways to Develop Strategic Writers*, Upper Saddle River, NJ: Pearson-Merrill-Prentice Hall.

UKLA/PNS (United Kingdom Literacy Association/Primary National Strategy) (2004) *Raising Boys' Achievements in Writing,* Royston, Hertfordshire: UKLA. Available at: http://www.standards.dfes.gov.uk/primary/publications/literacy/1094843/pns_ukla_boys094304report.pdf (accessed 15 March 2006).

Chapter 11

Developing spelling skills

> We must remember that children who learn to spell with accuracy and
> confidence in the primary grades master the orthographic patterns that
> underpin future success in writing and reading the English language.
>
> (Brown and Morris 2005: 182)

For many low-achieving students, spelling continues to present a problem long
after reading skills have improved. In part, this problem arises in the English
language because it is impossible to spell every word by a simple translation of
sound to single letter (Goswami 2005). Spencer (2002: 16) observes that:

> In a perfect orthography there would be one letter for each sound and the
> number of sounds would exactly match the number of letters. This is not
> the case with English, although some languages do approach this degree of
> correspondence. English words usually have more letters than sounds, and it
> is this discrepancy (the phonetic difference) which is one of the main factors
> linked to spelling difficulty.

But children's difficulties can also be due to the fact that too little time and attention
have been devoted to the explicit teaching of spelling skills and strategies. For
almost twenty years, beginning in the early 1980s, instruction in spelling ceased to
feature prominently in the primary school curriculum, due mainly to the influence
of whole-language philosophy on literacy teaching. However, in recent years the
systematic teaching of spelling has enjoyed something of a renaissance due to a
growing awareness that children will not necessarily become adequate spellers
if they are left to discover spelling principles for themselves. The current view
is that taking a systematic approach to spelling and word study is essential, and
leads to measurable improvement in students' spelling ability (Graham and Harris
2005a; Kreis 2005).

Whole-language perspectives on spelling

The advent of whole-language philosophy in the 1980s saw the teaching of spelling become fully integrated into children's daily writing activities rather than being treated as a subject in its own right. It was argued that spelling instruction must be kept within a meaningful context at all times, and students can be helped individually and informally to learn to spell the words they need to use when they write. This integrated approach is deemed to be a 'natural' way of acquiring spelling skill and is therefore regarded by whole-language exponents as preferable to any form of direct teaching based on the content of a predetermined word list. Instead, children are taught – in theory anyway – the precise information they need at the exact moment they need it.

Whole-language philosophy still exerts a very powerful influence over primary school teaching in many countries today; but used alone, this fully integrated approach to spelling proves to be inadequate for many children. In classrooms containing 28 or more children it is virtually impossible to find the necessary time to devote to such a personalised approach. Even if a few moments can be devoted to each child within the writing lesson, helping a child with a spelling difficulty for a fleeting moment inevitably results in very superficial coverage of any specific spelling principle. Dealing with words and spelling principles only as they are needed also results in undesirable fragmentation of learning experience. For example, a child told briefly how to spell the word 'fight' in her story may not recognise by analogy that it belongs to the word family comprising *right, sight, might, tight, light, bright, flight*, etc. An essential part of understanding how words are constructed involves students in recognising that many words share predictable letter patterns. It does not make sense to leave students to acquire this important knowledge through incidental learning.

Interventionist perspectives on spelling

In contrast to the whole-language exponents, those who lean instead toward a more skills-based approach believe that children require direct teaching of spelling skills and strategies. They agree that spelling should not be taught in a decontextualised manner, and that the instruction that is given must help children spell words they require for authentic writing purposes – but they emphasise that spelling is a skill that needs to be taught explicitly using principles of modelling, imitation, feedback and abundant practice.

Those who subscribe to skill-based teaching recognise the vital importance of teaching children efficient strategies for analysing and remembering unfamiliar words and for generating correct spelling patterns. The aim is to help children become strategic spellers (Wheatley 2005). It is clear that even without instruction most children do begin to develop their own unique strategies for spelling difficult words (Dahl *et al.* 2003), but some of their strategies are not effective and contribute to on-going problems. More will be said in a moment about the teaching of spelling strategies.

Developmental stages in spelling acquisition

It is important for teachers to be aware of the normal stages of development through which children pass on their way to becoming proficient spellers (Manning and Underbakke 2005). Students pass through these stages at different rates, and it is unrealistic to expect a student to achieve a level of independence or accuracy in spelling that is beyond his or her current developmental level. The stages have been described in the following way – although the exact title for each stage has differed among the various researchers (Bissex 1980; Scharer and Zutell 2003):

Stage 1: Prephonetic

At this stage the child 'plays' at writing (often using capital letters) in imitation of the writing of others. There is no connection between these scribbles and speech sounds or real words.

Stage 2: Phonetic

At this stage the child relies mainly upon phonemic awareness. In the child's spelling there is evidence of an emerging knowledge of letter–sound correspondences, picked up through incidental learning. The invented words are quite recognisable as children begin to apply basic phonic principles as they write. Sometimes the phoneme they identify is equated with the letter name rather than the sound, as for example in 'rsk' (ask), 'yl' (while), 'lefnt' (elephant).

Towards the end of the phonetic stage, approximations move much nearer to regular letter–sound correspondences, as in 'sed' (said) or 'becos' (because). But even at this stage some children have difficulty identifying the second or third consonant in a letter-string, and may write 'stong' (strong) or 'bow' (blow). Or they may fail to identify correctly a sound within the word and may write incorrect letters, as in 'druck' (truck), 'jriv' (drive), 'sboon' (spoon), 'dewis' (juice).

It should be noted that the majority of individuals with poor spelling have reached this phonetic stage in their development but have not progressed beyond it. They now need to be taught to use strategies such as visual checking of words and spelling by analogy in order to move to the next stage. Activities involving word analysis are also useful in helping the student to recognise letter patterns within words (orthographic units).

Stage 3: Transitional

At this stage there is clear evidence of a more sophisticated understanding of word structure. The child has become aware of within-word letter strings and syllable junctures. Common letter sequences, such as -ough, -ious, -ea-, -ai-, -aw-, -ing, etc., are used much more reliably. The children who are gaining real mastery over spelling at this stage also begin to spell by analogy, using words they know already in order to spell words they have never written before.

Stage 4: Independence

At this stage the child has mastery of quite complex grapho-phonic principles, and also uses visual imagery more effectively when writing and checking familiar words. Flexible use is made of a wide range of spelling, proofreading, self-help and self-correcting strategies.

In general, the invented spellings produced by children provide a useful window into their current phonological knowledge and their thought processes related to encoding written language (Bissaker and Westwood 2006; Scharer and Zutell 2003). In an ideal situation, teachers would gear spelling instruction to match children's current knowledge and ability. When spelling instruction and content are differentiated according to individual capabilities, the results are usually very positive (e.g. Brown and Morris 2005; Massengill 2006). But in reality this is not easy to do in the context of whole-class mixed-ability teaching.

Do we spell by eye, by ear, by hand, or by brain?

The answer to the question, 'Do we spell by eye, ear, hand or brain?', is almost certainly that we use all these resources on the way to becoming proficient spellers. However, for many years teachers have regarded the encoding of words as predominantly a *visual* processing skill (Manning and Underbakke 2005). For this reason, if students were fortunate enough to receive guidance in spelling, the strategies they were taught were mainly concerned with improving visual memory for word forms, for example, the 'look-cover-write-check' strategy. Much less importance has been attached to *auditory* processing strategies due to the erroneous belief that 'sounding out' words will lead to too many errors due to the irregularity of English spelling. Indeed, some teachers actively dissuade students from attending closely to the sound values heard within spoken words since the individual letters used to represent these sounds may not be entirely predictable. It is argued that because up to three words in every ten are not written precisely as they sound, with perfect letter-to-sound translations, it is not beneficial to teach children to utilise phonic information when spelling. Counter to this argument is evidence to suggest that learning to read and learning to spell, particularly in the beginning stages, are far more closely related to auditory-processing abilities than we previously believed. In the early stages of teaching children to read, the teaching of basic phonics should deliberately incorporate teaching of spelling as well as word recognition. Knowledge of phonics enhances early spelling because it enables children to relate the sounds they can hear in a spoken word to the letter or letters required to represent that sound in the written form (Nyholm 2002).

Let us consider the general contributions made to spelling by visual perception, auditory perception, hand movements and the brain.

Visual perception: spelling by eye

Very proficient spellers appear to make great use of visual information when writing words. It is obvious that visual clues are extremely important for accurate spelling. The most common way of checking one's own spelling and detecting errors is to look carefully at the written word and ask oneself, 'Does this word look right?' Strategies that involve the deliberate use of visual imagery, such as look-say-cover-write-check, are very effective for the learning of what are termed 'irregular' words, those with unpredictable letter-to-sound correspondences. To this extent we certainly do learn to spell by eye. The effective use of visual perception in learning to spell causes the student to build up a memory bank of visual images of words and of common letter strings. The knowledge in this store can be called upon whenever the student attempts to write an unfamiliar word.

Learning to spell by eye does not mean, however, that learners simply acquire the ability to spell by seeing words as they read – just 'looking' at words does not seem to be enough for most learners (Graham 2000). It is necessary for them to examine a word very carefully, with every intention of trying to commit its internal configuration to memory. As this behaviour does not come naturally to every learner, it is important that any student who lacks this experience be given the necessary instruction and practice. By implication, this may mean devoting specific time and attention to word study, over and above any help given to individual students as they write. It is most unlikely that such an important skill as word analysis could be adequately developed through incidental learning alone.

The current viewpoint is that spelling actually involves the coordinated use of several different complementary processes, strategies and modalities, including listening carefully to the component sounds and syllables within the word and developing kinaesthetic images of the most commonly written words.

Auditory perception: spelling by ear

Research has indicated that in the early stages of learning to read and spell it is important that a child can identify the different sound units within spoken words (phonemic awareness). The basic knowledge upon which successful reading and spelling develop seems to depend upon the child's awareness that spoken words can be broken down into smaller units and that these units can be represented by letters. In order to spell, young children in the first years of schooling rely on auditory perception to a much greater extent than older children, simply because they have not yet had as much exposure to letter patterns through daily reading and writing experiences. Building a memory bank of visual images of words and letter strings takes time and experience. The extent to which early attempts at spelling do rely upon attention to sounds in words and to letter–sound correspondences is evident in children's early attempts at inventing spelling.

When spelling a word there is actually a complementary association between auditory perception and visual perception. The process of writing an unfamiliar word requires the child first to identify the sound units within the word and then to match these sound units with appropriate letter clusters stored as visual images in what is termed 'orthographic memory'. Having identified the sound values in the word, and having represented these units on paper by writing the specific letters in sequence, visual perception is then used to check that what the student writes on paper also 'looks right' – for example, *brekfirst* should be recognised visually as an incorrect letter pattern for the word *breakfast*.

Motor memory: spelling by hand

Since the spelling of a word is typically produced by the physical action of writing, it is fair to assume that kinaesthetic memory may also be involved in learning to spell. Indeed, the rapid speed and high degree of automaticity with which a competent speller encodes a very familiar word directly from its meaning to its graphic representation, supports the view that motor memory is involved. Nichols (1985: 3) suggested that, 'Spelling is remembered best in your hand. It is the memory of your fingers moving the pencil to make a word that makes for accurate spelling.' The frequent action of writing may be one of the ways of establishing in orthographic memory the stock of images of words and letter strings. The process of building up orthographic images in memory is also facilitated by the study of word families with common letter sequences, for example, 'gate, date, late, fate, mate, etc.' (Worthy *et al.* 2001).

It is often recommended that we should not think of spelling words letter-by-letter but rather by concentrating upon the groups of letters that form common units in many words. This has some implications for the way in which we teach handwriting in the early years of schooling. Some evidence exists to support the notion that it is beneficial to teach young children to join letters together almost from the beginning of their instruction in handwriting, rather than teaching print script first and linked script much later. It is believed that joining the letters together in one smooth action helps children develop an awareness of common letter strings (Cripps 1990).

The brain's contribution to spelling

Obviously, the brain plays the central role in generating and checking plausible spelling alternatives. The learning of new words and the analysis of unfamiliar words prior to writing are both brain-based (cognitive) activities. The brain coordinates and integrates various sources of perceptual information to help predict the spelling of a word. Working out the most probable way to spell an unfamiliar word requires the writer to consider the meaning of the word (or the separate morphemes that make up the word), to reduce the word to sound units, to select feasible letter groups to represent those sounds, and to compare and contrast the written word (or part of the word) mentally with a known word (Nunes and Bryant 2004).

It is also the brain that makes the decision whether to apply auditory, visual, or some other strategy to encode the word. The ability to recall and apply spelling rules and strategies, or to recognise when a word is an exception to a rule, reflects a cognitive aspect of spelling. Similarly, devising some form of mnemonic to help one recall a particularly difficult word illustrates a cognitive solution to a problem.

The relative contributions of vision, audition, hand movement, and cognition

The extent to which visual perception, auditory perception, kinaesthetics and cognition contribute to the act of spelling a particular word seems to depend upon how familiar the word is to the writer. Unfamiliar words appear to require an analysis into their component sounds before an attempt can be made to write them. What has been written can then be checked for accuracy in terms of visual appearance. For example, when trying to spell the word 'work', the /w/ and the /rk/ can probably be encoded from their sound values, but the writer's orthographic visual memory has to be checked for the information that the vowel is o and not e in work. Very familiar, high-frequency words, such as 'and', 'the' and 'are', are probably written mainly from kinaesthetic memory and checked simultaneously for visual appearance.

Individual differences among spellers

Four types of imagery appear to be used in spelling a word:

- visual – the way the word looks;
- auditory – the way the word sounds;
- kinaesthetic – the way the word feels when written;
- speech-motor – the way the word articulates when spoken.

It seems that some students rely much more heavily on one type of imagery than on another and may need to be taught to use other types of imagery if possible. For example, dyslexic students are often found to be particularly weak in phonological skills and may rely too heavily on faulty visual memory for recall of letter patterns. Training them in phonemic awareness and the application of basic phonic knowledge appears to have a positive effect on spelling ability.

Examination of the written work produced by students with difficulties can reveal a great deal about their current skills and specific needs in spelling. One of the most common problems is the tendency of the student to be over-dependent on phonic knowledge and therefore to write irregular words as if they are phonemically regular. They appear to have remained at the phonetic stage of development for too long. Close examination of a student's exercise books, or the use of dictated word lists, will quickly reveal the extent to which the individual has this problem. Students producing these errors seem to lack the necessary strategies for carefully checking the visual appearance of a word, and will fail to identify the errors even when encouraged to proofread their material.

Teaching spelling by the visual-emphasis approach

The visual approach to spelling requires the student to memorise the overall appearance of words and the correct sequence of letters. Rather than attending to sounds and syllables within the word, the student attempts to store a visual image of the word, or key parts of the word, in long-term memory. Research has suggested that children can be trained to focus more attentively on words and to improve their visual imagery for letter sequences. Writing a word many times may also help the learner store the correct image of that word.

To improve visual processing of words, one of the simplest aids to make and use is the flashcard. These cards are particularly useful for teaching irregular words and for students who need to be weaned away from a predominantly phonetic approach to spelling – for example, students who have reached a plateau at the phonetic stage. The words are introduced to the student on cards measuring about 30 cm × 10 cm. The word is pronounced clearly and attention is drawn to any particular features in the printed word that may be difficult to recall later. The child is encouraged to make a 'mental picture' of the word, and examine it. Some teachers say, 'Use your eyes like a camera. Take a picture of the word. Close your eyes and imagine you can still see the word.' With the eyes closed the child is then told to trace the word in the air. After a few seconds the student writes the word from memory, articulating it clearly as he or she writes. The word is then checked against the flashcard. The writing of the whole word avoids the inefficient letter-by-letter copying habit that some students have developed.

The general look-cover-write-check approach is based on the principle of learning words by giving attention to their visible sequences of letters, rather than using letter-to-sound correspondences. Some teachers add the word 'say' to the strategy, making it 'look-say-cover-write-check' to accommodate the importance of clear articulation for accurate spelling.

The visual strategy in action involves the following steps:

- Look very carefully at the word.
- Say the word clearly. Try to remember every detail.
- Cover the word so that it cannot be seen.
- Write the word from memory, pronouncing it quietly as you write.

- Check your version of the word with the original. If it is not correct, go back through the steps again until you can produce the word accurately.
- For some students, finger tracing over the word may help with assimilation and retention of the letter sequence.
- Teachers should check for recall several days and weeks later.

The look-say-cover-write-check approach is far better than any rote learning or recitation procedure for learning to spell. It gives the student an independent system that can be applied to the study of any irregular words set for homework or to corrections or omissions from free writing. Students can work in pairs where appropriate, to check that the procedure is being followed correctly by the partner.

The look-say-cover-write-check strategy, although regarded as a visual learning method, almost certainly is effective because students are identifying groups of letters that represent pronounceable parts of words (orthographic units). From the earlier chapter on reading skills we know that this is precisely the type of information that is also essential for swift and efficient reading.

Several computer programs designed to develop spelling skills are on the market. Teachers should ensure that the way in which the words are presented on the screen causes the students to attend carefully to the sequence and clusters of letters, and requires the student to type the complete word from memory each time. Programs that focus too much attention on spelling letter-by-letter or inserting missing letters into spaces are far less effective.

Applying phonic principles

It is unnecessary and inappropriate to use the look-cover-write-check strategy if the target word could be written correctly from its sounds. The phonemic approach encourages students to attend carefully to sounds and syllables within regular words and to write the letters most likely to represent these sounds. While it is true that some 30 per cent of English words are not phonemically regular, some 70 per cent of words do correspond reasonably well with their letter-to-sound translations, particularly if *groups* of letters are recognised as representing larger sound units (e.g. *–ite; -eed; pre-; dis-*). The phonic knowledge necessary for effective spelling goes well beyond knowing the sound associated with each single letter. It is necessary to draw on knowledge of letter groups that represent pronounceable parts of words. When students have acquired this level of proficiency, the percentage of words that can be spelled as they sound increases very significantly. As Templeton (2003a: 48) states: 'The spelling system of English makes sense – most of the time'.

Spelling from meaning

Templeton (2003b) suggests that teachers should help children understand that words related in meaning are frequently also related in spelling. Cramer (1998: 148) describes an approach to spelling that stresses a link between meaning and spelling. He states:

> The spelling–meaning connection is not complex. It consists of the fact that words that are related in meaning are often closely related in the way they are spelled. Thus if you know the meaning and spelling of *heal* you have a good shot at spelling *health*. Notice that the sound of the word *heal* by itself and the sound of *heal* in *health* are quite different. *Heal* has a long /e/ sound; *heal* in *health* has the short /e/ sound. So why are they spelled the same? Because spelling them the same way preserves the spelling–meaning connection between the two words. If this were not so, the English spelling system would be more arbitrary and more complex.

To facilitate the study of words related by meaning, students can be helped to compile word families sharing a common root or base. Dictionary skills can be used to identify such words. Worthy *et al.* (2001) suggest that this type of activity is valuable because it helps to make spelling more predictable by relating it to meaning.

The morphemic approach

An approach that specifically capitalises on linking spelling with meaning is the morphemic approach. In this approach, children are taught to apply knowledge of sub-units of meaning within a word. The smallest unit of meaning is termed a morpheme, and the written version of a morpheme is known as a morphograph. For example, the word 'throw' contains only one morpheme, but 'throwing' contains two. The word 'unhappiness' (un-happ[y]-ness) contains three morphemes. The latter example also illustrates the use of a rule (changing y to i) when combining certain morphemes. When using a morphemic approach, teachers need to teach these rules.

Perhaps the best-known programme using a morphemic approach is *Spelling Through Morphographs* (Dixon and Englemann 1996). The materials are appropriate for students from Year 4 upwards and can be used with adults. In 140 lessons, the students learn all the key morphographs and the basic rules of the spelling system. Whole-language enthusiasts would reject such an approach, but *Spelling Through Morphographs* has proved particularly valuable for students with learning difficulties.

Spelling rules

Some experts advocate teaching spelling rules to students; but students with learning difficulties find most rules too obscure to be of help when they are faced with a particular word to spell. Worthy *et al.* (2001) indicate that teaching of rules and generalisations rarely works. In many cases, rather than drilling complex rules it is easier to help students spell the specific words they need for their writing and to teach them strategies to use when learning new words.

Some educators working with students with learning disabilities suggest that rules may be of some value for older students of above-average intelligence (Darch *et al.* 2000). They can understand the rule or principle and can appreciate when it might be applied. Even in these cases, the rules should be simple and have few exceptions (e.g. 'i' before 'e' except after 'c'– *receive*; words ending with 'e', drop the 'e' when adding an ending that begins with a vowel – *hope, hoping*; words ending in a single vowel and consonant, double the consonant before adding an ending that begins with a vowel – *stop, stopped, stopping*).

Activities such as Word Sorts (see below) can be used to help students discover rules and principles for themselves. This process is much more effective than any attempt at rote learning and memorising a taught rule.

Dictation

Although the regular use of dictation has fallen out of favour in many schools, it is sometimes suggested that dictation develops listening skills and concentration, and at the same time gives students experience of spelling words in context. It is recommended that the material to be dictated should be presented for children to study *before* it is dictated. In this way there is an opportunity to clarify meaning and to point out any difficult words.

Another approach encourages proofreading and self-correction. An unseen passage at an appropriate level of difficulty is dictated for students to write. They are then given a period of time to check and alter any words that they think are incorrect, perhaps using a different coloured pen. The teacher then checks the work and can observe two aspects of the student's performance. First, it is useful to look at the words the child has been able to correct (or at least knows to be wrong). Second, the teacher can record words that were in fact wrong but were not noticed by the student. If, based on their level of difficulty, these words should be known by the student, the teacher must make every effort to teach their correct spelling since they have become firmly set as incorrect responses. Kervin (2002) suggests that proofreading is useful for developing children's awareness of correct and incorrect word forms.

The use of 'phonic dictation', where the teacher deliberately stresses the sequence of sounds in a word or breaks a word into syllables, can be helpful in developing a student's sensitivity to the phonemic characteristics of words

(Savage 2004). Such work at a very simple level can be incorporated into phonological training activities described in earlier chapters.

Should spelling lists be used?

The notion that lists can be compiled that contain words that all students should know and use at a particular year or grade level has, to some extent, been abandoned. However, spelling lists continue to form the core of many spelling programmes, and some teachers strongly recommend their use for specific word study purposes (e.g. Beckham-Hungler and Williams 2003; Hammond 2004). The limitation of formal lists is that they usually fail to supply a particular word just when the student needs to use it for writing or proofreading. In addition, having one common word list for all students in the class ignores the fact that children are at different stages of spelling development and therefore have different learning needs (Manning and Underbakke 2005).

The question most often asked by teachers is, 'Do students learn to spell best from lists?' If the question refers to lists of words that students actually use and need when writing, the answer is certainly 'yes'. If the lists are based on other criteria – for example, words grouped according to visual, phonemic or morphemic similarity – the decision to use such a list with a particular student or group of students must be made in the light of their specific learning needs. It is known that rote learning words from a standard list does not generally result in any transfer of skill to everyday writing (Beckham-Hungler and Williams 2003). The most useful list from the point of view of the weakest spellers will be one compiled according to personal writing needs and common errors. A copy of this list can be kept in the back of the student's exercise book and used when he or she is writing a rough draft or proofreading a final draft of a piece of work (Thibodeau 2002).

'Word Walls' represent another excellent method of ensuring that words children need in their daily writing are readily to hand (Allen 2005). Words are written in blackboard-size writing so that children can locate them and use them as necessary. Vocabulary is added regularly to the Word Wall as each new topic is studied.

The value of lists comprising word families is that they represent yet another way of helping students establish awareness of common orthographic sub-units (e.g. onset and rime units; syllables). This awareness will help a student take a more rational approach to tackling an unfamiliar word, for example by using analogy to move from the known to the unknown (Kirkbride and Wright 2002).

Developing strategic spellers

Students have become truly independent in their spelling when they can look at an unfamiliar word and select the most appropriate strategy to use for learning that word. For example, they need to be able to look at a word and decide for themselves whether it is phonemically irregular or regular. For an irregular word they may need to apply the look-cover-write-check strategy, coupled perhaps with repeated writing of the word. For some irregular words they may also need to call upon knowledge of the simple principle about doubling letters, or dropping or changing a letter. If the word is phonemically regular they need to recognise that they can spell it easily from its component sounds. When students can operate at this level of judgement, the shift is from rote learning to an emphasis on studying words rationally.

This level of independence does not come easily to all students. Many individuals need to be taught how to learn new material. Some students, left to their own devices, fail to develop any systematic approach. They may just look at the word. They may recite the spelling alphabetically. They may copy letter-by-letter rather than writing the whole word. They may use no particular strategy at all, believing that learning to spell the word is beyond them. Any serious attempt to help children with spelling difficulties must involve determining *how* they set about learning a word or group of words. Where a student has no systematic approach it is essential that he or she be taught one.

Cognitive and metacognitive approaches to spelling teach students specific self-regulatory strategies to use when learning new words or checking the accuracy of spelling at the proofreading stage of writing. For example, they are taught to ask themselves:

- How many syllables do I hear in this word?
- Do I have the right number of syllables in what I have written?
- Do I know any other words that sound like this word?
- Does this word look correct? I'll try it again.
- Does this look better?

As with all other examples of strategy training described in this book, the teacher's role is to model effective strategies, to 'think aloud', and demonstrate ways of going about the task of spelling, checking and self-correcting. Based on classroom observation of teachers, O'Sullivan (2000) reported that the most effective teachers of spelling helped children develop a variety of spelling strategies – phonic and visual – and drew their attention to spelling patterns through analogy with other known words.

Simultaneous Oral Spelling (SOS)

This approach was first developed by Gillingham and Stillman in 1960. It has been applied very successfully for remediation of spelling problems in individual tutorial settings and is appropriate for any age level beyond beginner (Weeks *et al.* 2002). The approach involves five steps:

- Select the word you wish to learn, and have the teacher pronounce it clearly.

- Pronounce the word clearly yourself while looking carefully at the word.
- Say each syllable in the word (or break a single-syllable word into onset and rime).
- Name the letters in the word twice.
- Write the word, naming each letter as you write it.

Note that the *letter name* is used, not its common sound. This makes the method particularly appropriate for older students, who may be embarrassed by 'sounding out' words.

Repeated writing

The practice of having a student correct an error by writing the correct version of the word several times is believed by some teachers to serve no useful purpose. They consider that it is a form of rote learning that can be carried out without conscious effort on the part of the learner, and that words practised in this way are not remembered later.

It is true that if the student is thinking of other things or is distracted by noise or activity while carrying out the repeated writing, the procedure is of little or no value. However, repeated writing of a target word can be very helpful indeed if (i) the learner has every intention of trying to remedy an error and (ii) if he or she is attending fully to the task. It is one way in which kinaesthetic images of words can be more firmly established. Only a few words (usually *no more than three*) should be practised in any one session (Schlagal 2002).

Old Way/New Way method

Lyndon (1989) identified the psychological construct of 'proactive inhibition' as a possible reason for the failure of many conventional remedial methods to help a student 'unlearn' incorrect responses, such as habitual errors in spelling. Proactive inhibition (or proactive interference) is the term used to describe the situation where previously learned information interferes with one's ability to remember new information or to acquire a new response. What the individual already knows, even erroneous information, is protected from change.

Lyndon's approach, called 'Old Way/New Way', uses the student's error as the starting point for change. A memory of the old way of spelling the word is used to activate later an awareness of the new (correct) way of spelling the word. The following steps and procedures are used in the 'Old Way/New Way' approach:

- Student writes the word in the usual (incorrect) form.
- Teacher and student agree to call this the 'old way' of spelling that word.
- Teacher shows student a 'new way' (correct way) of spelling the word.
- Attention is drawn to the similarities and differences between the old and the new forms.

- Student writes the word again in the old way.
- Student writes the word in the new way, and states clearly the differences.
- Repeat five such writings of old way, new way and statement of differences.
- Write the word the new way six times, using different colour pens or in different styles.
- Older students may be asked to write six different sentences using the word in its 'new' form.
- Revise the word or words taught after a two-week interval.
- If necessary, repeat this procedure every two weeks until the new response is firmly established.

Word Sorts

Students are provided with word cards containing the words to be studied and compared. The words might be: *sock, black, truck, lock, rack, trick, track, block, lick, sack, stick, flock, flick, suck*. The students are asked, 'What is the same about these words?' The response might be that the words all end with /ck/. The words might now be categorised in other ways by sorting the cards into groups (for example, words ending in /ock/; words ending in /ack/). At a more advanced level, Word Sorts could involve words that are grouped according to the meaning–spelling connection, as discussed above – for example, *played, playfully, replay, player, playground, horseplay*.

The use of Word Sorts is strongly advocated by Joseph (2002) as a valuable investigative approach to help children discriminate among orthographic features within and across words. Bhattacharya and Ehri (2004) suggest that comparing and contrasting words in this way helps older students discover basic spelling rules; and Massengill (2006) reports positively on their use with adults with spelling difficulties.

Useful resources and activities involving Word Sorts can be found in Invernizzi *et al.* (2004) or Bear *et al.* (2006).

Programming for individual students

When planning an individualised programme in spelling, the following points should be kept in mind.

- Apply the basic diagnostic questions and procedures described in Chapter 8.
- Daily attention will be needed for the least able spellers, with weekly revision and regular testing for maintenance.
- Collect a list of words frequently needed by students to whom you are giving special help. Use this list for regular review and assessment.

- Try to obtain from teachers in secondary schools important vocabulary lists from specific subject areas: e.g. *ingredients, temperature, chisel, theory, science, hydrochloric, equation,* etc. These can be a useful focus of study for older students.
- Within each tutorial session, students should always work on specific words misspelled in free writing lessons as well as on more general word lists or word families.
- When making a correction to a word, a student should rewrite the whole word not merely erase the incorrect letters.
- Repetition and overlearning are important, so it is useful to have a range of games, word puzzles and computer tasks available to reinforce the spelling of important words. The games and activities must be closely matched to the objectives of the intervention programme.
- A visual record of improvement, such as an individual progress chart or graph, can help to indicate the number of new words mastered each week.
- The value of having students spell words aloud without seeing them or writing them is very questionable because spelling is a visual, auditory and motor activity. The visual appearance of the word as it is being written provides important clues to the speller. These clues are absent when the word is spelled aloud unseen.
- A neat, careful style of handwriting that can be executed swiftly and easily by the student is an important factor associated with good spelling. It cannot be inferred that good handwriting *per se* causes good spelling, but laboured handwriting and uncertain letter formation almost certainly inhibit the easy development of spelling habits at an automatic response level.

Additional practical advice on activities to improve spelling skills can be found in the books listed here under *Further reading*.

Further reading

Bear, D.R., Invernizzi, M. and Johnston, F. (2006) *Words Their Way: Word Sorts for Emergent Spellers*, Upper Saddle River, NJ: Pearson-Merrill-Prentice Hall.
Ganske, K. (2006) *Word Sorts and More: Sound, Pattern and Meaning Explorations K-3*, New York: Guilford.
Gentry, J.R. (2004) *The Science of Spelling*, Portsmouth, NH: Heinemann.
Invernizzi, M., Johnston, F. and Bear, D. (2004) *Words their Way: Word Sorts for Within Word Pattern Spellers*, Upper Saddle River, NJ: Pearson-Merrill.
Johnston, F., Invernizzi, M. and Bear, D.R. (2005) *Words Their Way: Word Sorts for Syllables and Affixes Spellers*, Upper Saddle River, NJ: Pearson.
Marten, C. and Graves, D.H. (2003) *Word Crafting: Teaching Spelling, Grades K-6*, Portsmouth, NH: Heinemann.
McGuiness, D. (2004) *Early Reading Instruction: What Science Really Tells us About How to Teach Reading*, Cambridge, MA: MIT Press.
Simon, L. (2004) *Strategic Spelling: Every Writer's Tool*, Portsmouth, NH: Heinemann.

Sipe, R.B., Putnam, D., Reed-Nordwall, K., Roseware, T. and Walsh, J. (2003) *They Still Can't Spell? Understanding and Supporting Challenged Spellers in Middle and High School*, Portsmouth, NH: Heinemann.

Westwood, P.S. (2005) *Spelling: Approaches to Teaching and Assessment* (2nd edn), Melbourne: Australian Council for Educational Research.

Wheatley, J.P. (2005) *Strategic Spelling: Moving Beyond Word Memorization in the Middle Grades*, Newark, DE: International Reading Association.

Chapter 12

Developing numeracy and mathematical problem-solving skills

Many students have difficulty in acquiring and using mathematics skills. About 6% to 7% of the students in general education classes show evidence of a serious mathematics difficulty.

(Lerner and Kline 2006: 477)

As Lerner and Kline (2006) indicate, many children with and without disabilities or learning difficulties experience major problems learning mathematics. In this chapter, some of the possible reasons for this situation will be discussed and procedures will be described for assessing students' abilities in basic mathematical skills. Attention will also be given to identifying appropriate teaching methods to help overcome learning difficulties.

Contemporary perspectives on mathematics teaching

As a result of the reforms in mathematics education that started in many countries in the late 1980s, schools were required to implement a *constructivist* teaching approach, often referred to as activity-based, problem-based, or 'process maths'. Rather than using traditional didactic methods with a focus on developing children's arithmetic skills, teachers were encouraged to create learning situations that provide opportunities for children to discover mathematical relationships, solve real problems and construct meaning (National Council of Teachers of Mathematics 2005). In constructivist approaches, the emphasis is on helping students move beyond practising routine calculations to a much deeper understanding of mathematical processes and problems (Xin *et al.* 2005b). It is believed that these constructivist methods are more effective in fostering development of higher-order cognitive skills and strategies.

In theory at least, constructivist approaches would appear to have much to offer in teaching mathematics; but it must be acknowledged that the exclusive use of constructivist approaches has been seriously questioned (e.g. Kroesbergen *et al.* 2004). The critics suggest that constructivist theory makes unreasonable assumptions concerning children's ability to discover, conceptualise, and remember mathematical relationships for themselves. There is also major concern over the reduced attention given to developing children's fluency and automaticity in basic number skills. It is suggested by some advocates of constructivist methods that, for example, children do not require skills in computational procedures in order to understand mathematics. Others refute such claims (Desimone *et al.* 2005).

So, the notion has been challenged that mathematics can be taught successfully by an entirely immersion approach (Jones and Southern 2003; Klein *et al.* 2005). The evidence seems to indicate that not all children make good progress under approaches that require learners to discover essential principles for themselves and acquire vital skills through incidental learning. Some students clearly make much better progress in mathematics when they are directly taught (Ellis 2005; Farkota 2005). In general, research on teacher effectiveness in the area of mathematics supports the use of a structured approach within a carefully sequenced programme. Evidence seems to prove that the most effective teachers provide systematic instruction in mathematics in such a way that genuine understanding accompanies mastery of number skills and the acquisition of problem-solving strategies.

In countries where the highest achievement levels in mathematics occur (e.g. Japan, Korea, Singapore, Hong Kong), teachers have not moved wholeheartedly into student-centred activity methods. Typically, mathematics lessons in these countries reveal that teachers maintain fairly close control over the learning process, but they ensure that all students participate in interactive whole-class lessons to solve problems and apply new skills. The emphasis is certainly still upon constructing meaning, but not through the medium of unstructured activities. Lessons are typically clear, accurate and rich in examples and demonstrations of a particular concept, process or strategy. The teacher takes an active role in stimulating students' thinking, imparting relevant information, and teaching specific skills. In the UK, the arrival of the interactive electronic whiteboard (IWB) has provided an incentive for teachers to refine their presentation skills and capitalise on the potential of ICT, while at the same time increasing student participation (Smith *et al.* 2006; University of Hull 2006).

In countries such as Britain and Australia, where national strategies for enhancing numeracy are in operation, the recommendation is for daily intensive lessons, using an interactive whole-class teaching approach. Lessons are conducted at a reasonably fast pace and incorporate a high degree of student participation and practice. The evidence is that the daily lessons have had beneficial impact on students' skills and confidence (Kyriacou 2005), but many teachers still don't find the interactive fast-paced teaching easy to implement. Nor are they particularly skilled yet in ensuring that students think more deeply and critically about the mathematics they are learning.

The emerging perspective at this time is that effective teaching and learning in mathematics requires not only student-centred investigative activities but also a good measure of teacher-directed explicit instruction (Hay *et al.* 2005; Fleischner and Manheimer 1997). The amount of explicit instruction required varies from student to student and from concept to concept, with direct teaching being of most benefit for students with learning difficulties (Baker *et al.* 2002; Pincott 2004). The perspective presented in this chapter reflects this conclusion.

Whole-class teaching and group work

Although there is increasing support for interactive whole-class teaching in mathematics (e.g. Wilson *et al.* 2006), the use of a direct teaching approach does not mean that teachers should abandon the use of group work or collaborative learning in the classroom. Lessons with well-planned group work do facilitate student achievement, interest, and motivation. Group activities that involve students in discussion and sharing of ideas appear to help individuals negotiate a better understanding of key concepts and processes (*socio-constructivism*).

It should be noted however that certain students don't seem to gain as much as others from small group processes, particularly those students who remain passive and allow others to make decisions and do most of the work. Students with learning difficulties appear often to receive too much help from their partners during group activities in mathematics. Teachers need to recognise this potential problem and attempt to structure group work in such a way that all students can usefully participate (see Chapter 6).

Another difficulty associated with group work in mathematics is the paucity of curriculum materials specifically designed for collaborative learning. It is usually left to the teacher to develop appropriate resources; and the additional work involved may result in some teachers opting out of this pattern of organisation.

Learning difficulties in mathematics

It is suggested that 5 to 7 per cent of students have significant difficulties in learning basic mathematical concepts and skills (Fuchs and Fuchs 2005). A much higher percentage of students are observed to be low achievers in mathematics, displaying a poor attitude towards the subject and having no confidence in their own ability to improve. Some students exhibit anxiety in situations where they are expected to demonstrate competence in applying mathematical skills. While a very small number of these students may have a specific learning disability related to mathematics (*dyscalculia*) (Temple 2001; Westwood 2004b), most have simply encountered difficulties with mathematics learning for a variety of different reasons.

Some of the factors associated with learning difficulty in mathematics include:

- insufficient or inappropriate instruction (Farkota 2005; Pincott 2004);
- pacing of the curriculum outstripping the students' ability to assimilate new concepts and skills; they fall behind and become discouraged (Harniss *et al.* 2002);

- little or no differentiation of learning activities, problems, and assessment tasks to match students' differing abilities (Maccini and Gagnon 2006);
- too little structuring of discovery learning or process maths situations, so students fail to abstract or remember anything from them (Fleischner and Manheimer 1997);
- the teacher's use of language in explaining mathematical relationships or in posing questions may not match the students' level of comprehension (Cawley *et al.* 2001);
- abstract symbols are introduced too early in the absence of concrete materials or real-life examples (Lerner and Kline 2006);
- reading difficulties contributing significantly to learning difficulties in mathematics (Gersten *et al.* 2005);
- the students' grasp of simple relationships in numbers to 10 or 20 may not be fully developed before larger numbers involving complications of place value are introduced (Ross 2002);
- too little time spent in developing automaticity with number facts, leading later to slowness and inaccuracy in processes and problems (Riccomini 2005).

It is important that any child with learning difficulties in mathematics should be identified as soon as possible and given appropriate support (Mazzocco and Thompson 2005). Early intervention programmes for children with learning difficulties do exist – for example, *Mathematics Recovery* (Wright 2003) and *Numeracy Recovery* (Dowker 2005). *Mathematics Recovery* involves 30 minutes a day of individualised assessment-based instruction for low-achieving children aged 6 to 7 years. *Numeracy Recovery* also targets 6- to 7-year-old children, but involves 30 minutes of instruction per week over a period of approximately 30 weeks. Both programmes give attention to such fundamental skills as counting, numeral recognition, grouping, solving simple addition and subtraction problems, and the beginnings of place value. The DfES (2005) has also produced special materials to help children with learning difficulties in basic number skills. The earlier such interventions are implemented the more likely it is that young children can develop sound 'number sense', procedural skills, and basic concepts. Intensive intervention, particularly when it incorporates computer-aided practice and application, can definitely enhance the basic number skills of early primary students (Fuchs *et al.* 2005).

What should be taught?

In the same way that views have changed in recent years on how best to teach mathematics to students with special needs, views are changing too on *what* should be taught to these students. Traditionally, students with learning problems were usually placed in the lowest-ability group and given a watered-down version of the mainstream curriculum. Sometimes (particularly in secondary school classes) a 'functional' curriculum would be developed with a title such as 'social maths' or 'real-life maths'. The belief was that students with special needs required an alternative to the mainstream programme, with the content significantly reduced in both depth and quantity, and focused clearly on numeracy skills required in adult life. However, it is argued now that students with special needs, like all other students, are entitled to engage in an interesting, challenging, relevant and inclusive mathematics curriculum (Cawley et al. 2001; Harniss et al. 2002). The suggestion now is that the content of the mathematics course should be reduced as little as possible for lower-ability students in order to maintain sufficient interest and challenge. This is an admirable notion, but is far from simple to put into practice. The dilemma remains unresolved concerning what should and should not be included in the curriculum for students with significant learning problems.

The *National Numeracy Strategy Framework* in Britain states that:

> The needs of pupils regarded as 'special' are not essentially different from those of other children. Instead of focusing on differences, you might emphasize the links with the needs of all learners, and use them productively to improve learning opportunities for all children.
>
> (DfEE 1999: 21)

To help make mathematics more interesting and relevant to a diverse range of students, it has been suggested that it should also be integrated into other school subjects, particularly into literacy learning, social studies, environmental education and the sciences. For example, the value of using mathematical concepts and skills within the context of reading and writing has been stressed very strongly (Martinez and Martinez 2001). A contextualised approach appears to enhance student motivation and involvement, and also increases the likelihood that mathematical concepts and skills will generalise to other situations and uses. However, such an approach does not imply that basic skills of numeracy are devalued or left to incidental learning. It is clear that mastery of basic number skills and development of sound 'number sense' must be given high priority in any early mathematics programme (Berch 2005; Riccomini 2005).

A diagnostic approach

There are many reasons why some students experience difficulty in mastering the facts, concepts and operations in arithmetic and applying these successfully to problem solving. As with reading, writing and spelling, the first step toward intervention should be to ascertain what the student can already do in this area of the curriculum, to locate any specific gaps which may exist, and to determine what he or she needs to be taught next. In other words, the diagnostic model presented in Chapter 8 can be applied to the assessment of skills in arithmetic, and can guide programme planning in mathematics interventions.

The first step in the diagnostic evaluation of mathematical skills might involve formal testing of the student to determine the level at which he or she is functioning. A comprehensive picture of a student's range of knowledge and skills can be obtained from teacher-made tests. These tests reflect the content of the curriculum being taught. Curriculum-based assessment is now widely acknowledged as a positive approach for teachers to use when linking assessment to instructional design.

Teacher-made tests can be supplemented with information gleaned from teachers' anecdotal records and from examination of the student's exercise books, worksheets or portfolio. The nature of a student's errors over a period of time can be appraised and follow-up diagnostic tests assessing proficiency in particular processes could be used (Riccomini 2005). As Hay *et al.* (2005: 6) remark: 'Children's numeracy errors reflect the processes involved in their thinking and serve useful diagnostic functions for programming'.

Teachers can construct their own 'informal mathematical skills inventory' containing test items covering key concepts, knowledge and skills presented in earlier years together with essential material from the current year. Such an inventory can indicate precisely what the student can and cannot do, and will assist with the ordering of priorities for teaching.

Concrete to abstract

Various levels of abstraction are involved in diagnostic work in mathematics. Identification of these levels will help a teacher answer the question 'What can the student do in mathematics if given a little help and guidance?' The levels are concrete, semi-concrete and abstract. At the *concrete level* the student may be able to solve a problem or complete a process correctly if allowed to manipulate real objects. At the *semi-concrete level* pictorial representations of the objects, together with symbols or tally marks, will be sufficient visual information to ensure success. At the *abstract level* the student can work with symbols only. During the diagnostic work with the student, the teacher may move up or down within this hierarchy from concrete to abstract in an attempt to discover the level at which the child can succeed with each concept.

Informal diagnostic interviews

The main goal in teaching mathematics to all students is the development of everyday problem-solving skills, and therefore diagnosis of a student's current ability in this domain should have high priority. Close investigation of strategies used by a student in carrying out a computation or solving a problem can be achieved in a *diagnostic interview*. Using appropriate calculations or problems as a focus, discussion between teacher and student can reveal much about the student's level of confidence, flexibility of thinking and underlying knowledge.

Teachers should probe for understanding in the following areas when appraising a student's problem-solving abilities:

- detecting what is called for in a problem;
- identifying relevant information;
- selecting correct procedure;
- estimating an approximate answer;
- computing the answer;
- checking the answer.

It may be helpful to keep the following thoughts in mind when attempting to discover the student's functional level. By referring to any items the student fails to solve in a test or during deskwork, consider:

- Why did the student get this item wrong?
- Can he or she carry out the process if allowed to use concrete aids, count on fingers, use a number line or calculator?
- Can he or she explain to me what to do? Ask the student to work through the example step by step. At what point does the student misunderstand?

The value of this procedure cannot be over-stressed. If a student explains how he or she tackles the problem, the teacher can pick up at once the exact point of confusion, and can teach from there. Too often in remedial intervention situations teachers quickly re-teach the whole process, but still fail to help the student recognise and overcome the precise point of difficulty.

In many ways, assessing problem-solving skills and strategies in mathematics has much in common with assessing comprehension in reading. Additional information on teaching problem-solving strategies is provided later in the chapter.

Three levels of assessment

The following three levels of assessment may help a teacher design appropriate assessment materials. It is likely that the first two levels will be the most applicable for students with learning difficulties, including students with intellectual disability.

Level I

If the student's performance in basic number is very poor, consider the following areas of knowledge and ability. At this stage almost all the assessments need to be made at an individual level, using appropriate concrete materials such as toys, blocks, pictures, number cards.

- Check the student's grasp of *vocabulary* associated with number relationships (e.g. 'bigger', 'altogether', 'less', 'share', etc.).
- Check the student's *conservation of number.*

Then check the following knowledge and skills in the following order.
Can the student:

- sort objects given one attribute (colour, size, shape, etc.)?
- sort objects given two attributes?
- produce equal sets of objects by one-to-one matching?
- count correctly objects to 10? 20?
- recognise numerals to 10? 20?
- place number symbols in correct sequence to 10? 20?
- write numerals correctly from dictation to 10? 20?
- understand ordinal values (fifth, tenth, second, etc.)?
- perform simple addition with numbers below 10 (e.g. $3 + 5 = $). With counters? In written form?
- perform subtraction with numbers below 10 (e.g. $8 - 5 = $). With counters? In written form?
- count-on in a simple addition problem?
- answer simple oral problems involving addition or subtraction with numbers below 10?
- recognise coins and paper money (lp 2p 5p 10p 50p £1 or 5¢ 10¢ 20¢ 50¢ $1.00 $2.00)?

Level 2

If the student's performance in number is slightly better than Level 1, consider the following areas. Harniss *et al.* (2002) refer to some of the basic principles listed below as 'big ideas' – they underpin much of the understanding at the next level.
Can the student:

- carry out simple mental addition with numbers below 20?
- carry out simple mental problem-solving without use of finger-counting or tally marks?
- carry out simple subtraction mentally as above? Is there a marked difference between performance in addition and subtraction?
- perform both vertical and horizontal written forms of simple addition?
- understand the *commutative law* in addition (i.e. that the order of items to be totalled does not matter)? Does the child see for example that $5 + 3$ and $3 + 5$ are bound to give the same total? When counting-on to obtain a total in such problems, does the child always count the smaller number on to the larger; or are these problems always solved from left to right?

- understand *additive composition* (i.e. all the possible ways of producing a given set or total)? For example, 5 is $4 + 1$, $3 + 2$, $2 + 3$, $1 + 4$, $5 + 0$.
- understand the complementary or reversible character of addition and subtraction ($7 + 3 = 10$, $10 - 7 = 3$, $10 - 3 = 7$)?
- watch an operation demonstrated using concrete material and then record this in written form?
- translate a written equation into a practical demonstration (e.g. using Unifix cubes to demonstrate $12 - 4 = 8$)?
- listen to a simple real-life situation described in words and then work the problem in written form? (Seven people were waiting at the bus stop. When the bus came only three could get on. How many were left to wait for the next bus?) Use numbers below 20. Can the child work problems at this level mentally?
- recognise and write numerals to 50?
- tell the time: read a digital clock correctly? Read an analogue clock to the nearest hour and half-hour?
- recite the days of the week?
- recite the months of the year?

Level 3

If students are able to succeed with most of the items in the previous levels, or if they seem reasonably competent in most areas of basic number work, consider these questions.

Can the student:

- read and write numbers to 100? To 1000? Can he or she read and write sums of money correctly?
- halve or double numbers mentally?
- add money mentally? Give change by the counting-on method?
- recite the multiplication tables correctly and answer random facts from these tables?
- perform the correct procedures for addition of hundreds, tens, units (HTU) and thousands, hundreds, tens and units (ThHTU). Without carrying? With carrying in any column?
- understand place value with T U? With H T U? With Th H T U?
- perform the subtraction algorithm, without exchanging in any column? With exchanging? It is important to note the actual method used by the child to carry out subtraction. Is it 'decomposition' using only the top line of figures; or the 'equal addition' method using top and bottom lines? Perform the correct steps in the multiplication algorithm? To what level of difficulty?
- perform the correct steps in the division algorithm? To what level of difficulty?

- recognise fractions: $\frac{1}{2}, \frac{1}{4}, 3\frac{1}{2}, 7\frac{1}{4}, 5\frac{3}{10}, 0.8, 5.9$ etc.?
- read and interpret correctly simple word problems?

The following sections present some teaching points for the most basic levels of number work. Children with learning difficulties, including those with intellectual disability, may benefit from application of the following principles within their programmes.

Teaching and learning at the concrete and semi-concrete levels

The use of structural equipment such as Dienes MAB, Cuisenaire Rods and Unifix is strongly advocated in the early stages of any student's mathematics programme. In theory, using such material provides a bridge between concrete experience and abstract reasoning by taking learners through experiences at the intermediate levels of semi-concrete (not the real object but another object or picture used to represent it) to the semi-abstract (the use of the first stages of symbolic representation such as tally marks). Using concrete material appears to help children construct deeper mathematical understanding. Structural material is particularly important for students with learning difficulties and learning disabilities as it helps them to store visual representations of number relationships.

The use of apparatus is also helpful for making word problems more visual and concrete, and for establishing an understanding of place value. However, it must be recognised that such materials have to be used effectively if students are to form necessary connections between the material and the underlying concepts and processes they are designed to illustrate. Problems arise if students come to rely too much on apparatus and do not progress to the next pencil-and-paper level of processing number relationships.

Counting

Counting is perhaps the most fundamental of all early number skills. Counting can assist with the development of conservation of number because it facilitates comparing of groups. If a child has not acquired accurate counting of real objects the skill must be taught by direct instruction. The problem is often that the student fails to make a correct one-to-one correspondence between the spoken number and the objects touched in order. If the physical act of counting a set of objects appears difficult for a student with a disability, manual guidance of his or her hands may be needed. For young children the use of 'finger plays' and 'number rhymes or songs' may assist with the mastery of counting.

Counting of actual objects will eventually be extended to encompass the 'counting-on' strategy for addition, and the 'counting-back' strategy for subtraction, in the absence of real objects. These strategies may have to be taught directly to certain students.

Recognition of numerals

The cardinal value of number symbols should be related to a wide variety of sets of objects. Teachers can make numeral-to-group matching games (for example, the numeral 11 on a card to be matched with eleven birds, eleven kites, eleven cars, eleven dots, eleven tally marks, etc.). Also useful are teacher-made lotto cards containing a selection of the number symbols being taught or overlearned (1 to 10, or 1 to 20, or 25 to 50, etc.). When the teacher holds up a flashcard and says the number, the student covers the numeral on the lotto card. At the end of the game the student must say each number aloud to the teacher as it is uncovered on the card. Later, these same lotto cards can be used for basic addition and subtraction facts, the numerals on the cards now representing correct answers to some simple question from the teacher (5 add 4 makes ...? The number 1 less than 8 is ...?).

Activities with number cards can also be devised to help students sort and arrange numerals in correct sequence from 1 to 10, 1 to 20, etc. The early items in the Unifix mathematics apparatus can be useful at this stage (e.g. the inset pattern boards, number indicators, number line to 20).

The writing of numerals should be taught in parallel to the above activities. Correct formation of numerals should be established as thoroughly as correct letter formation in handwriting: this will reduce the incidence of reversals of figures in written recording.

Written recording

There is a danger that some very young students or those with moderate learning difficulties will be expected to deal with symbolic number recording too early. Pictorial recording, tally marks and dot patterns are all very acceptable forms of representation for the young or developmentally delayed child. Gradually, the writing of number symbols will accompany picture-type recording and then finally replace it, by which time the cardinal values of the numerals are understood. It is important that written recording should evolve naturally from concrete experiences. In the same way that 'emergent writing' occurs in the literacy domain so too 'emergent number skills' are evident in the numeracy domain.

Number facts

Functional knowledge in arithmetic involves two major components: mastery of number facts that can easily be retrieved from memory (to $9 + 9$ and 9×9), and a body of knowledge about computational procedures. Both components are needed in typical arithmetic problem-solving situations.

Many students with learning disabilities have difficulties learning and recalling number facts and tables, so require extra attention devoted to this key area (Dowker 2005; Gersten *et al.* 2005). Number facts (e.g. $5 + 4 = 9$) are involved in all steps of the sub-routines carried out in complex computations, so they need to be recalled with a high degree of automaticity. Hay *et al.* (2005: 7) confirm that, 'Automatic, accurate access to basic number facts is essential for fluent computational processing'. It is therefore vital that students be helped to develop automatic recall of facts rather than having to calculate with fingers each time they are needed.

Being able to recall number facts easily is important for two main reasons: it makes calculation easier and it allows time for the deepening of understanding (Westwood 2003). Knowing number facts is partly a matter of learning through repetition (remembered through constant exposure and practice) and partly a matter of grasping a rule (e.g. that zero added to any number doesn't change it: 3 + 0 = 3, 13 + 0 = 13, etc.; or if 7 + 3 = 10 then 7 + 4 must be 'one more than 10', etc.). Regular practice will help develop the necessary automaticity. Burns (2005) reviewed a number of studies and concluded that teaching through drill tasks can lead to better retention of basic skills and later to improved performance in more advanced skills. Burns comments that children who lack prerequisite skills for attempting higher-order tasks must first master these skills in order to move to higher levels.

Pocket calculators

The pocket calculator provides a means of bypassing the computational weakness of some students. There is a valid argument that time spent on drilling mechanical arithmetic is largely wasted if students cannot remember the same steps later when working through a calculation. The use of the calculator as a permanent alternative is totally defensible in such cases (Huinker 2002). The instructional time saved can then be devoted to helping the students select the correct type of operation needed to solve particular problems.

Computation and algorithms

Once young students have evolved their own meaningful forms of recording in the early stages one must move on to the introduction of conventional forms of vertical and horizontal computation. A student should be able to watch as a bundle of ten rods and two extra ones are added to a set already containing a bundle of ten rods and three extra ones and then write the operation as

12 + 13 = 25 or

$$\begin{array}{r} 12 \\ + 13 \\ \hline 25 \end{array}$$

The reverse of this procedure is to show the student a 'number sentence' (e.g. $20 - 13 = 7$) and ask him or her to demonstrate what this means using some form of concrete materials. Dienes MAB blocks are particularly useful for this purpose. Unifix blocks, being larger in size, are more appropriate for children with poor manipulative skills.

This stage of development is likely to require careful structuring over a long period of time if students with learning difficulties are not to become confused. The careful grading of the examples, and the amount of concrete practice provided at each stage, are crucial for long-term mastery. Once students reach this stage of applying the basic algorithms for addition (with and without carrying), subtraction (with and without exchanging), multiplication and division, the demands on their thinking and reasoning increase rapidly. According to Hay *et al.* (2005: 7): 'Students' lack of understanding of the number system, place value and renaming often underlies numeracy difficulties'.

It is, of course, traditional to teach students verbal self-instructions (cues) when carrying out the steps in a particular calculation. For example, using the decomposition method for this subtraction problem the student would be taught to verbalise the steps in some way similar to the wording below.

$5^7 8^1 1$ The child says: 'Start with the units. I can't take 9 from 1 so I must
$-1\ 3\ 9$ borrow a ten
———   and write it next to the 1 to make 11. Cross out the 8 tens and write 7.
$4\ 4\ 2$ Now I can take 9 from 11 and write 2 in the answer box.
     Then, 7 take away 3, leaves 4 in the tens box.
     In the hundreds column, 5 take away 1 leaves 4. Write 4 in the answer box.
     My answer is 442.'

A support teacher or parent who attempts to help a student in this area of school work must liaise closely with the class teacher in order to find out the precise verbal cues ('scripts') that are used in teaching the four processes, so that exactly the same words and directions are used in the remedial programme to avoid confusion. Verbal cueing is only required during the time a child is first mastering a new algorithm. Once mastered, the algorithmic procedure becomes automatic and verbal cueing fades.

Learning these scripts has fallen somewhat into disrepute in recent years. It is felt by some experts that these methods inhibit the thinking of more-able students and may prevent them from devising insightful and rapid methods of completing a calculation. It is argued that mindlessly following an algorithm may represent nothing more than mechanical responses based on rote learning. However, without the verbal cues for working through a calculation, lower-ability students are likely to remain totally confused and utterly frustrated.

It is important that students also be taught other strategies for solving addition and subtraction problems, preferably those which will help to develop insight into the structure and composition of the numbers involved. For example, if the student is faced with 47 + 17 = ?, he or she is encouraged to think of this regrouped as a set of (40 + 7) added to a set of (10 + 7). The tens are quickly combined to make 50, and the two 7's make 14. Finally 14 combined with 50 is obviously 64. Fewer errors seem to occur with this method than with the 'carry ten under the line' type of vertical addition. This is almost certainly because the approach is meaningful and does help to develop insight into the structure of number. It can also be easily demonstrated using MAB blocks or similar concrete materials.

With subtraction the procedure may be illustrated thus:

(53 – 27 =)   53 can be regrouped as 40 + 13
                27 can be regrouped as 20 + 7
                Deal with the tens first: 40 – 20 = 20
                Now the second step: 13 – 7 = 6
                We are left with 26.

Once this method is established with understanding it appears to result in fewer errors than either 'decomposition' or 'equal addition' methods for subtraction. The equal addition method has fallen out of favour in recent years. It was once considered the best method to use for students with learning difficulties because it led to fewer errors when tackling difficult subtraction problems involving zeros in the top line.

Dole (2003) recommends the Old Way/New Way method to help children remedy specific errors in carrying out calculations. The Old Way/New Way method has already been described in connection with remedying spelling errors (Chapter 11). It is believed that this method helps a learner internalise and remember the correct algorithmic procedure by overcoming the negative influence of proactive inhibition. Dole recommends the following teaching steps:

- Student performs the calculation incorrectly on whiteboard.
- Teacher asks if he can call this the 'Old Way' of calculating.
- Teacher demonstrates the correct way of calculating, and calls it the 'New Way'.
- Student and teacher together compare and discuss the differences.
- Student performs the Old Way again, then the New Way again, and clearly points out and describes the differences.
- Student repeats five more Old Way/New Way cycles, each time comparing and contrasting the two models.

Developing problem-solving skills and strategies

The whole purpose of mathematics education is to acquire information, skills, and strategies that enable an individual to solve problems that may present themselves during school time, working life, at home, or during leisure. Children need therefore to be taught how and when to use computational skills and problem-solving strategies for authentic purposes. However, as Kroesbergen and Van Luit (2003) point out, from the teacher's point of view, instructing students in problem-solving strategies is not easy, compared with teaching them basic arithmetic processes. Similarly, from the learner's perspective, solving a problem involves much more than simply applying a pre-taught algorithm. Non-routine problems need to be analysed, explored for possible procedures to use, and then the final result checked for feasibility.

Students with learning difficulties commonly display helplessness and confusion when faced with mathematics problems in word form. They begin by having difficulty reading the words in the problem, or with comprehending the exact meaning of specific terms. The fact that they do not really understand what they are being asked to find out obviously compounds their difficulty in selecting which process or processes to use. Their most obvious weakness is their total lack of any effective strategy for approaching a mathematical task (Hay *et al.* 2005). Their inability and lack of success leads to loss of confidence and diminution of their feeling of self-esteem. Most students with these difficulties need to be taught a range of effective problem-solving and task-approach strategies (Furner *et al.* 2005). The aim is to teach them how to process the information in a problem without a feeling of panic or hopelessness. They need to be able to sift the relevant from the irrelevant information and impose some degree of structure on the problem.

How do we solve problems?

Although described differently by different writers, it is generally accepted that there are recognisable and teachable steps through which an individual passes when solving mathematical problems. These steps can be summarised as:

- interpretation of the problem to be solved;
- identification of processes and steps needed;
- translation of the information into an appropriate algorithm (or algorithms);
- calculation;
- evaluation of the result.

It is recognised that in addition to the cognitive skills involved in these five steps there are also significant metacognitive components. These components include the self-monitoring and self-correcting questions the learner uses when processing a problem. For example:

- 'What needs to be worked out in this problem?' (identify the problem).
- 'How will I try to do this?' (select or create a strategy).
- 'Can I picture this problem in my mind?' (visualise).

- 'Is this working out OK?' (self-monitoring).
- 'How will I check if my solution is correct ?' (evaluation).
- 'I need to correct this error and then try again' (self-correction).

When teaching a problem-solving strategy the teacher needs to:

- model and demonstrate effective use of the strategy for solving routine and non-routine problems;
- 'think aloud' as various aspects of the problem are analysed and possible procedures for solution identified;
- reflect upon the effectiveness of the procedure and the validity of the result obtained.

A problem-solving strategy might, for example, use a particular mnemonic to aid recall of the procedure. For example, in the mnemonic 'RAVE CCC' the word RAVE can be used to identify the first four possible steps to take:

- R = Read the problem carefully.
- A = Attend to words that may suggest the process to use (for example, *share, altogether, less than*).
- V = Visualise the problem, and perhaps make a sketch or diagram.
- E = Estimate the possible answer.

Then the letters CCC suggest what to do next:

- C = Choose the numbers to use.
- C = Calculate the answer.
- C = Check the answer against your estimate.

Once students have been taught a particular strategy they must have an opportunity to apply the strategy themselves under teacher guidance and with feedback. Finally they must be able to use the strategy independently and to generalise its use to other problem contexts. The sequence for teaching problem solving to students with learning difficulties therefore follows a sequence beginning with direct teaching, followed by guided practice, and ending with student-centred control and independent use.

Since there is evidence that students can be helped to become more proficient at solving problems, teachers of students with learning difficulties need to devote more time to this area of work. As mentioned already, perhaps the students' use of pocket calculators will enable teachers to spend more time on this, rather than restricting students to a diet of mechanical arithmetic. Calculators do not inhibit the development of students' computational skills; and children who are permitted to use calculators often develop a better attitude towards mathematics.

Additional teaching points to consider when improving the problem-solving abilities of students with learning difficulties include:

- pre-teaching any difficult vocabulary associated with specific word problems so that comprehension is enhanced;
- providing cues (such as directional arrows) to indicate where to begin calculations and in which direction to proceed;
- linking problems to the students' own life experiences;
- giving children experience in setting their own problems for others to solve;
- stressing self-checking and praising self-correction.

In a review of interventions reported by Xin and Jitendra (1999) the following approaches all proved to be effective in improving students' ability to solve problems:

- computer-assisted instruction (CAI);
- training in visualisation;
- metacognitive training;
- use of diagramming;
- use of manipulatives;
- estimating;
- use of calculators;
- attending to key words.

The results from their review suggested that CAI, the use of visual representations (e.g. drawing a picture or diagram), explicit strategy training and metacognitive training (e.g. teaching the students to self-question and self-instruct using previously taught steps), all proved to be helpful in advancing students' problem-solving skills. It is clear that for students with learning difficulties it is necessary to provide many more examples than usual to establish, and then strengthen, the application of a particular strategy (Lerner and Kline 2006).

The text by Booker *et al.* (2004) is particularly useful in helping teachers to understand more about the processes involved in solving problems, with some excellent examples provided.

Further reading

Booker, G., Bond, D., Sparrow, L. and Swan, P. (2004) *Teaching Primary Mathematics* (3rd edn), Melbourne: Pearson-Longman.

Chinn, S. (2004) *The Trouble with Maths: A Practical Guide to Helping Learners with Numeracy Difficulties*, London: RoutledgeFalmer.

DfES (Department for Education and Skills: UK) (2005) *Targeting Support: Implementing Interventions for Children with Significant Difficulties in Mathematics*, Norwich: HMSO.

Dowker, A. (2004) *What Works for Children with Mathematical Difficulties?* Research Report RR554, London: DfES. Available at: http://www.dfes.gov.uk/research/data/uploadfiles/RR554.pdf (accessed 25 May 2006).

Montague, M. and Jitendra, A.K. (2006) *Teaching Mathematics to Middle School Students with Learning Difficulties*, New York: Guilford Press.

Tucker, B.F., Singleton, A.H. and Weaver, T.L. (2006) *Teaching Mathematics to All Children* (2nd edn), Upper Saddle River, NJ: Pearson-Prentice Hall.

Watson, A., Houssart, J. and Roaf, C. (eds) (2005) *Supporting Mathematical Thinking*, London: Fulton.

Wright, R.J., Martland, J. and Stafford, A.K. (2006) *Early Numeracy: Assessment for Teaching and Intervention* (2nd edn), London: Paul Chapman.

Wright, R.J., Stanger, G., Stafford, A.K. and Marland, J. (2006) *Teaching Number in the Classroom with 4–8 Year Olds*, Thousand Oaks, CA: Paul Chapman.

Chapter 13

Adapting curriculum and instruction

> Adaptive teaching is an educational approach that clearly recognizes differences between learners – especially cognitive differences or other specific characteristics. Teachers accept that their students differ in capabilities and take these differences as the starting point for teaching and learning.
>
> (Van den Berg *et al.* 2001: 246)

In Britain, the statutory 'inclusion statement' contained within the revised National Curriculum requires teachers to provide all children, regardless of ability or disability, with effective learning opportunities (QCA 2005). All children must receive relevant and appropriately challenging schoolwork, tailored as far as possible to their differing aptitudes and abilities. The principle of differentiation thus applies to teaching across the full spectrum of ability, including children with disabilities, learning difficulties, language differences, and children with gifts and talents. It is intended that the curriculum be differentiated in terms of its subject matter, teaching methods, activities, and assessment procedures to suit the diverse learning characteristics among the children (Van Garderen and Whittaker 2006). In the simplest of terms, differentiation can be defined as teaching things differently according to observed differences among learners. To achieve this goal and reduce obstacles to learning, Idol (2006: 94) calls for teachers to use more 'multi-layered lessons and differentiated curricula'.

It must be acknowledged from the start that differentiation is never a simple matter in practice. Teachers may believe *in principle* that their teaching should be adapted to address students' individual needs and differences, but in reality they have great difficulty translating this belief into positive action (Westwood 2001). Effective differentiation invariably places heavy demands on teachers' time, knowledge, ingenuity and organisational skills (Pettig 2000; Raveaud 2005).

In this chapter, some generic principles for developing inclusive practice through differentiation will be discussed, together with specific suggestions for adapting curriculum content and resources, modifying teaching approaches, and tailoring assessment procedures.

Differentiation

The starting point for differentiation involves acknowledging that children do differ from one another in many educationally significant ways, and then planning and teaching lessons so that those differences are taken into account. It is argued that when differentiation occurs all students can make optimum progress.

The main advocates for differentiated instruction in the US, Tomlinson and Strickland (2005), refer to *personalising* instruction to take account of students' current levels of ability, prior knowledge, strengths, weaknesses, learning preferences and interests in order to maximise their opportunities to learn. To achieve a personalised approach it is necessary to respond to individual differences among students by (for example):

- setting individualised objectives for learning;
- modifying curriculum content to match more closely the cognitive level of the students;
- providing different paths to learning to suit differing learning preferences;
- varying time allocation for classroom tasks to take account of students' differing rates of learning;
- adapting instructional resource materials;
- encouraging students to produce their work in different forms or through different media;
- using flexible groupings of students;
- varying the amount of guidance and assistance given to individual students.

Most advocates of an adaptive approach to teaching consider the above eight areas to be the major focus for differentiated practice (e.g. Dettmer *et al.* 2005; Ford 2005; Hollas 2005). Each area will be discussed more fully, but first it is important to stress the *simplicity principle*.

Keep it simple

The whole process of applying differentiation in the classroom can sound very daunting for teachers because the professional literature describes many different ways of adapting instruction and modifying curricula. Although in theory there are many strategies for meeting students' different needs, in practice it is not always feasible or desirable to apply more than one such strategy at a time, particularly in large classes. The following advice from Deschenes *et al.* (1999: 13) is well worth noting:

> Adaptations are most effective when they are simple, easy to develop and implement, and based on typical assignments and activities. Adapting in this way is feasible for the classroom teacher because it is relatively unobtrusive,

requiring little extra time for special planning, materials development, and/or instruction.

So, adaptations and modifications should not be used unless absolutely necessary, and should be faded as soon as possible in order to offer a child more realistic challenges through regular activities, tasks and resources. It is important to ensure that a differentiated curriculum does not become an *impoverished* curriculum, with lower-ability students always receiving less demanding and less interesting work than more-able students.

Specific examples of differentiation

The mnemonic CARPET PATCH summarises the main ways in which teachers might adapt their approach in order to establish more inclusive classroom practice and meet their students' individual needs.

C = *Curriculum content:* The curriculum to be studied may be increased or decreased in terms of depth and complexity. Aspects of the curriculum may be sequenced into smaller units and presented in smaller steps. Lesson content may draw more on students' own interests.

A = *Activities:* Teachers can vary the difficulty level of the tasks and activities the students are required to undertake in the lesson. Activities may be undertaken via different pathways (e.g. computer programs, discussion, textbooks, apparatus).

R = *Resource materials:* Teachers could select or create a variety of different texts and instructional materials for students to use (e.g. some requiring less reading or writing).

P = *Products from the lessons:* Teachers can plan for students to produce different types of output from a lesson, according to their abilities, interests and aptitudes.

E = *Environment:* The classroom can be set up to support more individualised or group work. Use may be made of learning centres, computer-assisted learning, or resource-based learning.

T = *Teaching strategies:* Teachers can adopt particular ways of teaching designed to stimulate the poorly motivated students; or they may use more explicit and direct forms of instruction for certain groups in the classroom. Teachers may use tactics such as differentiated questioning, more frequent revising, practising, prompting, cueing, according to individual needs and responses from students. They may also set individual learning contracts for students.

P = *Pace:* Teachers may vary the rate at which teaching takes place, or the rate at which students are required to complete tasks and produce outputs.

A = *Amount of assistance:* Teachers can vary the amount of help given to individuals during a lesson. They may encourage peer assistance and collaboration among students.

T =   *Testing and grading:* Teachers may vary the ways of assessing students' learning and may modify grading to reflect effort and originality as well as the standard achieved.

C =   *Classroom grouping:* Teachers can use various ways of grouping students within the class to allow for different activities to take place, under differing amounts of teacher direction (e.g. peer tutoring, partner activities, team learning).

H =   *Homework assignments:* Teachers may give some students homework that involves additional skill practice at the same level of difficulty, while others have extension tasks involving application, critical thinking, and reflection.

Much longer lists of differentiation strategies do exist, but they tend to become unrealistic in their demands on teachers' time and ingenuity. At a more practical level, teachers will find the book *Modifying Schoolwork* valuable (Janney and Snell 2004).

Starting points

Kameenui and Simmons (1999) recommend that teachers begin to plan for differentiated instruction by focusing on essential core concepts or skills they would hope *all* students will learn from the lesson or series of lessons. They refer to this as identifying the 'big ideas'. Planning and differentiating the topic then becomes a process of creating many different ways the students can encounter these big ideas through a variety of coherent experiences matched to their abilities. For example, some students may encounter new ideas through reading about them in books; some may understand them best if they encounter them visually through direct experience or via video; others may gain most from talking with peers about the issues or problems; some will understand new ideas best by creating their own pictures or models; and some will acquire the concepts most easily through direct teaching. As a general rule, all students in the group will learn best if provided with a variety of activities and pathways. To avoid fragmentation of the total learning experience the teacher must not lose sight of the big ideas for the topic, regardless of the many and varied activities and tasks set for students.

Several writers have described appropriate procedures for adapting curriculum and instruction (e.g. Deschenes *et al.* 1999; Dettmer *et al.* 2005; Hoover and Patton 2005). The steps they identify can be summarised as:

- selecting the subject or topic to be taught;
- identifying the specific content to be included;
- prescribing the learning goals and objectives for the majority of students in the class;
- deciding on the way the lesson will be organised and conducted for most students;

- identifying any students who will need modifications to the general lesson format;
- modifying the objectives for these students, if necessary;
- preparing any necessary adaptations (e.g. shorter assignments, easier textbook, extra use of concrete materials);
- teaching the lesson, and making any necessary additional changes while teaching;
- providing extra assistance to certain students while the lesson is in progress;
- planning appropriate methods for assessing students' learning, based on the goals and objectives for the lesson.

When planning the differentiated objectives for the lesson it is usually helpful to have in mind the three sentence starters:

- All students will ...
- Some students will ...
- A few students may ...

These subheadings help teachers identify the essential core of knowledge and skills that *all* students will be expected to master (the 'big ideas'), possibly through different activities and varied pathways. Some students will achieve more than this core; and a few may achieve one or two higher-order objectives through extension activities (Kenward 1997).

In terms of organisation for the lesson, it is important to consider how students will be grouped and how the available time will be used most effectively (Ford 2005). Planning needs to include consideration of strategies for facilitating the delivery of additional help to certain students during the lesson (e.g. via peer assistance, a learning support assistant, or from the teacher).

The following questions may need to be answered concerning any student requiring adaptations:

- Does the student have the prerequisite skills for this work (e.g. adequate reading ability)?
- Can the student work without constant supervision?
- Can the student work cooperatively with others?
- What is the attention span of the student?
- Does the student have any behaviour problems?
- What will represent appropriate work output from this student?
- What feasible modifications to the activities or resources will need to be made?
- Will the assessment procedure have to be modified for this student?

Modifying curriculum content

Modifying curriculum content usually implies that:

- Students with learning difficulties are required to cover less material in the lesson; the tasks or activities they attempt are usually easier to accomplish.
- In the case of gifted or more-able students, the reverse would be true; they might cover more content and in greater depth.
- For certain students in the class, the objectives set for the lesson might involve mastery of fewer concepts and the application of easier skills.
- The nature of the learning tasks set for the students will be matched to their learning rate and abilities; some tasks may take a longer time to complete than others.
- Differentiated content for homework assignments could be used as one way of meeting the needs of gifted and able students, as well as those of students with difficulties.

Some descriptions of differentiation in action refer to matching the demands of curriculum content and the learning activities themselves to the ability levels of the children. A different viewpoint argues that differentiation should be less about changing the content of activities but much more about providing alternative pathways and giving extra individual assistance as and when necessary to enable all students to study the same curriculum content and achieve satisfactory outcomes (e.g. Dettmer *et al.* 2005).

Several potential problems exist when modifying the curriculum. Reducing the complexity and demands of the curriculum and setting easier objectives may sound like very good advice; but watering down the curriculum in this way can have the long-term effect of increasing the achievement gap between students with learning difficulties and other students. By reducing the demands placed on students of lower ability we may be exaggerating the effect of individual differences and perpetuating inequalities among students. It can be argued, particularly in countries with national curricula, that rather than reducing our expectations for what students can achieve we should be finding ways of providing students with sufficient assistance to ensure that they can achieve the same core objectives applicable to the majority of the school population (Raveaud 2005). Obviously this argument cannot easily be extended to cover students with moderate to severe disabilities integrated in inclusive classrooms. In such cases it will be necessary to modify significantly the demands of the mainstream curriculum to match more closely the students' cognitive level (Silva and Morgado 2004). In many countries this is achieved through the medium of an individual education plan (IEP) and the provision of additional services.

Adapting resources

One of the main areas where modifications are recommended to improve access to the curriculum is that of instructional resources (Janney and Snell 2004). The resource materials used within a lesson (texts, worksheets, exercises, blackboard notes, computer software) may need to be modified, and apparatus or equipment may need to be provided for some students (e.g. blocks for counting in mathematics; pages taped to the desktop for a student with gross motor difficulties; a 'talking' calculator for a student with impaired vision; a pencil with a thick grip for a student with poor hand coordination).

When preparing print materials for students with learning difficulties the following strategies may be helpful:

- Simplify the language (use short sentences, substitute simple words for difficult terms).
- Pre-teach any new vocabulary (if a difficult word cannot be simplified, ensure that it is looked at and discussed before students are expected to read it unaided).
- Provide clear illustrations or diagrams.
- Improve legibility of print and layout. If necessary, enlarge the size of print.
- Remove unnecessary detail.
- Present information in small blocks of text, rather than dense paragraphs.
- Use bullet points and lists rather than paragraphs, where possible.
- Make printed instructions or questions clear and simple.
- Use cues or prompts where responses are required from the students (e.g. provide the initial letter of the answer, or use dashes to show the number of words required in the answer).
- Highlight important terms or information (e.g. use underlining, or print the words in bold type or colour).
- Modify sentence construction to facilitate comprehension. (Active voice is easier to process than passive voice, e.g. 'The teacher draws a line' rather than 'A line was drawn by the teacher'.)

Applying some of the strategies listed above will often be sufficient to allow a student with a mild disability or a literacy problem to access text elements of the curriculum without the need for further adaptation. Evidence indicates, however, that in general teachers do not engage in much modification of resource materials, possibly through lack of time or lack of knowledge and skills (Chan *et al*. 2002). There is a danger that differentiation is attempted merely by providing graded worksheets. While there may be occasions where the use of graded worksheets is appropriate and helpful, their frequent use can label a student as belonging to a particular ability group. It is also relevant to heed the warning from Robbins (1996: 33) that differentiation should not lead to 'death by a thousand worksheets'!

Use of too many worksheet assignments in class can produce poorer outcomes than the use of direct teaching. Based on classroom evidence from research into mathematics teaching in British primary schools, Reynolds and Muijs (1999: 21) reported that:

> ... there was often an over-reliance on worksheets and published [texts]. While these were not necessarily poor in themselves, they simply isolated pupils in ways that made it difficult for them to receive any sustained, direct teaching at all. In other words, more often than not complex arrangements for individual work were self-defeating; they dissipated rather than intensified the quality of the teaching and reduced the opportunities for children to learn.

On the issue of using simplified resources, an interesting finding has been that, in general, students *don't like* to use modified materials or to be given easier tasks (Hall 1997). Students with special needs, particularly those in the secondary and upper primary age range, want to have the same activities, books, homework, grading criteria, and grouping practices as their classmates – but they generally appreciate any extra help the teacher may give them while attempting that work. Students do not like to be given simplified tasks, materials or tests because these practices mark them out as 'different' and undermine their status in the peer group. Adolescents in particular are acutely sensitive to peer-group reactions, and they may deeply resent being treated as if they are lacking in ability.

Regarding the simplification of language and content in print materials, Sperling (2006) warns that in our efforts to make learning tasks easier we sometimes reduce the instructional content in text to simple isolated facts that are actually more difficult for children to understand and to link with prior knowledge, because the information is not embedded in a well-argued and cohesive presentation.

Adapting instruction

Adapting instruction covers all the major and minor changes that may be made to the way teaching occurs in the classroom. It includes the method of instruction, how students are grouped, the nature of their participation in the lesson, the interactions between teacher and students, and interactions among the students themselves.

When teaching and learning processes are modified, some of the following strategies may be used:

- The teacher may re-teach some concepts or information to some students, using simpler language and more examples.
- Questions asked during the lesson may be pitched at different levels of difficulty for different individuals.
- Closer monitoring of the work of some students may take place throughout the lesson.

- The teacher may use particular tactics to gain and maintain the interest of poorly motivated students.
- Feedback may be given in more detail or less detail, according to the students' needs.
- The rate at which the students are expected to work may be varied, with extra time allowed for some students to complete tasks.
- The teacher may give more assistance or less assistance to individual students according to their needs.
- Extra practice may be provided for students who need it, often via differentiated homework assignments.
- Extension work may be set for the most able students, requiring mainly independent study, investigation, and application.
- The ways in which students are grouped for specific purposes (e.g. by ability, interest, friendships) may also be part of differentiation within the teaching process. The aim may be to encourage cooperation and peer assistance; or to facilitate the matching of learning tasks to students' ability levels; or to help the teacher to give more assistance to certain students.
- Classroom learning centres may be set up, individual contract systems established, and computer-assisted instruction (CAI) may be used.

There is evidence to suggest that teachers are much better at using the modifications to teaching process described above than they are at modifying curriculum content (Chan *et al.* 2002). They appear to find teaching process modifications more natural and much easier to accomplish within their personal teaching style. For example, skilled teachers do tend to provide additional help to students when necessary, they do use differentiated questioning, and they do make greater use of descriptive praise, encouragement and rewards during lessons. These are all strategies that can be applied while the teacher is still following a common curriculum with the whole class – and for this reason they are regarded as the most feasible adaptations for teachers to make. They certainly provide a very sound starting point for any teacher moving from a formal, whole-class method of instruction to a more personalised approach. What we know about the dynamics of change processes in education suggests that change is most likely to occur when teachers are required to take small steps in a new direction rather than giant leaps, and when they can build on their current practices.

Differentiating student output

The term 'student output' refers here to the products from the learning process. Often these will be tangible products such as written work, graphics, or models; but sometimes the 'product' refers to other forms of evidence of learning such as an oral report, a performance, a presentation to the group, participation in discussion, or the answering of oral questions.

Differentiating the products of learning may mean that:

- Each student is not expected to produce exactly the same amount or quality of work as every other student.
- A student may be asked to produce work in a different format; for example, an audio recording, a drawing or poster, rather than an essay.
- The student may complete a multiple-choice exercise rather than prepare a project involving extensive writing.
- Individual students might negotiate what they will produce, and how they will produce it, in order to provide evidence of their learning in a particular topic.

Whether or not teachers expect students to produce different amounts and varying qualities of work, they will of course do so – and have always done so. The potential danger in setting out from the start to accept less work or an inferior quality of work from some students, is that this strategy represents a lowering of expectations that can result in a self-fulfilling prophecy. The students produce less and less, and we in turn expect less and less of them. A different perspective suggests that teachers need to help students achieve more, not less, in terms of work output than they would have achieved without support.

The second suggestion of encouraging quite different products can be applied more easily in some subject areas rather than in others. For example, in social studies, language arts, expressive arts, and environmental education it is quite feasible and desirable to differentiate the product and encourage diversity in what the students produce. On the other hand, in mathematics for example, it is more difficult to find acceptable variations in the way that students can demonstrate their mastery of key understandings and skills.

Differentiation of product should never be seen as offering a 'soft option'. It should never lead to a student consistently managing to avoid tasks he or she does not like to complete.

Differentiation of assessment and grading

'Assessment' refers to any process used to determine how much learning, and what quality of learning, has occurred for each student in the class. Assessment provides an indication of how effective a particular episode of teaching and learning has been. The process of assessment also highlights anything that may need to be taught again, revised, or practised further by some students. 'Grading' refers to the fairly common practice of indicating the quality of the work a student has produced for assessment purposes. Often a letter grade (e.g. A, B, C, D) is used, or the work may be given a mark out of 10 or 100. In some countries there has been a trend away from this form of grading in favour of more descriptive comments and written feedback.

Descriptions of differentiation usually include reference to modifying assessment procedures for students with disabilities or learning difficulties (Rieck and Wadsworth 2005). This is deemed necessary because these students may have problems in demonstrating what they know and can do if the assessment method requires them to use language, literacy, numeracy or motor skills they don't possess. In the UK, the Qualification and Curriculum Authority (QCA) has introduced a 'Level P' into the assessments related to the National Curriculum, thus allowing teachers to record the small increments of progress made by students with moderate to severe disabilities. For these students the standard methods of assessment at Level 1 are inappropriate. A similar system operates in Australia in connection with the National Profiles for all major areas of the curriculum. In that country, assessment of students with disabilities may be done against criteria described within the National Profiles as 'Towards Level 1'.

Modifications to assessment processes include such options as:

- simplifying the assessment task for some students;
- shortening the task;
- allowing a longer time for some students to complete the task or test;
- allowing a student with special needs to have some assistance in performing the task (e.g. questions read to the student; student dictating answers to a scribe);
- enabling the student to present the work in a different format (e.g. scrapbook rather than essay).

Classroom tests are one of the ways in which teachers routinely assess the progress of their students. Students with special needs may require modification to test formats, or additional time allowed to complete the test. Some may need a variation in the mode of responding.

Standard adaptations for test formats include:

- enlarging the print;
- leaving more space for the student to write the answer;
- using more variety in question type (e.g. short answer, multiple-choice, sentence completion, gapped paragraphs, matching formats);
- rewriting the instructions in simple language, and highlighting key points;
- keeping directions brief and simple;
- providing prompts such as: *Begin the problem here.*

Modifications to test administration procedures include:

- using oral questioning and answering.
- using a scribe (someone else to write down what the student says);
- allowing the student to dictate the answers on to audiotape;
- giving short rest breaks during the test without penalty;
- allowing extra time to complete the test;
- avoiding any penalty for poor spelling or handwriting;
- allowing the student to use a laptop computer to complete the test;

- giving credit for drawings or diagrams if these help to indicate that the student knows the concept or information;
- spending adequate time making sure that *all* students understand the requirements before the test begins;
- reducing the anxiety that some students have in test situations;
- for some students, testing in an environment other than the classroom (e.g. social worker's office, withdrawal room) may help the student relax and do his or her best.

Some ways of modifying grading to take account of learning difficulties include:

- using 'Satisfactory/Unsatisfactory' as the yardstick for grading a subject;
- reporting achievement not as a grade but as the number of specific objectives achieved in the course. This becomes a more *descriptive* report and can include indications of areas still needing to be improved as well as what was achieved;
- providing two grades for every subject – one grade represents 'effort' while the other grade represents 'achievement' (e.g. D for achievement; A for effort);
- recording results in numerical form (e.g. achievement: 66%; effort: 90%). Achievement is calculated from test scores or marks obtained for assignments. Effort is estimated rather more subjectively, but might also have specific criteria made known to the students before the course begins (e.g. 'You will receive 25 per cent if all classroom assignments are completed; 20 per cent for neatness and presentation; 30 per cent for participation during lessons; 25 per cent for all homework completed.').

Differentiation of grading procedures for students' work in inclusive classrooms is problematic. The main debate concerning modifications to grading systems for students with special needs tends to focus on 'fairness'. For example:

- Is it fair to judge the standard of work produced by a student with mild intellectual disability, or a student who is deaf, against the standard applying to students of average or good ability in the class?
- Is it fair to give a student of very limited ability a report card showing Ds and Fails when he or she has worked extremely hard? Doesn't this lower motivation and self-esteem?
- Is it fair to students who do not have learning difficulties or disabilities if we give 'good' grades to lower achievers simply based on the fact that they 'tried hard' and to encourage them?
- Is it fair to parents and employers to misrepresent a student's actual abilities and achievements on school reports by giving grades to encourage the student rather than to represent actual attainment? Shouldn't a grading system be the same for all students if it is to be fair and accurate?

For these and other similar questions there are no easy answers. Those who provide simplistic advice on adapting assessment procedures and grading criteria seem, at times, to be unaware of the complexity of some of the underlying dilemmas.

Accommodations for students with disabilities

The term 'accommodation' usually conveys the notion of making sure that students with disabilities can participate fully or partially in a particular lesson by varying the type of activities or the method of instruction, providing additional human and technical resources, giving extra support, modifying the ways in which the student will respond, or changing the classroom environment. Janney and Snell (2004: 39) suggest: 'Accommodations are provided to enable the student to gain access to the classroom or the curriculum.'

Many of the modifications and adaptations already described above are equally appropriate for students with disabilities. For example, simplifying objectives and tasks, frequently re-teaching important concepts and skills, allowing more time for students to complete work, encouraging different outputs from students, and facilitating peer assistance are all strategies that reduce or remove barriers to learning. Some students will also need additional support and modified equipment. The specific needs of students with disabilities are usually identified within their individual education plans (IEPs). The IEP should be seen as the main source of advice on the types of differentiation and adaptation needed by the students.

Technological accommodations often involve the use of assistive devices to help a student communicate or to produce work output (e.g. modified keyboards, a computer with a visual display and touch screen or with voice synthesiser, braillers for blind students, greatly enlarged text on a computer screen for a student with partial sight, radio-frequency hearing aids for students with impaired hearing). Less sophisticated aids might include school-made communication boards for students without speech, or symbol or picture-card systems for communicating. Technology has increased the mobility and independence of many students with severe physical disabilities. It is beyond the scope of this book to discuss assistive technology in detail. For practical advice on adaptations and modifications required for students with physical disabilities see Best *et al.* (2005). Other appropriate texts are listed under *Further reading*.

Differentiation is not easy

When advising teachers to become more responsive to individual differences among their students, it is important not to overlook the genuine difficulties involved in sustaining a differentiated approach (Chan *et al.* 2002; Graham and Harris 2005a; Pettig 2000). In Britain, Clare (2004: 1) wryly observes that, 'DfES publications are characterised by lots of exhortations to do it [differentiate], but little advice on what it is or how!' Similarly, Rose (2001: 147) remarks, 'The teaching methods and practices required for the provision of effective inclusion are easier to identify than they are to implement.'

Differentiation is of course essential if students with special educational needs are to be included fully in mainstream classes. Given that differentiation as a strategy within classroom teaching has the potential to increase success rates for all students and remove some of the barriers to learning for students with disabilities, it is hoped that teachers will continue to become more adaptive in their approach. Despite the difficulties mentioned in this chapter, many teachers already do a great deal to respond to their students' unique needs. If given appropriate guidance, teachers will continue to gain in expertise. Advisers, inspectors, and support personnel need to be aware of the ways in which classroom instruction can be adapted so that the advice they give to teachers is of practical value. They also need to be fully aware that teachers will not necessarily find it easy to implement such advice and will require much on-going support in moving in that direction. The problems, as well as the practices, have been addressed in this chapter.

Further reading

Bender, W.N. (2005) *Differentiating Math Instruction: Strategies that Work for K-8*, Thousand Oaks, CA: Corwin Press.

Cook, R.E., Klein, M.D. and Tessier, A. (2004) *Adapting Early Childhood Curricula for Children in Inclusive Settings* (6th edn), Upper Saddle River, NJ: Pearson-Merrill-Prentice Hall.

Haager, D. and Klingner, J.K. (2005) *Differentiating Instruction in Inclusive Classrooms*, Boston, MA: Allyn and Bacon.

Henley, M., Ramsey, R.S. and Algozzine, R.F. (2006) *Characteristics of and Strategies for Teaching Students with Mild Disabilities* (5th edn), Boston, MA: Pearson-Allyn and Bacon.

Janney, R. and Snell, M.E. (2004) *Modifying Schoolwork* (2nd edn), Baltimore, MD: Brookes.

Nunley, K.F. (2006) *Differentiating in the High School Classroom: Solution Strategies for 18 Common Obstacles*, Thousand Oaks, CA: Corwin Press.

QCA (Qualifications and Curriculum Authority: UK) (2001) *Planning, Teaching and Assessing the Curriculum for Pupils with Learning Difficulties: General Guidelines*, London: Department for Education and Employment.

Salend, S. (2005) *Creating Inclusive Classrooms* (5th edn), Upper Saddle River, NJ: Pearson-Merrill-Prentice Hall.

Tomlinson, C.A. and McTighe, J. (2006) *Integrating Differentiated Instruction and Understanding by Design: Connecting Content with Kids*, Alexandria, VA: Association for Supervision and Curriculum Development.

Wood, J.W. (2006) *Teaching Students in Inclusive Settings: Adapting and Accommodating Instruction* (5th edn), Upper Saddle River, NJ: Merrill-Prentice Hall.

Chapter 14

Teaching methods: an overview

There is no single instructional method that deserves sole claim to being 'best practice'. Of course, this comes as no surprise to teaching practitioners operating in the real worlds of their classrooms. Rather than single strategy solutions, the common wisdom of research in the field currently points to the need for balanced approaches to be employed to accommodate for the diverse needs of students.

(Ellis 2005: 44)

There are many ways of approaching the complex task of helping children with special needs acquire new knowledge, skills, strategies, attitudes and values across the curriculum. A teacher's decision to select a particular approach for use at a particular time must depend upon the nature of the lesson content, the learning objectives, and the characteristics of the students in the group. Learning difficulties may be created or exacerbated for some students if an inappropriate teaching approach is used.

Current evidence suggests that many problems associated with student learning can be directly traced to the method of instruction (Farkota 2005). For example, as discussed in Chapter 7, it is now generally believed that a whole-language approach, if used as the sole method for teaching reading and writing, is not entirely successful with every child. Some children make significantly better progress in literacy when directly taught the essential knowledge and skills required for decoding, spelling, and comprehending (e.g. Ehri 2003; Lyon 2005). Similarly, in the early stages of learning mathematics, some students experience much greater success when directly instructed and given practice with feedback from the teacher, rather than being expected to discover number concepts and algorithms through investigative problem-solving activities alone (Baker *et al.* 2002; Kroesbergen *et al.* 2004). As the opening quotation from Ellis (2005) suggests, there is no single method when used alone that is superior to all other methods for all purposes. One particular method of teaching cannot possibly suit all types of learning or all ages and abilities of students, so methods must be selected according to their goodness of fit for achieving specific learning objectives with particular students.

This chapter provides an overview of teaching methods, ranging from those that may be regarded as 'teacher directed' (or *instructive*) to those that are clearly more 'learner oriented' (or *constructive*). The strengths and weakness in each method will be summarised, with particular reference to achieving particular types of learning objectives and their suitability for teaching students with learning difficulties or disabilities.

Teacher-directed approaches

Expository teaching

Expository or didactic methods include demonstrating, lecturing, explaining, narrating, requiring students to read a textbook or manual, showing students an instructional video, or asking students to work through a computer program presenting new information. Expository teaching represents a method of presenting new information to learners in a form they can access and understand.

Expository teaching is used across the curriculum when introducing an overview of a new topic to a class, when clarifying a concept that has been misunderstood by students, when responding to issues raised by students, when setting out the steps in a new procedure or process, and when consolidating or reviewing learning at the end of a lesson or series of lessons. Expository teaching can be greatly enhanced by the use of appropriate visual support such as 'advance organisers', on-screen PowerPoint material, pictures, models, key points summarised on the whiteboard, by using bold type or colour to highlight textbook information, and providing students with supplementary notes. The most essential skill for a teacher to possess is the ability to explain things simply and clearly. This skill partly depends on the teacher's ability to appreciate the new topic from the perspective of a novice learning it for the first time.

Expository teaching has several potential weaknesses, particularly when used with students with learning difficulties. These weaknesses include:

- The method does not take account of individual differences among learners, such as prior knowledge, language background, literacy skills, experience or motivation.
- Teachers' presentations place a high premium on learners' ability to concentrate and to follow a line of thought. Students with learning difficulties are disadvantaged in lessons that rely entirely upon expository methods due to their inability to maintain listening attention in such a passive learning situation. If used too much, expository teaching can lead to boredom and disengagement.
- Expository methods require that learners have adequate linguistic skills, particularly a good vocabulary and adequate reading and writing (note-taking) skills. Students with learning difficulties often have poor language and literacy skills so they encounter problems understanding what the teacher

says, or they have difficulties processing what is written in the textbook. They also have difficulty taking notes during the lesson, so they are at a disadvantage later in follow-up homework assignments and independent study.

• Students with learning difficulties often lack confidence and assertiveness, so they are unlikely ever to ask the teacher questions, or seek clarification on a particular issue.

It would be rare indeed to find a primary or secondary teacher who uses expository teaching as their only approach. Almost any lesson at any age level requires active participation and input from the students. During the course of a single lesson a teacher may switch several times between teacher-directed activity and student-centred activity. The lesson may commence with direction instruction and explanation, but then change quickly to student-centred activity with the teacher adopting a more supportive or facilitative role. Then in the final stage of the lesson there is a return to teacher direction in order to consolidate learning and check for understanding. During a single lesson in a classroom the instructional techniques will generally reflect the skilful integration of both teacher-directed and student-centred learning methods.

Interactive whole-class teaching

Interactive whole-class teaching embodies some of the elements of expository teaching but facilitates very high levels of active participation and a high response rate from the students. The lesson operates using a two-way process in which the teacher explains, ask questions and challenges the students' thinking, but also encourages and responds to questions and points contributed frequently by the students. The students offer their own ideas, express their opinions, ask questions of the teacher and each other, explain their thinking, or demonstrate their methods (Dickinson 2003). Interactive whole-class teaching does not simply comprise verbal exchanges between teacher and students, and the teacher must make effective use of instructional media to gain and hold students' attention.

As mentioned in Chapter 12, in countries where students gain excellent results in international surveys of achievement, the teachers seem to employ interactive whole-class teaching methods very effectively. In Britain, interactive whole-class teaching has been advocated as one way for improving literacy and numeracy standards in primary schools. The approach is seen as much more productive than individual programming or unstructured groupwork. It is claimed that effective use of interactive whole-class teaching helps to close the 'learning gap' that usually appears between higher-achievers and lower-achievers when individualised 'work at your own pace' methods are used (Zhou 2001).

Some potential problems associated with interactive whole-class teaching include:

- The teacher needs to be very skilled in drawing all students into discussion, otherwise some students will not participate actively in the lesson.
- Unfortunately, some teachers appear to find this fast-paced, interactive method difficult to implement and sustain (Hardman *et al.* 2003).
- The pace of the lesson will be slowed unintentionally if teachers tell individual students to raise a hand if they wish to ask or answer a question. Not all teachers recognise the participation and motivation values of encouraging 'choral responding' (all students answering together sometimes) (Feldman and Denti 2004).
- At the other extreme, if the pace of the lesson is too brisk, students with learning difficulties tend to opt out.

Direct instruction

Direct instruction is the term applied to various forms of explicit and active teaching that convey the curriculum to students in a reasonably structured and systematic manner. Direct instruction is characterised by precise learning objectives, clear demonstrations, explanations and modelling by the teacher, followed by guided practice, and independent practice by the students. Teaching takes place at a brisk pace and learning is assessed regularly. Re-teaching and remediation are provided where necessary. Direct instruction of this type has proved to be very effective indeed in raising achievement levels in basic academic skills for all students, and is particularly beneficial for students with learning difficulties and those with intellectual disability (Ellis 2005; White 2005). Direct instruction is not exclusive and can be combined with many other approaches to teaching (Lerner and Kline 2006).

The most highly structured and carefully designed model using direct instruction is associated most closely with the work of Engelmann at the University of Oregon (e.g. Engelmann 1999). This highly teacher-directed form of curriculum delivery, based on behavioural learning principles, is usually referred to using the capitalised form – *Direct Instruction* (DI). DI is a system for teaching basic academic skills such as reading, spelling and arithmetic through the provision of carefully sequenced and scripted lessons (Carnine *et al.* 2006). DI was originally associated with the published programme called DISTAR (*Direct Instructional System for Teaching and Remediation*) for teaching basic skills to disadvantaged and at-risk children in the US; but DI programmes now include materials covering writing, spelling, comprehension, mathematics, and problem solving for a much wider age and ability range.

In a typical Direct Instruction session the young children are taught in small groups, based on ability. Usually, they are seated in a semicircle facing the teacher, who gains and holds their attention and follows the teaching steps clearly set out in the script. The scripted presentation ensures that all steps in the teaching sequence are followed, and that all questions and instructions are clear. Lessons are designed so that there is a very high rate of participation and responding by all children in the group. The teacher gives immediate feedback, correction and encouragement. Rather than requiring each child to 'raise a hand' to reply, much choral responding by the whole group is used as a strategy for motivating students and maximising participation (Feldman and Denti 2004).

The effectiveness of DI has been thoroughly evaluated over many years (e.g. Lockery and Maggs 1982; Shippen *et al.* 2005). Having reviewed the evidence, Schug *et al.* (2001: 12) conclude that:

> Direct Instruction has a strong research base confirming its positive effects on student learning. The supporting evidence arises from well-controlled experimental studies that validate the principles and the theory underlying Direct Instruction. In addition, small-scale pilot studies have documented the effectiveness of particular Direct Instruction programs in various classroom settings, and comprehensive evaluations have demonstrated the effectiveness of Direct Instruction more generally across classrooms and schools.

Since DI is highly effective, one would expect to find the method being widely used for teaching the foundation stages of academic skills; but this is not the case (Carnine 2000). While DI has enjoyed some popularity in special education settings it has had rather limited impact in mainstream schools. It appears that mainstream primary and early childhood teachers prefer to use child-centred methods that encourage children to learn at their own rate and in their own way. These teachers shy away from methods that appear prescriptive and structured. It is also clear that most teacher education institutions in the past twenty years have tended to omit coverage of DI in their methodology courses, instead devoting their full attention to methods that are child-centred and guided by constructivist learning theory.

The difficulties or limitations associated with the use of DI relate mainly to the teachers, not to students.

- The fact that DI must be implemented on a daily basis, using small group instruction rather than whole-class teaching can cause problems in scheduling and staffing.
- Many teachers, particularly in Britain and Australia, react very negatively towards DI, claiming that it is too highly structured, too rapidly paced, and has a narrow focus on skill acquisition.
- Teachers also claim that DI allows very little opportunity for a teacher or the students to be creative.

Student-centred approaches

Discovery learning

Discovery learning (DL) is one form of inquiry-based approach drawing heavily on constructivist learning theory. In DL, students construct knowledge about a topic largely through their own endeavours by accessing whatever human and material resources they may require. The emphasis is on the students being active investigators rather than passive recipients of information delivered to them by the teacher or textbook. In order to participate successfully in open discovery activities, learners must have adequate inductive reasoning ability to recognise principles or relationships emerging from their observations. In typical discovery situations in mathematics, science or social studies, examples and non-examples of specific concepts are available to the learners, and from these they must 'discover' the corresponding rule or relationship.

The two main forms of discovery learning are 'unstructured' discovery and 'guided' discovery. Unstructured discovery places learners in situations where they are given very little direction from the teacher and must decide for themselves the appropriate way to investigate a given topic or problem. At the end of the process they must reach their own conclusions and develop their conceptual understanding from their observations and data. This unstructured approach (often under the guise of 'problem-based learning') is sometimes used in secondary school science, mathematics and topics in social studies, but the outcome is not always good, particularly for students with poor literacy or study skills, weak self-management, and difficulties with inductive reasoning. Often students with learning difficulties do not have a clear idea of what they are expected to do, and they do not believe in their own ability to engage successfully with a problem by thinking in an active way. Eggen and Kauchak (2004) reviewed research on the effectiveness of discovery learning and concluded that some students develop serious misconceptions and can become confused and frustrated in unstructured discovery activities.

Guided discovery has a much tighter structure, and teachers have found that learning is more successful when the investigative process is explicitly taught and the students have the prerequisite skills (Tuovinen and Sweller 1999). The teacher sets clear objectives, provides initial explanation to help students begin the task efficiently, and may offer suggestions for a step-by-step procedure to find the target information or to solve the problem.

The major benefits of DL include the following:

- Learners are actively involved in the process of learning and the topics studied are often intrinsically motivating.
- The activities used in authentic discovery contexts are usually more meaningful than typical classroom exercises and textbook study.

- It is claimed that learners are more likely to remember concepts if they discover them. For example, there is some evidence that students with learning difficulties retain key information better in subjects such as science through carefully guided discovery learning (e.g. Bay *et al.* 1992).
- DL builds on learners' prior knowledge and experience.
- DL encourages independence in learning because learners acquire new investigative skills that can be generalised and applied in many other contexts.
- DL also fosters positive group-working skills.

The major problems associated with DL include:

- The approach can be very time-consuming, often taking much longer for information to be acquired than would occur with direct teaching.
- DL relies on learners having adequate literacy, numeracy, and independent study skills. Students may learn little of value from discovery activities if they lack adequate skills and prior knowledge for interpreting their 'discoveries' accurately.
- 'Activity' does not necessarily equate with 'learning'. Learners may be actively involved but may still not understand or recognise underlying concepts, rules or principles.
- Children with learning difficulties often have problems forming opinions, making predictions, or drawing conclusions based on evidence.
- Poor outcomes occur when teachers are not good at creating and managing discovery learning environments.
- Some teachers do not monitor activities effectively, so are not able to give individual encouragement and guidance (scaffolding) that is frequently needed by learners.

Project-based and resource-based learning

The project approach has been used in primary and secondary schools for many years. It lends itself easily to curriculum areas such as social studies, environmental education, geography, history, civics, science, mathematics and the languages, enabling students to apply and extend their knowledge. Project work can help students integrate ideas and information from these different subjects (Solomon 2003). Information technology can be fully utilised in project work, resulting in students learning both ICT skills and specific content knowledge simultaneously (OTEC 2005). The extended timeframe usually provided for project work allows students to plan carefully, revise, and reflect more deeply upon their learning.

There are many potential benefits from project work (Kraft 2005). Compared with traditional textbook teaching, project-based learning has the following advantages:

- It is an inclusive approach in that all learners can participate to the best of their ability.
- Projects promote meaningful learning, connecting new information to students' past experience and prior knowledge.
- The learning process involved in gathering data is valued as well as the product.
- Students are responsible for their own learning, thus increasing self-direction.
- Undertaking a project encourages decision-making and allows for student choice.
- Researching the topic develops deeper knowledge of subject matter.
- Learners use higher-order thinking and conceptual skills, in addition to acquiring facts.
- Information collection and presentation encourages various modes of communication and representation.
- Preparing the project helps students apply and improve basic reading, writing and ICT skills.
- Assessment is performance-based.
- If undertaken with a partner or in a group, project work increases team-working and cooperative skills.

Potential difficulties associated with project-based learning include:

- Some students lack adequate study skills for researching and collating information.
- When working on projects, some students may give the impression of productive involvement but may in fact be learning and contributing very little.
- When projects involve the production of posters, models, charts, recordings, photographs and written reports for display, there is a danger that these are actually 'window dressing' that hides a fairly shallow investigation and understanding of the topic.
- When different aspects of a topic are given to different group-members to research, there is a danger that individual members never really gain an overall understanding of the whole topic.

Resource-based learning (RBL) can be considered another form of inquiry method, closely associated with problem-based or issues-based learning, and underpinned by constructivist learning principles. In resource-based learning, as in project-based learning, students use books, community publications, reports, online information, and other resources to obtain the information they must then analyse and critique before organising it in an appropriate form for presentation. RBL is suited to most 'content' areas of the school curriculum and is said to be adaptable to students' different abilities.

The main aim of RBL is to foster students' autonomy in learning by providing opportunities for them to work individually or collaboratively while applying relevant study skills to investigate authentic topics. Typically, in RBL situations the teacher introduces an issue, topic or problem to be investigated through the use of relevant resources that are made immediately available. The teacher and students together clarify the nature of the task and set goals for inquiry; then students work individually or in groups to carry out the necessary investigation over a series of lessons. In some cases, it may be necessary to pre-teach researching skills such as locating information, extracting relevant data, summarising, locating websites, and taking notes.

Some of the advantages claimed for RBL include:

- The method motivates students and encourages self-directed learning and reflection.
- Students learn from their own active and creative processing of information using a range of authentic resources.
- Suitable RBL topics stimulate higher-order thinking (problem solving, reasoning, and critical evaluation).
- Through the use of print and electronic media, students' independent study skills are strengthened and extended in ways that may easily generalise to other learning contexts.
- RBL can foster enthusiasm for learning and can increase academic engagement time.

Potential difficulties associated with RBL are similar to those identified for discovery learning, namely:

- RBL generally requires a resource-rich learning environment, including easy access to reference books and computers.
- Effective engagement in RBL depends upon the students having adequate literacy, numeracy and independent study skills; they will learn little from RBL if they lack the prerequisite prior knowledge for interpreting new information.
- RBL demands reasonable initiative and self-management from the students.
- Teachers are not necessarily good at identifying suitable topics for RBL and collecting the necessary resources, resulting sometimes in poor outcomes.
- Teachers may not monitor activities effectively, so are not able to give encouragement and support that is frequently needed by learners.

Problem-based and issues-based learning

Lee (2001: 10) suggests that: 'Learning through problem-solving may be much more effective than traditional didactic methods of learning in creating in the student's mind a body of knowledge that is useful in the future'. This view sits well with constructivist theories of learning, and highlights the value of providing students with many genuine opportunities to apply knowledge and skills they may have been taught more directly. At the same time they will acquire new information, skills and insights by engaging in the problem-solving process.

In problem-based learning, students are presented with a real-life situation or issue that requires a solution or a decision leading to some form of action. With older learners, the problems are often intentionally 'messy' (ill-defined) in the sense that not all of the information required for solution is provided in the problem, and there is no clear path or procedure to follow (Kauchak and Eggen 2003).

Problem-based learning (PBL) and issues-based learning (IBL) are still not widely used in schools although they have become popular in higher education. PBL also features quite frequently in programmes for gifted students (Coleman 2001). Where schools have adopted PBL, its use is often related to issues identified in social studies or environmental education. As discussed in Chapter 12, a problem-solving approach has also been recommended for application in mathematics teaching; but teachers find it necessary to supplement such an approach by directly teaching students necessary computational skills.

The advantages of PBL and IBL are considered to be:

- The objectives are authentic, and link school learning with the real world.
- The process of tackling a problem is motivating for learners and empowers them to identify, locate, and use appropriate resources.
- PBL and IBL involve the active construction of new knowledge.
- Solving problems requires the integration of information and skills from different disciplines.
- Learning achieved through PBL and IBL is likely to be retained, and can be transferred to other situations.
- The method encourages self-direction in learning and prepares students to think critically and analytically.
- Problem-solving processes enhance communication skills and social skills necessary for cooperation and teamwork.

Some of the difficulties associated with using PBL and IBL from the perspective of students with learning difficulties include:

- Lack of specific subject knowledge about the topic or content of the problem.
- Limited experience in working collaboratively.
- Lack of confidence in working through problems without direction.
- Inability to identify and separate out irrelevant information from what is relevant for addressing the problem.
- Lack of flexibility in their thinking.

- A tendency to decide on a solution too early, and resist change later.
- Not all students like group work or discussion, preferring instead to work independently.

Cognitive apprenticeship

Conway (1997) explains that:

> Cognitive apprenticeship is a method of teaching aimed primarily at teaching the processes that experts use to handle complex tasks. The focus of this learning-through-guided-experience is on cognitive and metacognitive skills, rather than on the physical skills and processes of traditional apprenticeships. Applying apprenticeship methods to largely cognitive skills requires the externalization of processes that are usually carried out internally.

The notion of cognitive apprenticeship has been put forward as an ideal way in which we might help a learner gain expertise. Apprenticeship implies that the learner acquires knowledge and skills from an 'expert', partly as a result of direct teaching (instruction, demonstration, practice and feedback) and partly by incidental observation of what the expert does, thinks and says while engaged in a task (Collins *et al.* 1990). Learning takes place within the individual's 'zone of proximal development' – that is, it occurs while the learner is working on an authentic task slightly more difficult than he or she can manage to complete independently. The learner requires coaching and support from peers or the instructor in order to succeed. Gradually the amount of support provided to the learner is reduced (faded) until the individual can complete the task independently and can continue to increase in expertise. The most important element of cognitive apprenticeship is the passing on of mental strategies that form the key part of expertise related to approaching a task effectively and solving problems that may occur.

In Chapter 4, and elsewhere in this book, the importance and value in teaching students effective cognitive strategies has been stressed. A cognitive strategy is a mental plan of action that allows a student to approach a learning task systematically. Using such a strategy results in a much greater chance of success than would occur simply by trial and error methods. Cognitive strategies are involved in all learning activities that require thinking, planning and decision making – such as writing an essay, note-taking, researching a project, tackling a mathematical problem, or conducting a science experiment. An effective cognitive strategy enables learners to plan what they will do, implement their plan, monitor what they are doing, and modify their thoughts and actions if necessary as they proceed. The cognitive apprenticeship model represents an effective way of helping students acquire such strategies; and it is clear from the five points below that the model matches exactly the teaching process that is highly desirable in effective remedial teaching and tutoring.

The cognitive apprenticeship approach relies on:

- using authentic tasks or problems;
- modelling effective ways of approaching the task or problem (thinking aloud, demonstrating, self-questioning, self-correcting);
- feedback and coaching for the learner while engaging in the activity;
- discussion with the learner concerning his or her performance;
- gradual withdrawal of support as the learner becomes proficient.

The benefits of cognitive apprenticeships include:

- Students acquire effective strategies and tactics for attempting many types of task.
- A thoughtful and reflective approach to learning is encouraged.
- Collaboration, sharing and support among learners are encouraged.
- Teachers and instructors think much more deeply about the cognitive and metacognitive demands of the tasks they set for students.
- When working with lower-ability learners, teachers begin to understand their difficulties much more clearly and can provide precise assistance.

The difficulties involved in implementing cognitive apprenticeships include:

- Large class size is a major obstacle; implementation is much more viable in small tutorial groups and in one-to-one training contexts.
- Cognitive apprenticeship is not a relevant model for all types of learning. It is useful mainly when a teacher needs to teach students how to tackle fairly complex cognitive tasks.

The emphasis on using authentic tasks and contexts as the medium for teaching cognitive skills and strategies is echoed in approaches known as 'situated learning' (Vincini 2003) and 'anchored instruction' (Foster 2004). It is beyond the scope of this text to deal with these two approaches in detail. Suffice it to say that situated learning takes place in a setting that is functionally identical to where the learning will be applied in real life – for example, a workshop, on a fieldtrip, in a supermarket, on a bus, and so forth. Situated learning attempts to combat the criticism that almost all teaching in schools is 'inert' because it does not take place in real contexts where the particular knowledge or skills will be needed. The learner does not recognise its functional value, and is unlikely to recall it later for use at the appropriate time (Alexiades *et al.* 2001). This fact has been recognised for very many years in special schools; and perhaps special schools can be credited with the original concept of situated learning. Anchored instruction (AI) is an example of situated learning that uses real or simulated situations and data (often on video or CD-Rom) to create a variety of real-life scenarios depicting issues or problems that must be resolved. In a typical anchored instruction session, students identify relevant aspects of the problem and become actively involved in generating possible solutions. The scenarios serve to 'anchor' the learning in a realistic context to which the learners can relate.

The advantages of situated learning and anchored instruction include:

- Learning opportunities are provided in real or simulated contexts in which new knowledge or skills must be acquired for immediate use.
- Experts or mentors are available to provide learners with support.
- Instructional scaffolding and direct coaching are provided as necessary.
- Situated learning and AI represent motivating and active approaches to learning.
- If appropriate, supportive use can be made of current technology.
- Students are more likely to become confident and independent thinkers.
- Learning is likely to generalise more easily to new contexts.
- Collaboration is encouraged.

Difficulties include:

- For most teachers, the task of arranging and maintaining real-life learning situations adds considerably to their workload, and also demands ingenuity on their part.
- The teacher needs to be skilled in giving just the right amount of direction and support.
- It is difficult to avoid fragmentation of curriculum content.
- Assembling computer-simulated resources and links is demanding of time and technical expertise.
- Both situated learning and AI are most difficult to implement in schools and systems following prescriptive curricula with an emphasis on examination results.

Computer-based learning (CBL) and computer-assisted learning (CAL)

Computers and their associated software provide opportunities for improving the quality of educational programmes and enhancing students' participation. In general, the findings from research into the effectiveness of CBL and CAL have been positive (e.g. Linden *et al.* 2003; Minton 2002; Polkinghorne 2004; Prideaux *et al.* 2005). The appropriate use of CBL and CAL can exert positive influences on students' enthusiasm, motivation, and concentration – and these are important considerations when working with students who have learning difficulties or disabilities. In the remedial teaching field, CAL has become increasingly valued as a method for not only building automaticity in basic skills but also improving confidence, motivation and attention to task (Kennedy 2000). Polloway and Patton (1997) report that students with disabilities frequently display a positive attitude towards using computers, are eager to participate, and show improved levels of on-task behaviour.

Computers can deliver multi-media instructional programs covering virtually any area of the curriculum and geared to any age or ability level. In reality though, much of the learning in an average classroom will be achieved not by using CBL, but through other forms of presentation and study such as direct teaching, interactive whole-class teaching, group work, discussions, silent reading, and independent or collaborative project work. In such a context, CAL may be used only to support or enrich students' learning. An example might be using drill and practice software to help a certain student increase automaticity in number skills or spelling. Students can also use ICT to help them conduct investigations by searching for information online or completing independent projects (Kennedy 2000).

CBL and CAL have the following benefits:

- The mode of presentation ensures that learners make active, self-initiated responses and are 'in charge' of the learning situation.
- Students move toward greater independence and self-regulation in learning.
- Software can be matched to a student's ability level and is therefore one way of individualising or differentiating instruction.
- The learner usually gains immediate knowledge of results after every response; reinforcement, and any necessary corrective feedback, can be provided immediately.
- The student can usually control the pace of the lesson.
- Working at a computer is challenging, but non-threatening.
- CAL provides a private method of responding and self-correcting.
- Students can be provided with extra practice and overlearning to master basic skills.
- Most (but not all) students enjoy working at the computer more than using textbooks and print resources.
- Students can extend their computer competencies.
- The teaching of subjects such as science, social studies, mathematics, environmental education, and the arts can be enhanced by documentary or simulation programs and by giving access to Internet resources.

Difficulties associated with the use of CBL include:

- Students with literacy problems have difficulty comprehending verbal information on the screen.
- Some students lack prerequisite computer skills.
- Some teachers lack expertise in integrating CBL into the curriculum.
- There may be a shortage of computers in the school; or computers may only be available in a computer lab at limited times each week.

- Technical failures occur, resulting in lost time and frustration.
- There can be additional demands on teachers' planning and preparation time.
- A few students do not like to learn by ICT methods and prefer group interactions with peers and the teacher.

In the descriptions of methods above, the potential problems that may be encountered by children with learning difficulties have been identified. With this information in mind, teachers are in a better position to structure the methods with greater precision and to provide more active support for learning when required.

Further reading

Brophy, J. and Pinnegar, S. (eds) (2005) *Learning from Research on Teaching: Perspective, Methodology, and Representation*, Amsterdam: Elsevier JAI.

Carnine, D.W., Silbert, J., Kameenui, E., Tarver, S. and Jongjohann, K. (2006) *Teaching Struggling and At-risk Readers: A Direct Instruction Approach*, Upper Saddle River, NJ: Pearson-Prentice Hall.

Eggen, P.D. and Kauchak, D.P. (2006) *Strategies and Models for Teachers: Teaching Content and Thinking Skills* (5th edn), Boston, MA: Pearson-Allyn and Bacon.

Elliott, D.C. (2005) *Teaching on Target: Models, Strategies, and Methods That Work*, Thousand Oaks, CA: Corwin Press.

Ellis, L.A. (2005) *Balancing Approaches: Revisiting the Educational Psychology Research on Teaching Students with Learning Difficulties*, Melbourne: Australian Council for Educational Research.

Freiberg, H.J. and Driscoll, A. (2005) *Universal Teaching Strategies* (4th edn), Boston, MA: Pearson-Allyn and Bacon.

Kauchak, D. and Eggen, P.D. (2003) *Learning and Teaching: Research-based Methods* (4th edn), Boston, MA: Allyn and Bacon.

Moore, K.D. (2005) *Effective Instructional Strategies: From Theory to Practice*, Thousand Oaks, CA: Sage.

Muijs, D. and Reynolds, D. (2005) *Effective Teaching: Evidence and Practice* (2nd edn), London: Sage.

Olson, J.L. and Platt, J.C. (2004) *Teaching Children and Adolescents with Special Needs* (4th edn), Upper Saddle River, NJ: Pearson-Merrill-Prentice Hall.

Ormrod, J.E. (2006) *Educational Psychology: Developing Learners* (5th edn), Upper Saddle River, NJ: Pearson-Merrill-Prentice Hall.

References

Alberto, P.A. and Troutman, A.C. (2006) *Applied Behavior Analysis for Teachers* (7th edn), Upper Saddle River, NJ: Pearson-Merrill-Prentice Hall.

Alexiades, J., Gipson, S. and Morey-Nase, G. (2001) 'Deconstructing "the classroom": situating learning with the help of the World Wide Web'. In A. Herrmann and M.M. Kulski (eds) *Expanding Horizons in Teaching and Learning.* Proceedings of the 10th Annual Teaching Learning Forum, 7–9 February 2001. Perth: Curtin University of Technology. Available at: http://lsn.curtin.edu.au/tlf/tlf2001/alexiades.html (accessed 7 May 2006).

Allen, D., James, W., Evans, J., Hawkins, S. and Jenkins, R. (2005) 'Positive behavioural support: definition, current status and future directions', *Tizard Learning Disability Review*, 10, 2: 4–11.

Allen, J. (2005) 'Making word-learning special', *Voices from the Middle*, 12, 4: 50–1.

Allington, R.L. (2001) *What Really Matters for Struggling Readers?* New York: Longman.

Andrews, R., Torgerson, C., Beverton, S., Freeman, A., Locke, T., Low, G., Robinson, A. and Zhu, D. (2006) 'The effect of grammar teaching on writing development', *British Educational Research Journal*, 32, 1: 39–55.

Antia, S.D., Reed, S. and Kreimeyer, K.H. (2005) 'Written language of deaf and hard-of-hearing students in public schools', *Journal of Deaf Studies and Deaf Education*, 10, 3: 244–55.

Antonacci, P.A. and O'Callaghan, C.M. (2006) *A Handbook for Literacy Instructional and Assessment Strategies, K–8*, Boston, MA: Pearson-Allyn and Bacon.

APA (American Psychiatric Association) (2000) *Diagnostic and Statistical Manual of Mental Disorders: Text Revised (DSM–IV–TR)*, Washington, DC: APA.

Ardoin, S.P., Martens, B.K., Wolfe, L.A., Hilt, A.M. and Rosenthal, B.D. (2004) 'A method for conditioning reinforcer preferences in students with moderate mental retardation', *Journal of Developmental and Physical Disabilities*, 16, 1: 33–51.

Atkinson, C., Regan, T. and Williams, C. (2006) 'Working collaboratively with teachers to promote effective learning', *Support for Learning*, 21, 1: 33–9.

Baker, L. and Welkowitz, L. (2005) *Asperger's Syndrome: Intervening in Schools, Clinics and Communities*, Mahwah, NJ: Erlbaum.

Baker, S., Gersten, R. and Lee, D.S. (2002) 'A synthesis of empirical research on teaching mathematics to low-achieving students', *Elementary School Journal*, 103, 1: 51–73.

Balajthy, E. (2005) 'Text-to-speech software for helping struggling readers', *Reading Online*, January 2005, 1–9. Available at: http://www.readingonline.org/articles/art_index.asp?HREF=balajthy2/index.html (accessed 4 June 2006).

Barrett, W. and Randall, L. (2004) 'Investigating the Circle of Friends approach: adaptations and implications for practice', *Educational Psychology in Practice*, 20, 4: 353–68.

Bartlett, L.D., Weisenstein, G.R. and Etscheidt, S. (2002) *Successful Inclusion for Educational Leaders*, Upper Saddle River, NJ: Merrill-Prentice Hall.

Barton-Arwood, S., Morrow, L., Lane, K. and Jolivette, K. (2005) 'Project IMPROVE: improving teachers' ability to address students' social needs', *Education and Treatment of Children*, 28, 4: 430–43.

Batshaw, M.L. (ed.) (2002) *Children with Disabilities* (5th edn), Baltimore, MD: Brookes.

Bay, M., Staver, J., Bryan, T. and Hale, J. (1992) 'Science instruction for the mildly handicapped: direct instruction versus discovery teaching', *Journal of Research in Science Teaching*, 29: 555–70.

Bear, D.R., Invernizzi, M. and Johnston, F. (2006) *Words Their Way: Sorts for Emergent Spellers*, Upper Saddle River, NJ: Pearson-Merrill-Prentice Hall.

Beck, I.L. (2006) *Making Sense of Phonics: The Hows and Whys*, New York: Guilford Press.

Beckham-Hungler, D. and Williams, C. (2003) 'Teaching words that students misspell: spelling instruction and young children's writing', *Language Arts*, 80, 4: 299–309.

Beirne-Smith, M., Patton, J.R. and Kim, S.H. (2006) *Mental Retardation: An Introduction to Intellectual Disabilities* (7th edn), Upper Saddle River, NJ: Pearson-Merrill-Prentice Hall.

Bender, W.N. (2004) *Learning Disabilities: Characteristics, Identification, and Teaching Strategies* (5th edn), Boston, MA: Allyn and Bacon.

Berch, D.B. (2005) 'Making sense of number sense: implications for children with mathematical disabilities', *Journal of Learning Disabilities*, 38, 4: 333–9.

Berger, A. and Morris, D. (2001) *Implementing the Literacy Hour for Pupils with Learning Difficulties* (2nd edn), London: Fulton.

Berry, R.A.W. (2006) 'Beyond strategies: teacher beliefs and writing instruction in two primary inclusion classrooms', *Journal of Learning Disabilities*, 39, 1: 11–25.

Best, S.J., Heller, K.W. and Bigge, J.L. (eds) (2005) *Teaching Individuals with Physical or Multiple Disabilities* (5th edn), Upper Saddle River, NJ: Pearson-Merrill-Prentice Hall.

Bhattacharya, A. (2006) 'Syllable-based reading strategy for mastery of scientific information', *Remedial and Special Education*, 27, 2: 116–23.

Bhattacharya, A. and Ehri, L. (2004) 'Graphosyllabic analysis helps adolescent struggling readers read and spell words', *Journal of Learning Disabilities*, 37, 4: 331–48.

Biddle, B.J. and Berliner, D.C. (2002) 'Small class size and its effects', *Educational Leadership* 59, 5: 12–23.

Biemiller, A. (1994) 'Some observations on beginning reading instruction', *Educational Psychologist*, 29, 4: 203–9.

Biggs, J. (1995) 'Motivating learning'. In J. Biggs and D. Watkins (eds) *Classroom Learning*, Singapore: Prentice Hall.

Birsh, J.R. (2005) *Multisensory Teaching of Basic Language Skills* (2nd edn), Baltimore, MD: Brookes.

Bishop, V.E. (2004) *Teaching Visually Impaired Children* (3rd edn), Springfield, IL: Thomas.

Bissaker, K. and Westwood, P.S. (2006) 'Diagnostic uses of the South Australian spelling test', *Australian Journal of Learning Disabilities*, 11, 1: 25–33.

Bissex, G. (1980) *GYNS AT WRK: A Child Learns to Write and Read*, Cambridge, MA: Harvard University Press.

Blachman, B.A., Ball, E.W., Black, R. and Tangel, D.M. (2000) *Road to the Code: A Phonological Awareness Program for Young Children*, Baltimore, MD: Brookes.

Blum, P. (2001) *A Teacher's Guide to Anger Management*, London: RoutledgeFalmer.

Booker, G., Bond, D., Sparrow, L. and Swan, P. (2004) *Teaching Primary Mathematics* (3rd edn), Melbourne: Pearson-Longman.

Bradley, R., Danielson, L. and Doolittle, J. (2005) 'Response to intervention', *Journal of Learning Disabilities*, 28, 1: 485–6.

Bremer, C.D. and Smith, J. (2004) 'Teaching social skills', *Institute on Community Integration Information Brief*, 3, 5: 1–6. Available at: http://www.eric.ed.gov/ERICDocs/data/ericdocs2/content_storage_01/0000000b/80/2e/17/78.pdf   (accessed 17 April 2006).

British Institute of Learning Disabilities (2004) *Fact Sheet: What is a Learning Disability?* Available at: http://www.bild.org.uk/pdfs/05faqs/ld.pdf (accessed 13 April 2006).

Brodkin, A. (2005) 'Still not making friends: between teacher and parent', *Early Childhood Today*, 20, 3: 21–3.

Brophy, J. (2004) *Motivating Students to Learn* (2nd edn), Mahwah, NJ: Erlbaum.

Browder, D.M., Wood, W., Test, D.W., Karvonen, M. and Algozzine, B. (2001) 'Reviewing resources on self-determination', *Remedial and Special Education*, 22, 4: 233–44.

Brown, J. and Morris, D. (2005) 'Meeting the needs of low spellers in a second-grade classroom', *Reading and Writing Quarterly*, 21, 165–84.

Bullis, M., Walker, H.M. and Sprague, J.R. (2001) 'A promise unfulfilled: social skills training with at-risk and antisocial children and youth', *Exceptionality*, 9 (1–2): 67–90.

Burden, R. and Snowling, M. (2005) *Dyslexia and Self-concept: Seeking a Dyslexic Identity*, London: Whurr.

Burns, M. (2005) 'Using incremental rehearsal to increase fluency of single-digit multiplication facts with children identified as learning disabled in mathematics computation', *Education and Treatment of Children*, 28, 3: 237–49.

Caldwell, P. (2006) *Finding you, Finding me: Using Intensive Interaction*, London: Jessica Kingsley.

Cameron, M., Depree, H., Walker, J. and Moore, D. (2002) 'Paired writing: helping beginning writers get started', *SET Research Information for Teachers*, 1: 49–52.

Canney, C. and Byrne, A. (2006) 'Evaluating Circle Time as a support to social skills development: reflections on a journey in school-based research', *British Journal of Special Education*, 33, 1: 19–24.

Cappellini, M. (2005) *Balancing Reading and Language Learning: A Resource for Teaching English Language Learners K–5*, Portland, ME: Stenhouse.

Carnine, D. (2000) *Why Education Experts Resist Effective Practices (and What it Would Take to Make Education More Like Medicine)*, Washington, DC: Thomas B. Fordham Foundation.

Carnine, D.W., Silbert, J., Kameenui, E.J. and Tarver, S.G. (2004) *Direct Instruction Reading* (4th edn), Upper Saddle River, NJ: Pearson-Prentice Hall.

Carnine, D.W., Silbert, J., Kameenui, E.J., Tarver, S.G. and Jongjohann, K. (2006) *Teaching Struggling and At-risk Readers: A Direct Instruction Approach*, Upper Saddle River, NJ: Pearson-Merrill-Prentice Hall.

Cartledge, G. (2005) 'Learning disabilities and social skills: reflections', *Learning Disability Quarterly*, 28, 2: 179–81.

Carver, R.P. (2000) *The Causes of High and Low Reading Achievement*, Mahwah, NJ: Erlbaum.

Catellano, C. (2005) *Making it Work: Educating the Blind or Visually Impaired Student in the Regular School*, Greenwich, CT: Information Age Publishing.

Cawley, J., Parmar, R., Foley, T., Salmon, S. and Roy, S. (2001) 'Arithmetic performance of students: implications for standards and programming', *Exceptional Children*, 67, 3: 311–28.

Chalk, J.C., Hagan-Burke, S. and Burke, M.D. (2005) 'The effects of self-regulated strategy development on the writing process for high school students with learning disabilities', *Learning Disability Quarterly*, 28, 1: 75–87.

Chan, C., Chang, M.L., Westwood, P.S. and Yuen, M.T. (2002) 'Teaching adaptively: how easy is "differentiation" in practice? A perspective from Hong Kong', *Asian-Pacific Educational Researcher*, 11, 1: 27–58.

Chan, L. and Dally, K. (2000) 'Review of literature'. In W. Louden, L. Chan, J. Elkins, D. Greaves, H. House, M. Milton, S. Nichols, M. Rohl, J. Rivalland and C. van Kraayenoord (eds) *Mapping the Territory: Primary Students with Learning Difficulties in Literacy and Numeracy*, Canberra: Department of Education, Training and Youth Affairs.

Chandler-Olcott, K. and Hinchman, K.A. (2005) *Tutoring Adolescent Literacy Learners: A Guide for Volunteers*, New York: Guilford Press.

Chang, C.C. and Westwood, P.S. (2001) 'The effects of ability grouping on low-achievers' motivation and teachers' expectations: a perspective from Hong Kong', *Hong Kong Special Education Forum*, 4, 1: 27–48.

Charles, C.M. and Senter, G.W. (2005) *Elementary Classroom Management* (4th edn), Boston, MA: Pearson-Allyn and Bacon.

Chilvers, D. and Cole, A. (2006) 'Using a sensory approach with children who challenge', *Support for Learning*, 21, 1: 30–2.

Clare, J. D. (2004) 'Differentiation'. A discussion paper available at *Greenfield School Website*. Available at: http://www.greenfield.durham.sch.uk/differentiation.htm (accessed 19 May 2006).

Clarren, S.K. (2003) 'Fetal alcohol syndrome'. In M.L. Wolraich (ed.) *Disorders of Development and Learning* (3rd edn), Hamilton, Ontario: Decker.

Clay, M.M. (1985) *The Early Detection of Reading Difficulties* (3rd edn), Auckland: Heinemann.

Clay, M.M. (1993) *Reading Recovery: A Guidebook for Teachers in Training*, Auckland: Heinemann.

Coffield, F., Moseley, D., Hall, E. and Ecclestone, K. (2004) *Should We Be Using Learning Styles? What Research Has to Say to Practice*, London: Learning and Skills Development Centre.

Cohen, D. and Jaderberg, L. (2005) 'Social skills for primary pupils', *Special Children*, 166 (n.p.).

Colbert, P. and van Kraayenoord, C. (2000) 'Mapping of provisions: states, systems and sectors'. In C. van Kraayenoord, J. Elkins, C. Palmer, F. Rickards and P. Colbert (eds)

Literacy, Numeracy and Students with Disabilities, vol. 2, Canberra: Commonwealth of Australia.

Cole, C.L. (2000) 'Self-management'. In C.R. Reynolds and E. Fletcher-Janzen (eds) *Encyclopedia of Special Education* (2nd edn), New York: Wiley.

Coleman, M.R. (2001) 'Curriculum differentiation: sophistication', *Gifted Child Today Magazine*, 24, 2: 24–5.

Collins, A., Brown, J.S. and Newman, S.E. (1990) 'Cognitive apprenticeship: teaching the crafts of reading, writing and mathematics'. In L.B. Resnick (ed.) *Knowing, Learning and Instruction: Essays in Honor of Robert Glaser*, Hillsdale, NJ: Erlbaum.

Combs, M. (2006) *Readers and Writers in Primary Grades: A Balanced and Integrated Approach K–4* (3rd edn), Upper Saddle River, NJ: Pearson-Merrill-Prentice Hall.

Congress of USA (2002) *Public Law 107–110: No Child Left Behind Act of 2001*, 107th Congress of United States of America. Available at: http://www.ed.gov/legislation/ESEA02/107–110.pdf (accessed 2 February 2006).

Conroy, M.A., Asmus, J.M., Sellers, J.A. and Ladwig, C.N. (2005) 'The use of an antecedent-based intervention to decrease stereotypic behavior in a general education classroom: a case study', *Focus on Autism and Other Developmental Disabilities*, 20, 4: 223–30.

Conway, J. (1997) *Educational Technology's Effect on Models of Instruction*. Available at: http://copland.udel.edu/~jconway/EDST666.htm (accessed 20 April 2006).

Cooney, K. and Hay, I. (2005) 'Internet-based literacy development for middle school students with reading difficulties', *Literacy Learning: The Middle Years*, 13, 1: 36–44.

Cooper, J.D. and Kiger, N.D. (2006) *Literacy: Helping Children Construct Meaning*, Boston, MA: Houghton Mifflin.

Cragg, L. and Nation, K. (2006) 'Exploring written narrative in children with poor reading comprehension', *Educational Psychology*, 26, 1: 55–72.

Cramer, R.L. (1998) *The Spelling Connection: Integrating Reading, Writing and Spelling Instruction*, New York: Guilford Press.

Cramer, R.L. (2004) *The Language Arts: A Balanced Approach to Teaching Reading, Writing, Listening, Talking, and Thinking*, Boston, MA: Pearson-Allyn and Bacon.

Cripps, C. (1990) 'Teaching joined writing to children on school entry as an agent for catching spelling', *Australian Journal of Remedial Education*, 22, 3: 11–15.

Croll, P. and Moses, D. (2000) *Special Needs in the Primary School: One in Five?* London: Cassell.

Crozier, S. and Sileo, N.M. (2005) 'Encouraging positive behaviour with social stories', *Teaching Exceptional Children*, 37, 6: 26–31.

Cullen-Powell, L., Barlow, J. and Bagh, J. (2005) 'The Self-discovery Programme for children with special educational needs in mainstream primary and secondary schools', *Emotional and Behavioural Difficulties*, 10, 3: 189–201.

Cunningham, P., Moore, S., Cunningham, J. and Moore, D. (2004) *Reading and Writing in Elementary Classrooms: Research-based K–4 Instruction* (5th edn), Boston, MA: Pearson-Allyn and Bacon.

Curtin, M. and Clarke, G. (2005) 'Listening to young people with physical disabilities' experiences of education', *International Journal of Disability, Development and Education*, 52, 3: 195–214.

Cushing, L.S., Clark, N.M., Carter, E.W. and Kennedy, C.H. (2005) 'Access to the general education curriculum for students with significant cognitive disabilities', *Teaching Exceptional Children*, 38, 2: 6–13.

Cuskelly, M. (2004) 'The evolving construct of intellectual disability: is everything old new again?', *International Journal of Disability, Development and Education*, 51, 1: 117–22.

Cuvo, A.J., May, M.E. and Post, T.M. (2001) 'Effects of living room, Snoezelen room, and outside activities on stereotypic behaviors and engagement by adults with profound mental retardation', *Research in Developmental Disabilities*, 22, 3: 183–204.

Dahl, K. and Associates (2003) 'Connecting developmental word study with classroom writing: children's descriptions of spelling strategies', *The Reading Teacher*, 57, 4: 310–19.

Darch, C., Soobang, K., Johnson, S. and James, H. (2000) 'The strategic spelling skills of students with learning disabilities: the results of two studies', *Journal of Instructional Psychology*, 27, 1: 15–27.

Davies, A. and Ritchie, D. (2004) *Teaching Handwriting, Reading and Spelling Skills* (THRASS), Chester: THRASS (UK).

Dempsey, I. and Foreman, P. (2001) 'A review of educational approaches for individuals with autism', *International Journal of Disability, Development and Education*, 48: 103–16.

Deschenes, C., Ebeling, D. and Sprague, J. (1999) *Adapting the Curriculum in Inclusive Classrooms*, New York: National Professional Resources.

Deshler, D.D. (2005) 'Adolescents with learning disabilities: unique challenges and reasons for hope', *Learning Disability Quarterly*, 28, 2: 22–4.

Desimone, L.M., Smith, T., Baker, D. and Ueno, K. (2005) 'Assessing barriers to the reform of US mathematics instruction from an international perspective', *American Educational Research Journal*, 42, 3: 501–35.

DEST (Department of Education, Science and Training: Australia) (2005) *Teaching Reading: National Inquiry into the Teaching of Literacy*, Canberra: Government Printing Service, Commonwealth of Australia.

Dettmer, P., Thurston, L. and Dyck, N. (2005) *Consultation, Collaboration and Teamwork for Students with Special Needs* (5th edn), Boston, MA: Pearson-Allyn and Bacon.

DETYA (Department of Education, Training and Youth Affairs: Australia) (1998) *Literacy for All: The Challenge for Australian Schools*, Canberra: Commonwealth Government Publishing Service.

DfEE (Department for Education and Employment: Britain) (1998) *The National Literacy Strategy: Framework for Teaching*, London: HMSO.

DfEE (Department for Education and Employment: Britain) (1999) *The National Numeracy Strategy*, London: DfEE.

DfEE (Department for Education and Employment: Britain) (2001) *Explanatory Notes to Special Educational Needs and Disability Act*, London: Queen's Printer of Acts of Parliament.

DfES (Department for Education and Skills: Britain) (2002) *The National Literacy and Numeracy Strategies: Including all Children in the Literacy Hour and Daily Mathematics Lesson*, London: DfES.

DfES (Department for Education and Skills: Britain) (2004a) *Removing Barriers to Achievement*, Annersley: DfES Publications.

DfES (Department for Education and Skills: Britain) (2004b) 'Behaviour and Education Support Teams (BESTs)'. In *Removing Barriers to Achievement: The Government's Strategy for SEN*, London: DfES.

DfES (Department for Education and Skills: Britain) (2005) *Targeting Support: Implementing Interventions for Children with Significant Difficulties in Mathematics*, Norwich: HMSO.

DfES (Department for Education and Skills: Britain) (2006a) *Special Educational Needs – What Does it Mean?* Available at: http://www.teachernet.gov.uk/wholeschool/sen/parentcarers/mychild/ (accessed 11 April 2006).

DfES (Department for Education and Skills: Britain) (2006b) *Special Educational Needs (SEN) Policy.* Available at: http://www.teachernet.gov.uk/management/atoz/s/senpolicy/ (accessed 11 April 2006).

Dickinson, P. (2003) 'Whole class interactive teaching', *SET Research for Teachers*, 1: 18–21. Wellington: New Zealand Council for Educational Research.

Dix, S. (2006) '"What did I change and why did I change it?" Young writers' revision practices', *Literacy*, 40, 1: 3–10.

Dixon, R. and Englemann, S. (1996) *Spelling Through Morphographs*, Desoto, TX: SRA-McGraw Hill.

Dixon, R.M., Marsh, H.W. and Craven, R.G. (2004) 'Interpersonal cognitive problem-solving intervention with five adults with intellectual impairment'. In H.W. Marsh, J. Baumert, G. Richards and U. Trantwein (eds) *Self-concept, Motivation and Identity: Where to From Here?* Proceedings of 3rd International Biennial SELF Research Conference, Berlin, 4–7 July 2004.

Dole, S. (2003) 'Applying psychological theory to helping students overcome learned difficulties in mathematics: an alternative approach to intervention', *School Psychology International* 24, 1: 95–114.

Doveston, M. and Keenaghan, M. (2006) 'Improving classroom dynamics to support students' learning and social inclusion: a collaborative approach', *Support for Learning*, 21, 1: 5–11.

Dowker, A. (2005) 'Early identification and intervention for students with mathematics difficulties', *Journal of Learning Disabilities*, 38, 4: 324–32.

Dymond, S.K. and Orelove, P. (2001) 'What constitutes effective curriculum for students with severe disabilities?' *Exceptionality*, 9, 3: 109–22.

Earl, L., Watson, N., Levin, B., Leithwood, K., Fullan, M. and Torrance, N. (2003) *Watching and Learning 3: Final Report of the External Evaluation of the Implementation of the National Literacy and Numeracy Strategies*, London: DfES.

Ee, J. and Soh, K.C. (2005) 'Teacher perceptions on what a functional curriculum should be for children with special need', *International Journal of Special Education*, 20, 2: 6–18.

Eells, J.M. (2000) 'Cloze technique'. In C.R. Reynolds and E. Fletcher-Janzen (eds) *Encyclopedia of Special Education* (2nd edn), New York: Wiley.

Eggen, P. and Kauchak, D. (2004) *Educational Psychology: Windows on Classrooms* (6th edn), Upper Saddle River, NJ: Pearson-Merrill.

Ehri, L.C. (2003) '*Systematic Phonics Instruction: Findings of the National Reading Project'*. Seminar paper for Standards and Effectiveness Unit, Department of Education and Skills, London. Available at: http://www.standards.dfes.gov.uk/pdf/literacy/lehri_phonics.pdf (accessed 27 March 2006).

Eke, R. and Lee, J. (2004) 'Pace and differentiation in the Literacy Hour: some outcomes of an analysis of transcripts', *Curriculum Journal*, 15, 3: 219–31.

Elbaum, B., Vaughn, S., Hughes, M. and Moody, S. (2000) 'How effective are one-to-one tutoring programs in reading for elementary students at risk for reading failure? A meta-analysis of intervention research', *Journal of Educational Psychology*, 92: 605–19.

Eldredge, J.L. (2005) *Teach Decoding: Why and How* (2nd edn), Upper Saddle River, NJ: Pearson-Merrill-Prentice Hall.

Elksnin, L.K. and Elksnin, N. (1995) *Assessment and Instruction of Social Skills* (2nd edn), San Diego, CA: Singular Publishing.

Elliott, C., Pring, T. and Bunning, K. (2002) 'Social skills training for adolescents with intellectual disabilities: a cautionary note', *Journal of Applied Research in Intellectual Disabilities*, 15, 1: 91–6.

Ellis, L.A. (2005) *Balancing Approaches: Revisiting the Educational Psychology Research on Teaching Students with Learning Difficulties*, Melbourne: Australian Council for Educational Research.

Engelmann, S. (1999) 'The benefits of direct instruction: affirmative action for at-risk students', *Educational Leadership*, 57, 1: 77–9.

Erion, J. and Ronka, C.S. (2005) 'Improving reading fluency with parent tutoring', *Teaching Exceptional Children*, 37, 3: 31.

Ezell, H.K. and Justice, L.M. (2005) *Shared Storybook Reading: Building Children's Language and Emergent Literacy Skills*, Baltimore, MD: Brookes.

Farkota, R. (2005) 'Basic math problems: the brutal reality!', *Learning Difficulties Australia Bulletin*, 37, 3: 10–11.

Fasting, R.B. and Lyster, S.H. (2005) 'The effects of computer technology in assisting the development of literacy in young struggling readers and spellers', *European Journal of Special Needs Education*, 20, 1: 21–40.

Feldman, K. and Denti, L. (2004) 'High-access instruction: practical strategies to increase active learning in diverse classrooms', *Focus on Exceptional Children*, 36, 7: 1–11.

Feng, S. and Powers, K. (2005) 'The short- and long-term effect of explicit grammar instruction on fifth graders' writing', *Reading Improvement*, 42, 2: 67–72.

Fitzgerald, J. and Shanahan, T. (2000) 'Reading and writing relations and their development', *Educational Psychologist*, 35, 1: 39–50.

Fleischner, J.E. and Manheimer, M.A. (1997) 'Math intervention for students with learning disabilities: myths and realities', *School Psychology Review*, 26, 3: 397–413.

Flood, J., Lapp, D. and Fisher, D. (2005) 'Neurological Impress Method Plus', *Reading Psychology*, 26: 147–60.

Foorman, B.R., Schatschneider, C., Eakin, M.N., Fletcher, J.M., Moats, L.C. and Francis, D.J. (2006) 'The impact of instructional practices in Grades 1 and 2 on reading and spelling achievement in high poverty schools', *Contemporary Educational Psychology*, 31, 1: 1–29.

Forbes, S. and Briggs, C. (2003) *Research in Reading Recovery*, vol. 2, Portsmouth, NH: Heinemann.

Ford, M.P. (2005) *Differentiation Through Flexible Grouping: Successfully Reaching All Readers*, Naperville, IL: Learning Point Associates [ERIC document: ED489 510].

Foster (2004) *Anchored instruction*. Available at: http://coe.sdsu.edu/eet/articles/anchoredinstruc/index.htm (accessed 20 April 2006).

Fountas, I.C. and Pinnell, G.S. (1996) *Guided Reading*, Portsmouth, NH: Heinemann.

Fountas, I.C. and Pinnell, G.S. (2001) *Guiding Readers and Writers in Grades 3–6*, Portsmouth, NH: Heinemann.

Fountas, I.C. and Pinnell, G.S. (2006) *Leveled Books (K–8): Matching Texts to Readers for Effective Teaching*, Portsmouth, NH: Heinemann.

Fox, C.L. and Boulton, M.J. (2005) 'The social skills problems of victims of bullying: self, peer and teacher perceptions', *British Journal of Educational Psychology*, 75, 2: 313–28.

Fox, G. (2003) *A Handbook for Learning Support Assistants* (2nd edn), London: Fulton.

Frederickson, N. and Furnham, A.F. (2004) 'Peer-assessed behavioural characteristics and sociometric rejection: differences between pupils who have moderate learning difficulties and their mainstream peers', *British Journal of Educational Psychology*, 74, 3: 391–410.

Frederickson, N., Warren, L. and Turner, J. (2005) 'Circle of Friends – an exploration of impact over time', *Educational Psychology in Practice*, 21, 3: 197–217.

Friend, M.P. and Bursuck, W.D. (2006) *Including Students with Special Needs: A Practical Guide for Classroom Teachers* (4th edn), Boston, MA: Pearson-Allyn and Bacon.

Fuchs, L.S. and Fuchs, D. (2005) 'Enhancing mathematical problem solving for students with disabilities', *Journal of Special Education*, 39, 1: 45–57.

Fuchs, L.S., Compton, D., Fuchs, D., Paulsen, K., Bryant, J. and Hamlett, C.L. (2005) 'Responsiveness to intervention: preventing and identifying mathematics disability', *Teaching Exceptional Children*, 37, 4: 60–3.

Furner, J.M., Yahya, N. and Duffy, M.L. (2005) 'Teach mathematics: strategies to reach all students', *Interventions in School and Clinic*, 41, 1: 16–23.

Galbraith, A. and Alexander, J. (2005) 'Literacy, self-esteem, and locus of control,' *Support for Learning*, 20, 1: 28–34.

Gersten, R., Jordan, N.C. and Flojo, J.R. (2005) 'Early identification and interventions for students with mathematics difficulties', *Journal of Learning Difficulties*, 38, 4: 293–304.

Gest, S.D. and Gest, J.M. (2005) 'Reading tutoring for students at academic and behavioral risk: effects on time-on-task in the classroom', *Education and Treatment of Children*, 28, 1: 25–47.

Gettinger, M. and Stoiber, K.C. (1999) 'Excellence in teaching: review of instructional and environmental variables'. In C.R. Reynolds and T.B. Gutkin (eds) *The Handbook of School Psychology* (3rd edn), New York: Wiley.

Gilbert, M.B. (2004) 'Grammar and writing skills: applying behaviour analysis'. In D.J. Moran and R.W. Malott (eds) *Evidence-based Educational Methods*, San Diego, CA: Elsevier Academic.

Gillingham, A. and Stillman, B. (1960) *Remedial Teaching for Children with Specific Disability in Reading, Spelling and Penmanship*, Cambridge, MA: Educators Publishing Service.

Glass, L., Peist, L. and Pike, B. (2000) *Read! Read! Read! Training Effective Reading Partners*, Thousand Oaks, CA: Corwin Press.

Goddard, A. (1995) 'From product to process in curriculum planning: a view from Britain', *Journal of Learning Disabilities*, 28, 5: 258–63.

Goldsworthy, C.L. (2001) *Sourcebook of Phonological Awareness Activities*, San Diego, CA: Singular Publishing.

Good, T.L. and Brophy, J. (2003) *Looking in Classrooms* (9th edn), Boston, MA: Allyn and Bacon.

Goodman, K.S. (1967) 'Reading: a psycholinguistic guessing game', *Journal of the Reading Specialist*, 6: 126–35.

Goswami, U. (2005) 'Synthetic phonics and learning to read: a cross language perspective', *Educational Psychology in Practice*, 21, 4: 273–82.

Graham, L. and Bellert, A. (2005) 'Reading comprehension difficulties experienced by students with learning disabilities', *Australian Journal of Learning Disabilities*, 10, 2: 71–8.

Graham, S. (2000) 'Should the natural learning approach replace spelling instruction?' *Journal of Educational Psychology*, 92, 2: 235–47.

Graham, S. and Harris, K. (2005a) 'Improving the writing performance of young struggling writers: theoretical and programmatic research from the center on accelerating student learning', *Journal of Special Education*, 39, 1: 19–33.

Graham, S. and Harris, K.R. (2005b) *Writing Better: Effective Strategies for Teaching Students with Learning Difficulties*, Baltimore, MD: Brookes.

Grainger, J. and Frazer, T. (1999) 'Using private speech to overcome learned helplessness'. In A.J. Watson and L.R. Giorcelli (eds) *Accepting the Literacy Challenge*, Sydney: Scholastic.

Graves, D.H. (1983) *Writing: Teachers and Children at Work*, Exeter, NH: Heinemann.

Greenspan, S.I. and Wieder, S. (2006) *Engaging Autism: Using the Floortime Approach to Help Children Relate, Communicate and Think*, Cambridge, MA: Da Capo Press.

Gregg, N. and Mather, N. (2002) 'School is fun at recess: informal analyses of written language for students with learning disabilities', *Journal of Learning Disabilities*, 35, 1: 7–22.

Gregory, G.H. and Chapman, C. (2002) *Differentiated Instructional Strategies: One Size Doesn't Fit All*, Thousand Oaks, CA: Corwin Press.

Gresham, F.M. (2002) 'Social skills assessment and instruction for students with emotional and behavioral disorders'. In K.L. Lane, F.M. Gresham and T.E. O'Shaughnessy (eds) *Interventions for Children With or At Risk for Emotional and Behavioral Disorders*, Boston, MA: Allyn and Bacon.

Gresham, F.M., Sugai, G. and Horner, R.H. (2001) 'Interpreting outcomes of social skills training for students with high-incidence disabilities', *Exceptional Children*, 67, 3: 331–44.

Gunning, T.G. (2001) *Building Words: A Resource Manual for Teaching Word Analysis and Spelling Strategies*, Boston, MA: Allyn and Bacon.

Haggerty, N.K., Black, R.S. and Smith, G.J. (2005) 'Increasing self-managed coping skills through social stories and apron storytelling', *Teaching Exceptional Children*, 37, 4: 40–7.

Hall, K. (2004) 'Reflections on six years of the National Literacy Strategy in England: an interview with Stephen Anwyll, Director of NLS 2001–2004, *Literacy*, 38, 3: 119–25.

Hall, S. (1997) 'The problem with differentiation', *School Science Review*, 78, 284: 95–8.

Hallahan, D.P. and Kauffman, J. (2006) *Exceptional Learners* (10th edn), Boston, MA: Pearson-Allyn and Bacon.

Halsey, K., Gulliver, C., Johnson, A., Martin, K. and Kinder, K. (2005) *Evaluation of Behaviour and Education Support Teams*, Annersley: DfES/NFER.

Hammond, L. (2004) 'Getting the right balance: effective classroom spelling instruction', *Australian Journal of Learning Disabilities*, 9, 3: 11–18.

Hansen, S. (2002) '"Writing Sux". Boys and writing: what's the problem?', *SET Research Information for Teachers*, 1: 38–43.

Hardman, F., Smith, F. and Wall, K. (2003) 'Interactive whole-class teaching in the National Literacy Strategy', *Cambridge Journal of Education*, 33, 2: 197–215.

Hardman, M.L., Drew, C.J. and Egan, W.W. (2005) *Human Exceptionality: School, Community, and Family* (8th edn), Boston, MA: Pearson-Allyn and Bacon.

Harniss, M.K., Carnine, D.W., Silbert, J. and Dixon, R.C. (2002) 'Effective strategies for teaching mathematics'. In E.J. Kameenui and D.C. Simmons (eds) *Effective Teaching Strategies that Accommodate Diverse Learners* (2nd edn), Upper Saddle River, NJ: Merrill-Prentice Hall.

Hart, B. (2002) 'Anger management', *Special Children*, 143: 17–19.

Harwayne, S. (2001) *Writing Through Childhood*, Portsmouth, NH: Heinemann.

Hasbrouck, J. and Tindal, G.A. (2006) 'Oral reading fluency norms: a valuable assessment tool for reading teachers', *The Reading Teacher*, 59, 7: 636–44.

Hay, I., Elias, G. and Booker, G. (2005) 'Students with learning difficulties in relation to literacy and numeracy', *Schooling Issues Digest 2005/1*, Canberra: Australian Government Department of Education, Science and Training. Available at: http://dest. gov.au/schools/publications/digest (accessed 25 May 2006).

Hazler, R (1996) *Breaking the Cycle of Violence: Interventions for Bullying and Victimization*, Washington, DC: Accelerated Development.

Hegde, M.N. and Maul, C.A. (2006) *Language Disorders in Children: An Evidence-based Approach to Assessment and Treatment*, Boston, MA: Pearson-Allyn and Bacon.

Heilman, A.W. (2006) *Phonics in Proper Perspective* (10th edn), Upper Saddle River, NJ: Merrill-Prentice Hall.

Heller, K.W. and Bigge, J.L. (2005) 'Augmentative and alternative communication'. In S.J. Best, K.W. Heller and J.L. Bigge (eds) *Teaching Individuals with Physical or Multiple Disabilities* (5th edn), Upper Saddle River, NJ: Pearson-Merrill-Prentice Hall.

Heller, K.W., Forney, P.E, Alberto, P.A., Schwartzman, M.N. and Goeckel, T.M. (2000) *Meeting Physical and Health Needs of Children with Disabilities*, Belmont, CA: Wadsworth.

Heron, T.E., Villareal, D.M., Yao, M., Christianson, R.J. and Heron, K.M. (2006) 'Peer tutoring: applications in classrooms and specialized environments', *Reading and Writing Quarterly*, 22, 1: 27–45.

Herrell, A.L. and Jordan, M. (2006) *50 Strategies for Improving Vocabulary, Comprehension, and Fluency: An Active Learning Approach*, Upper Saddle River, NJ: Pearson-Merrill-Prentice Hall.

Hetzroni, O.E. and Shrieber, B. (2004) 'Word processing as an assistive technology tool for enhancing academic outcomes of students with writing disabilities in the general classroom', *Journal of Learning Disabilities*, 37, 2: 143–54.

HMSO (2003) *Every Child Matters*, Norwich: The Stationery Office.

Hollas, B. (2005) *Differentiating Instruction in Whole-group Settings*, Peterborough, NH: Crystal Springs Books.

Holverstott, J. (2005) 'Promote self-determination in students', *Intervention in School and Clinic*, 41, 1: 39–41.

Hoover, J.J. and Patton, J.R. (2005) 'Differentiating curriculum and instruction for English-language learners with special needs', *Intervention in School and Clinic*, 40, 4: 231–5.

Horner, S.L. and Gaither, S.M. (2004) 'Attribution retraining instruction with a second grade class', *Early Childhood Education Journal*, 31, 3: 165–70.

House of Commons Education and Skills Committee (Britain) (2005) *Teaching Children to Read*, London: HMSO.

Howley, M. and Arnold, E. (2005) *Revealing the Hidden Code: Social Stories for People with Autism Spectrum Disorders*, London: Jessica Kingsley.

Huinker, D.A. (2002) 'Calculators as learning tools for young children's explorations of number', *Teaching Children Mathematics*, 8, 6: 316–21.

Humphrey, N. and Brooks, A.G. (2006) 'An evaluation of a short cognitive-behavioural anger management intervention for pupils at risk of exclusion', *Emotional and Behavioural Difficulties*, 11, 1: 5–23.

Hutchinson, R. and Kewin, J. (1994) *Sensations and Disability: Sensory Environments for Leisure, Snoezelen, Education and Therapy*, Exeter: ROMPA.

Hyde, M. and Power, D. (2006) 'Some ethical dimensions of cochlear implantation for deaf children and their families', *Journal of Deaf Studies and Deaf Education*, 11, 1: 102–11.

Idol, L. (2006) 'Toward inclusion of special education students in general education', *Remedial and Special Education*, 27, 2: 77–94.

Invernizzi, M., Johnston, F. and Bear, D. (2004) *Words their Way: Word Sorts for Within Word Pattern Spellers*, Upper Saddle River, NJ: Pearson-Merrill.

Iversen, S., Tunmer, W. and Chapman, J.W. (2005) 'The effects of varying group size on the reading recovery approach to preventive early intervention', *Journal of Learning Disabilities*, 38, 5: 456–72.

Jacklin, A. and Farr, W. (2005) 'The computer in the classroom: a medium for enhancing social interaction with young people with autistic spectrum disorders', *British Journal of Educational Studies*, 32, 4: 202–10.

Jacobs, R.A. (2003) 'Myelodysplasia (Spina Bifida-Myelomeningocele)'. In M.L. Wolraich (ed.) *Disorders of Development and Learning* (3rd edn), Hamilton, Ontario: Decker.

Janney, R. and Snell, M.E. (2004) *Modifying Schoolwork* (2nd edn), Baltimore, MD: Brookes.

Jindal-Snape, D. (2005) 'Use of feedback from sighted peers in promoting social interaction skills', *Journal of Visual Impairment and Blindness*, 99, 7: 403–12.

Johnson, D. (2006) 'Listening to the views of those involved in the inclusion of pupils with Down's Syndrome into mainstream schools', *Support for Learning*, 21, 1: 24–9.

Johnson, D.W. and Johnson, F.P. (2003) *Joining Together: Group Theory and Group Skills* (8th edn), Boston, MA: Allyn and Bacon.

Johnston, R. and Watson, J. (2005) 'A seven years study of the effects of synthetic phonics teaching on reading and spelling attainment', *Insight 17*, Edinburgh: Scottish Executive Education Department. Available at: http://www.scotland.gov.uk/library5/education/sptrs-00.asp (accessed 2 April 2006).

Jones, E.D. and Southern, W.T. (2003) 'Balancing the perspectives on mathematics instruction', *Focus on Exceptional Children*, 35, 9: 1–16.

Jones, L. (2004) 'Least restrictive adaptation model: anything you need you can find in the kitchen drawer', *Re:View*, 36, 2: 63–9.

Jonson, K.F. (2006) *60 Strategies for Improving Reading Comprehension in Grades K–8*, Thousand Oaks, CA: Corwin Press.

Joseph, L.M. (2002) 'Facilitating word recognition and spelling using word boxes and word sort phonic procedures', *School Psychology Review*, 31, 1: 122–9.

Kaiser, A.P. and Grim, J.C. (2006) 'Teaching functional communication skills'. In M.E. Snell and F. Brown (eds) *Instruction of Students with Severe Disabilities* (6th edn), Upper Saddle River, NJ: Pearson-Merrill-Prentice Hall.

Kameenui, E. and Simmons, D. (1999) *Towards Successful Inclusion of Students with Disabilities: The Architecture of Instruction*, Reston, VA: Council for Exceptional Children.

Kauchak, D. and Eggen, P.D. (2003) *Learning and Teaching: Research-based Methods* (4th edn), Boston, MA: Allyn and Bacon.

Kauffman, J.M., Landrum, T.J., Mock, D.R., Sayeski, B. and Sayeski, K.L. (2005) 'Diverse knowledge and skills require a diversity of instructional groups: a position statement', *Remedial and Special Education*, 26, 1: 2–6.

Kavale, K.A. (2005) 'Identifying specific learning disability: is responsiveness to intervention the answer?', *Journal of Learning Disabilities*, 38, 6: 553–62.

Kavale, K.A and Mostert, M. (2004) 'Social skills interventions for individuals with learning disabilities', *Learning Disability Quarterly*, 27, 1: 31–43.

Kellett, M. and Nind, M. (2003) *Implementing Intensive Interaction in Schools: Guidance for Practitioners, Managers and Coordinators*, London: Fulton.

Kennedy, G. (2000) 'Students with special needs and the Web', *Australian Journal of Learning Disabilities*, 5, 3: 39.

Kenward, H. (1997) *Integrating Pupils with Disabilities in Mainstream Schools*, London: Fulton.

Kervin, L.K. (2002) 'Proofreading as a strategy for spelling development', *Reading Online*, 5, 10 (n.p.).

Kewley, G. (2005) *Attention Deficit Hyperactivity Disorder: What can Teachers Do?* (2nd edn), London: Fulton.

Kimball, J.W., Kinney, E.M., Taylor, B.A. and Stromer, R. (2004) 'Video enhanced activity schedules for children with autism: a promising package for teaching social skills', *Education and Treatment of Children*, 27, 3: 280–98.

Kirby, A., Davies, R. and Bryant, A. (2005) 'Do teachers know more about specific learning difficulties than general practitioners?', *British Journal of Special Education*, 32, 3: 122–6.

Kirkbride, S. and Wright, B.C. (2002) 'The role of analogy use in improving early spelling performance', *Educational and Child Psychology*, 19, 4: 91–102.

Klein, D., Braams, B.J., Parker, T., Quirk, W., Schmid, W. and Wilson, W.S. (2005) *The State of State Math Standards: 2005*, Washington, DC: Thomas Fordham Foundation.

Koegel, R.L. and Koegel, L.K. (2006) *Pivotal Response Treatments for Autism: Communication, Social and Academic Development*, Baltimore, MD: Brookes.

Konings, K., Wiers, R., Wiel, M. and Schmidt, H. (2005) 'Problem-based learning as a valuable educational method for physically disabled teenagers? The discrepancy between theory and practice', *Journal of Developmental and Physical Disabilities*, 17, 2: 107–17.

Kraft, N. (2005) *Criteria for authentic project-based learning*, Denver, CO: RMC Research Corporation. Available at: http://www.rmcdenver.com/useguide/pbl.htm (accessed 11 May 2006).

Kreis, K. (2005) 'Improving spelling abilities', *Literacy Learning: The Middle Years*, 13, 2: 35–41.

Kroesbergen, E.H. and Van Luit, J.E. (2003) 'Mathematics interventions for children with special educational needs', *Remedial and Special Education*, 24, 2: 97–114.

Kroesbergen, E.H., Van Luit, J.E.H. and Maas, C.J.M. (2004) 'Effectiveness of constructivist mathematics instruction for low-achieving students in The Netherlands', *Elementary School Journal*, 104, 3: 233–51.

Kyriacou, C. (2005) 'The impact of daily mathematics lessons in England on pupil confidence and competence in early mathematics: a systematic review', *British Journal of Educational Studies*, 53, 2: 168–86.

Lane, H.B., Pullen, P.C., Eisele, M.R. and Jordan, L. (2005) 'Preventing reading failure: phonological awareness assessment and instruction'. In Z. Fang (ed.) *Literacy Teaching and Learning: Current Issues and Trends*, Upper Saddle River, NJ: Pearson-Merrill-Prentice Hall.

Lane, K.L., Wehby, J.H. and Cooley, C. (2006) 'Teacher expectations of students' classroom behaviour across the grade span: which social skills are necessary for success?', *Exceptional Children*, 72, 2: 153–67.

Lee, C. (2001) 'Problem-based learning: a personal view', *Planet (Special Edition 2)*: 10.

Leech, G., Rayson, P. and Wilson, A. (2001) *Word Frequencies in Written and Spoken English: Based on the British National Corpus*, Harlow: Longman.

Lerner, J. and Kline, F. (2006) *Learning Disabilities and Related Disorders* (10th edn), Boston, MA: Houghton Mifflin.

Levin, J. and Nolan, J.F. (2004) *Principles of Classroom Management: A Professional Decision-making Model* (4th edn), Boston, MA: Pearson-Allyn and Bacon.

Levy, S.E. and Hyman, S.L. (2005) 'Novel treatments for autistic spectrum disorders', *Mental Retardation and Developmental Disabilities Research Reviews*, 11, 2: 131–42.

Lewis, R.B. and Doorlag, D.H. (2006) *Teaching Special Students in General Education Classrooms* (7th edn), Upper Saddle River, NJ: Pearson-Merrill-Prentice Hall.

Leyser, Y. and Kirk, R. (2004) 'Evaluating inclusion: an examination of parent views and factors influencing their perspectives', *International Journal of Disability, Development and Education*, 51, 3: 271–85.

Liboiron, N. and Soto, G. (2006) 'Shared story book reading with a student who uses alternative and augmentative communication: a description of scaffolding procedures', *Child Language Teaching and Therapy*, 21, 1: 69–95.

Lieberman, L.J. and Wilson, S. (2005) 'Effects of a sports camp practicum on attitudes toward children with visual impairments and deaf-blindness', *Re:View*, 36, 4: 141–53.

Lindberg, J.A., Kelley, D.E. and Swick, A.M. (2005) *Common-sense Classroom Management for Middle and High School Teachers*, Thousand Oaks, CA: Corwin Press.

Linden, L., Banerjee, A. and Duflo, E. (2003) 'Computer-assisted learning: evidence from a randomized experiment', *Poverty Action Lab Report 5*. Available at: http://www.povertyactionlab.com/papers/banerjee_duflo_linden.pdf (accessed 05 May 2006).

Liptak, G.S. (2005) 'Complementary and alternative therapies for cerebral palsy', *Mental Retardation and Developmental Disabilities Research Reviews*, 11, 2: 156–63.

Lloyd, S. and Wernham, S. (1995) *Jolly Phonics Workbooks*, Chigwell: Jolly Learning.

Lockery, M. and Maggs, A. (1982) 'Direct Instruction research in Australia: a ten-year analysis', *Educational Psychology*, 2, (3–4): 263–88.

Lovaas, O.I. (1993) 'The development of a treatment research project for developmentally disabled and autistic children', *Journal of Applied Behavior Analysis*, 26, 4: 617–30.

Lovitt, T.C. (2000) *Preventing School Failure: Tactics for Teaching Adolescents* (2nd edn), Austin, TX: ProEd.

Lucangeli, D. and Cabrele, S. (2006) 'Mathematical difficulties and ADHD', *Exceptionality*, 14, 1: 53–62.

Luckason, R., Borthwick-Duffy, S., Buntix, W., Coulter, D.L., Craig, E.M., Reeve, A., Schalock, R.L., Snell, M.E., Spitalnik, D.M., Spreat, S. and Tasse, M.T. (2002) *Mental Retardation: Definition, Classification and Systems of Supports* (10th edn), Washington DC: American Association on Mental Retardation.

Lyndon, H. (1989) 'I did it my way: an introduction to Old Way–New Way', *Australasian Journal of Special Education*, 13: 32–7.

Lyon, G.R. (2005) 'Dr Reid Lyon interviewed by Norman Swan on ABC Radio National', *Learning Difficulties Australia Bulletin*, 37, 2: 3–5.

Lyon, G.R., Shaywitz, S. and Shaywitz, B. (2003) 'Defining dyslexia, comorbidity, teachers' knowledge of language and reading', *Annals of Dyslexia*, 53: 1–14.

Maag, J.W. (2005) 'Social skills training for youth with emotional and behavioral disorders and learning disabilities: problems, conclusions, and suggestions', *Exceptionality*, 13, 3: 155–72.

Maccini, P. and Gagnon, J.C. (2006) 'Mathematics instructional practices and assessment accommodations of special and general educators', *Exceptional Children*, 72, 2: 217–34.

MacInnis, C. and Hemming, H. (1995) 'Linking the needs of students with learning disabilities to a whole language curriculum', *Journal of Learning Disabilities*, 28, 9: 535–44.

Magnusen, C.L. (2005) *Teaching Children with Autism and Related Spectrum Disorders: An Art and a Science*, London: Jessica Kingsley.

Manning, M. and Underbakke, C. (2005) 'Spelling development research necessitates replacement of weekly word lists', *Childhood Education*, 81, 4: 236–8.

Manset-Williamson, G. and Nelson, J.M. (2005) 'Balanced, strategic reading instruction for upper-elementary and middle school students with reading disabilities: a comparative study of two approaches', *Learning Disability Quarterly*, 28, 1: 59–74.

Margalit, M. (1995) 'Effects of social skills training for students with intellectual disability', *International Journal of Disability, Development and Education*, 42, 1: 75–85.

Mariotti, A.S. and Homan, S.P. (2005) *Linking Reading Assessment to Instruction* (4th edn), Mahwah, NJ: Erlbaum.

Marrone, A.S. and Schutz, P.A. (2000) 'Promoting achievement motivation'. In K.M. Minke and G.C. Bear (eds) *Preventing School Problems, Promoting School Success*, Bethesda, MD: National Association of School Psychologists.

Martinez, J.G.R. and Martinez, N.C. (2001) *Reading and Writing to Learn Mathematics*, Boston, MA: Allyn and Bacon.

Massengill, D. (2006) 'Mission accomplished – it's learnable now: voices of mature challenged spellers using a word study approach', *Journal of Adolescent and Adult Literacy*, 49, 5: 420–31.

Mazzocco, M.M. and Thompson, R.E. (2005) 'Kindergarten predictors of math learning disability', *Learning Disabilities Research and Practice*, 20, 3: 142–55.

McInerney, D.M. and McInerney, V. (2006) *Educational Psychology: Constructing Learning* (4th edn), Frenchs Forest, NSW: Prentice Hall.

McKinnon, D.H. and Gordon, C. (1999) 'An investigation of teachers' support needs for the inclusion of students with disabilities in regular classrooms', *Special Education Perspectives*, 8, 2: 3–14.

McMaster, K.L., Fuchs, D. and Fuchs, L.S. (2006) 'Research on peer-assisted learning strategies: the promise and the limitations of peer-mediated instruction', *Reading and Writing Quarterly*, 22, 1: 5–25.

Meadow, K.P. (2005) 'Early manual communication in relation to the deaf child's intellectual, social and communicative functioning', *Journal of Deaf Studies and Deaf Education*, 10, 4: 321–9.

Meese, R.L. (2001) *Teaching Learners with Mild Disabilities: Integrating Research and Practice* (2nd edn), Belmont, CA: Wadsworth-Thomson.

Merttens, R. and Robertson, C. (2005) 'Rhyme and Ritual: a new approach to teaching children to read and write', *Literacy*, 39, 1: 18–23.

Mesibov, G.B., Shea, V. and Schopler, E (2005) *The TEACCH Approach to Autism Spectrum Disorders*, New York: Kluwer Academic-Plenum.

Mesmer, H.A.E and Griffith, P.L. (2006) 'Everybody's selling it – but just what is explicit, systematic phonics instruction?' *The Reading Teacher*, 59, 4: 366–76.

Meyerson, M.J. and Kulesza, D.L. (2002) *Strategies for Struggling Readers: Step by Step*, Upper Saddle River, NJ: Merrill-Prentice Hall.

Miles, P.A., Stegle, K.W., Hubbs, K.G., Henk, W.A. and Mallette, M.H. (2004) 'A whole-class support model for early literacy: the Anna Plan', *The Reading Teacher*, 58, 4: 318–27.

Miller, C., Lacey, P. and Layton, L. (2003) 'Including children with special educational needs in the Literacy Hour: a continuing challenge', *British Journal of Special Education*, 30, 1: 13–20.

Minton, P. (2001) 'Effectively integrating the computer to teach children with literacy difficulties', *Australian Journal of Learning Disabilities*, 6, 1: 35–7.

Minton, P. (2002) 'Using information and communication technology to help dyslexics and others learn to spell', *Australian Journal of Learning Disabilities*, 7, 3: 26–31.

Monreal, S.T. and Hernandez, R.S. (2005) 'Reading levels of Spanish deaf students', *American Annals of the Deaf*, 150, 4: 379–87.

Moody, S.W., Vaughn, S., Hughes, M.T. and Fischer, M. (2000) 'Reading instruction in the resource room: set up for failure', *Exceptional Children*, 66, 3: 305–16.

Mooney, P., Ryan, J.B., Uhing, B.M., Reid, R. and Epstein, M.H. (2005) 'A review of self-management interventions targeting academic outcomes for students with emotional and behavioral disorders', *Journal of Behavioral Education*, 14, 3: 203–21.

Moore, C., Evans, D. and Dowson, M. (2005) 'The intricate nature of phonological awareness instruction', *Special Education Perspectives*, 14, 1: 37–54.

Moores, D.F. (2005) 'Cochlear implants: an update', *American Annals of the Deaf*, 150, 4: 327–8.

Moran, D.J. (2004) 'The need for research-based educational methods'. In D.J. Moran and R.W. Malott (eds) *Evidence-based Educational Methods*, San Diego, CA: Elsevier Academic.

Morgan, M. and Moni, K.B. (2005) 'Use phonics activities to motivate learners with difficulties', *Intervention in School and Clinic*, 41, 1: 42–5.

Morris, D. (2005) *The Howard Street Tutoring Manual: Teaching At-risk Readers in the Primary Grades* (2nd edn), New York: Guilford Press.

Morris, D. and Slavin, R.E. (2003) *Every Child Reading*, Boston, MA: Allyn and Bacon.

Morrow, L.M. and Woo, D.G. (2001) *Tutoring Programs for Struggling Readers*, New York: Guilford Press.

Mortimore, T. (2005) 'Dyslexia and learning style: a note of caution', *British Journal of Special Education*, 32, 3: 145–8.

Muter, V. and Snowling, C. (2004) *Early Reading Development and Dyslexia*, London: Whurr.

National Council of Teachers of Mathematics (US) (2005) *Overview: Principles for School Mathematics.* Available at: http://standards.nctm.org/document/chapter2/index.htm (accessed 20 March 2006).

National Reading Panel (US) (2000) *Teaching Children to Read: An Evidence-based Assessment of the Scientific Research Literature on Reading and its Implications for Reading Instruction*, Washington, DC: National Institute of Child Health and Human Development.

Neale, M. (1997) *Neale Analysis of Reading Ability: Manual for Schools* (2nd revised British edn), Windsor: NFER-Nelson.

Neale, M. (1999) *Neale Analysis of Reading Ability* (3rd edn, Australian Standardisation), Melbourne: ACER Press.

Nelson, N. and Calfee, R.C. (1998) *The Reading–Writing Connection*, Chicago, IL: National Society for the Study of Education.

Neufeld, P. (2006) 'Comprehension instruction in content area classes', *The Reading Teacher*, 59, 4: 302–12.

Neuhaus, G., Roldan, L., Boulware-Gooden, R. and Swank, P. (2006) 'Parsimonious reading models: identifying teachable subskills', *Reading Psychology*, 27, 1: 37–58.

Ng, L. (2006) *Annual Monitoring of Reading Recovery: Data for 2004*, Wellington: New Zealand Ministry for Education.

Nichols, R. (1985) *Helping Your Child Spell*, Earley: University of Reading.

Nicholson, T. (2006) 'How to avoid reading failure: teach phonemic awareness'. In McKeough, A., Lupart, J.L. Phillips, L.M. and Timmons, V. (eds) *Understanding Literacy Development: A Global View*, Mahwah, NJ: Erlbaum.

Norton, T. and Land, B.L.J. (2004) *Literacy Strategies: Resources for Beginning Teachers, 1–6*, Upper Saddle River, NJ: Pearson-Merrill-Prentice Hall.

Norwich, B. and Kelly, N. (2004) 'Pupils' views on inclusion: moderate learning difficulties and bullying in mainstream and special schools', *British Educational Research Journal*, 30, 1: 43–65.

Nunes, T. and Bryant, P. (2004) 'Morphological awareness improves spelling and vocabulary', *Literacy Today*, 38: 18–19.

Nyholm, M. (2002) 'Spelling and phonological knowledge: sounds right to me!', *Classroom*, 22, 2: 32–3.

O'Brien, C. (2005) 'Modifying learning strategies for classroom success', *Teaching Exceptional Children Plus*, 1, 3 (n.p.). Available at: http://escholarship.bc.edu/education/tecplus/vol1/iss3/3 (accessed 19 February 2006).

O'Connor, E.A. and Simic, O. (2002) 'The effect of Reading Recovery on special education referrals and placements', *Psychology in the Schools*, 39, 6: 635–46.

O'Sullivan, O. (2000) 'Understanding spelling', *Reading*, 34, 1: 9–16.

OECD (Organisation for Economic Cooperation and Development) (1999) *Inclusive Education at Work: Students with Disabilities in Mainstream Schools*, Paris: OECD Centre for Educational Research and Innovation.

OECD (Organisation for Economic Cooperation and Development) (2000) *Special Needs Education: Statistics and Indicators*, Paris: OECD Centre for Educational Research and Innovation.

Olweus, D. (1993) *Bullying at School*, Oxford: Blackwell.

Orelove, F., Sobsey, D. and Silberman, R.K. (2004) *Educating Children with Multiple Disabilities: A Collaborative Approach* (4th edn), Baltimore, MD: Brookes.

Ormrod, J.E. (2006) *Essentials of Educational Psychology*, Upper Saddle River, NJ: Pearson-Merrill-Prentice Hall.

Ostrosky, M.M., Laumann, B.M. and Hsieh, W.Y. (2006) 'Early childhood teachers' beliefs and attitudes about inclusion: what does the research tell us?' In B. Spodek and O.N.

Saracho (eds) *Handbook of Research on the Education of Young Children* (2nd edn), Mahwah, NJ: Erlbaum.

Oswald, K., Safran, S. and Johanson, G. (2005) 'Preventing trouble: making schools safer places using positive behavior supports', *Education and Treatment of Children*, 28, 3: 265–78.

OTEC (Oregon Technology in Education Council) (2005) *Learning Theories and Transfer of Learning*. Available at: http://otec.uoregon.edu/learning_theory. htm#Situated%20Learning (accessed 5 June 2006).

Pajares, F. and Urdan, T. (eds) (2006) *Self-efficacy Beliefs of Adolescents*, Greenwich, CT: Information Age Publishing.

Paris, S.G. and Paris, A.H. (2001) 'Classroom applications of research on self-regulated learning', *Educational Psychologist*, 36, 2: 89–101.

Paris, S.G. and Stahl, S.A. (eds) (2005) *Children's Reading Comprehension and Assessment*, Mahwah, NJ: Erlbaum.

Paris, S.G., Byrnes, J.P. and Paris, A.H. (2001) 'Constructing theories, identities and actions of self-regulated learners'. In B.J. Zimmerman and D.H. Schunk (eds) *Self-regulated Learning and Academic Achievement* (2nd edn), Mahwah, NJ: Erlbaum.

Pavri, S. (2006) 'Introduction: School-based interventions to promote social and emotional competence in students with reading difficulties', *Reading and Writing Quarterly*, 22, 2: 99–101.

Pavri, S. and Monda-Amaya, L. (2001) 'Social support in inclusive schools: student and teacher perspectives', *Exceptional Children*, 67, 3: 391–411.

Petersen, M.C. and Whitaker, T.M. (2003) 'Cerebral palsy'. In M.L. Wolraich (ed.) *Disorders of Development and Learning* (3rd edn), Hamilton, Ontario: Decker.

Pettig, K.L. (2000) 'On the road to differentiated practice', *Educational Leadership*, 58, 1: 14–18.

Phillips, D. (2004) 'Writing with a word processor', *SET Research Information for Teachers*, 3: 6–9.

Piaget, J. (1963) *Origins of Intelligence in Children*, New York: Norton.

Pickering, S.J. and Gathercole, S.E. (2004) 'Distinctive working memory profiles in children with special educational needs', *Educational Psychology*, 24, 3: 393–408.

Pickles, P.A. (2004) *Inclusive Teaching, Inclusive Learning: Managing the Curriculum for Children with Severe Motor Learning Difficulties* (2nd edn), London: Fulton.

Pierangelo, R. and Giuliani, G. (2006) *Learning Disabilities: A Practical Approach to Foundations, Assessment, Diagnosis and Teaching*, Boston, MA: Pearson-Allyn and Bacon.

Pincott, R. (2004) 'Are we responsible for our children's maths difficulties?' In B.A. Knight and W. Scott (eds) *Learning Difficulties: Multiple Perspectives*, Frenchs Forest, NSW: Pearson.

Polkinghorne, J. (2004) 'Electronic literacy: Part 1 and Part 2', *Australian Journal of Learning Disabilities*, 9, 2: 24–7.

Pollington, M.F., Wilcox, B. and Morrison, T.G. (2001) 'Self-perception in writing: the effects of writing workshop and traditional instruction on intermediate grade students', *Reading Psychology*, 22: 249–65.

Polloway, E.A. and Patton, J.R. (1997) *Strategies for Teaching Learners with Special Needs* (6th edn), Upper Saddle River, NJ: Merrill-Prentice Hall.

Poulou, M. (2005) 'The prevention of emotional and behavioural difficulties in schools: teachers' suggestions', *Educational Psychology in Practice*, 21, 1: 37–52.

Pressley, M. (2006) *Reading Instruction that Works: The Case for Balanced Teaching* (3rd edn), New York: Guilford Press.

Pressley, M. and Hilden, K. (2006) 'Teaching reading comprehension'. In A. McKeough, L.M. Phillips, V. Timmons and J.L. Lupart (eds) *Understanding Literacy Development: A Global View*, Mahwah, NJ: Erlbaum.

Prideaux, A., Marsh, K.A. and Caplygin, D. (2005) 'Efficacy of the Cellfield Intervention for reading difficulties: an integrated computer-based approach targeting deficits associated with dyslexia', *Australian Journal of Learning Disabilities*, 10, 2: 51–62.

Prizant, B.M., Wetherby, A.M., Rubin, E., Laurent, A. and Rydell, P. (2005) *The SCERTS Manual: A Comprehensive Educational Approach for Children with Autism Spectrum Disorders*, Baltimore, MD: Brookes.

Pullen, P.C., Lane, H.B., Lloyd, J.W., Nowak, R. and Ryals, J. (2005) 'Effects of explicit instruction on decoding of struggling first grade students: a data-based case study', *Education and Treatment of Children*, 28, 1: 63–75.

QCA (Qualifications and Curriculum Authority) (2005) *The National Curriculum.* Available at: http://www.nc.uk.net/nc/contents/Ma-home.htm (accessed 15 April 2006).

Rappley, M.D. (2005) 'Attention Deficit-Hyperactivity Disorder', *New England Journal of Medicine*, 352, 2: 165–73.

Rasinski, T. and Padak, N. (2004) *Effective Reading Strategies: Teaching Children who Find Reading Difficult* (3rd edn), Upper Saddle River, NJ: Pearson-Merrill-Prentice Hall.

Raveaud, M. (2005) 'Hares, tortoises and the social construction of the pupil: differentiated learning in French and English primary schools', *British Educational Research Journal* 31, 4: 459–79.

Rea, P.J., McLaughlin, V.L. and Walther-Thomas, C. (2002) 'Outcomes for students with learning disabilities in inclusive and pullout programs', *Exceptional Children*, 68, 2: 203–22.

Reading Recovery Council of North America (2002) *What Evidence Says About Reading Recovery: Executive Summary*, Columbus, OH: RRCNA.

Reid, D.H. and Green, C.W. (2006) 'Preference-based teaching: helping students with severe disabilities enjoy learning without problem behaviours', *Teaching Exceptional Children Plus*, 2, 3 (n.p.). Available at: http://escholarship.bc.edu/education/tecplus/vol2/iss3/art2 (accessed 19 February 2006).

Reschly, D.J. (2005) 'Learning disabilities identification: primary intervention, secondary intervention, and then what?', *Journal of Learning Disabilities*, 38, 6: 510–15.

Reynolds, D. and Muijs, D. (1999) 'Contemporary policy issues in the teaching of mathematics'. In I. Thompson (ed.) *Issues in Teaching Numeracy in Primary Schools*, Buckingham: Open University Press.

Riccomini, P.J. (2005) 'Identification and remediation of systematic error patterns in subtraction', *Learning Disability Quarterly*, 28, 3: 233–42.

Rieck, W.A. and Wadsworth, D.E. (2005) 'Assessment accommodations: helping students with exceptional learning needs', *Intervention in School and Clinic*, 41, 2: 105–9.

Robbins, B. (1996) 'Mathematics'. In B. Carpenter, R. Ashdown and K. Bovair (eds) *Enabling Access: Effective Teaching and Learning for Pupils with Learning Difficulties*, London: Fulton.

Roeser, R.J. and Downs, M.P. (2004) *Auditory Disorders in School Children* (4th edn), New York: Thieme.

Rogers, B. (2004) 'Making a discipline plan', *Classroom*, 24, 2: 24–5.

Rose, J. (2005) *Independent Review of the Teaching of Early Reading: Interim Report*, London: Department for Education and Skills.

Rose, R. (2001) 'Primary school teacher perceptions of the conditions required for including pupils with special educational needs', *Educational Review*, 53, 2: 147–56.

Rosenshine, B. and Meister, C. (1994) 'Reciprocal teaching: a review of research', *Review of Educational Research*, 64, 4: 479–530.

Ross, S.R. (2002) 'Place value, problem solving and written assessment', *Teaching Children Mathematics*, 8, 7: 419–23.

Rustemier, S. and Vaughn, M. (2005) *Are LEAs in England abandoning inclusive education?* Press Release from Centre for Studies on Inclusive Education, 8 July 2005. Available at: http://inclusion.uwe.ac.uk/csie/segregationstats2005.htm (accessed 20 May 2006).

Sabbatino, E. (2004) 'Students with learning disabilities construct meaning through graphic organizers: strategies for achievement in inclusive classrooms', *Learning Disabilities: A Multidisciplinary Journal*, 13, 2: 69–74.

Sabornie, E. and deBettencourt, L.U. (2004) *Teaching Students with Mild and High-incidence Disabilities at the Secondary Level* (2nd edn), Upper Saddle River, NJ: Merrill-Prentice Hall.

Saddler, B. (2005) 'Sentence combining: a sentence-level writing intervention', *The Reading Teacher*, 58, 5: 468–71.

Salend, S.J. (2005) *Creating Inclusive Classrooms: Effective and Reflective Practices for All Students* (5th edn), Upper Saddle River, NJ: Pearson-Merrill-Prentice Hall.

Sample, K.J. (2005) 'Promoting fluency in adolescents with reading difficulties', *Intervention in School and Clinic*, 40, 4: 243–6.

Savage, J.F. (2004) *Sound it Out: Phonics in a Comprehensive Reading Program* (2nd edn), New York: McGraw Hill.

Scharer, P.L. and Zutell, J. (2003) 'The development of spelling'. In N. Hall, J. Larson and J. Marsh (eds) *Handbook of Early Childhood Literacy*, London: Sage.

Schlagal, B. (2002) 'Classroom spelling instruction: history, research and practice', *Reading Research and Instruction*, 42, 1: 44–58.

Schug, M.C., Tarver, S.G. and Western, R.D. (2001) 'Direct instruction and the teaching of early reading', *Wisconsin Policy Research Institute Report*, 14, 2: 1–31.

Sewell, K. (2000) *Breakthroughs: How to Reach Students with Autism*, Verona, WI: Attainment Company.

Shapiro, M., Parush, S., Green, M. and Roth, D. (1997) 'The efficacy of the "Snoezelen" in the management of children with mental retardation who exhibit maladaptive behaviours', *The British Journal of Developmental Disabilities*, 43, 2: 140–55.

Shippen, M.E., Houchins, D.E., Steventon, C. and Sartor, D. (2005) 'A comparison of two direct instruction reading programs for urban middle school students', *Remedial and Special Education*, 26, 3: 175–82.

Silva, J.C. and Morgado, J. (2004) 'Support teachers' beliefs about the academic achievement of students with special educational needs', *British Journal of Special Education*, 31, 4: 207–14.

Silverstone, B., Lang, M.A., Rosenthal, B.P. and Faye, E.E. (2000) *The Lighthouse Handbook on Vision Impairment and Vision Rehabilitation*, Oxford: Oxford University Press.

Simpson, R.L. (2005) 'Evidence-based practices and students with autism spectrum disorders', *Focus on Autism and Other Developmental Disabilities*, 20, 3: 140–9.

Siperstein, G.N. and Rickards, E.P. (2004) *Promoting Social Success: A Curriculum for Children with Special Needs*, Baltimore, MD: Brookes.

Skidmore, D. (2004) *Inclusion: The Dynamic of School Development*, Maidenhead: Open University Press.

Slavin, R.E. (2004) 'Built to last: long-term maintenance of "Success for All"', *Remedial and Special Education*, 25, 1: 61–6.

Slavin, R.E. and Madden, N.A. (2001) *One Million Children: Success for All*, Thousand Oaks, CA: Corwin Press.

Smart, D., Prior, M., Sanson, A. and Oberklaid, F. (2005) 'Children with reading difficulties: a six-year follow-up from early primary to secondary school', *Australian Journal of Learning Disabilities* ,10, (3–4): 63–75.

Smith, D. (2004) *Success in the Literacy Hour*, London: Fulton.

Smith, F., Hardman, F. and Higgins, S. (2006) 'The impact of interactive whiteboards on teacher–pupil interaction in the National Literacy and Numeracy Strategies', *British Educational Research Journal*, 32, 3: 443–57.

Smith, N.B. (1969) 'The many faces of reading comprehension', *The Reading Teacher*, 23: 249–59 and 291.

Smith-Burke, M.T. (2001) 'Reading Recovery: a systematic approach to early intervention'. In L.M. Morrow and D.G. Woo (eds) *Tutoring Programs for Struggling Readers*, New York: Guilford Press.

Snell, M.E. and Brown, F. (eds) (2006) *Instruction of Students with Severe Disabilities*, Upper Saddle River, NJ: Pearson-Merrill-Prentice Hall.

Soan, S. (2004) *Additional Educational Needs: Inclusive Approaches to Teaching*, London: Dulton.

Solomon, G. (2003) 'Project-based learning: a primer', *TechLearning*, 23, 6. Available at: http://www.techlearning.com/content/about/archives/volume23/jan.html (accessed 11 March 2006).

Søvik, N. (2003) *Writing: On Developmental Trends in Children's Manual and Compositional Writing*, Hauppauge, NY: Nova Science.

Sparzo, F.J. and Walker, S.C. (2004) 'Managing behavior in the inclusive classroom'. In J.S. Choate (ed.) *Successful Inclusive Teaching: Proven Ways to Detect and Correct Special Needs* (4th edn), Boston, MA: Allyn and Bacon.

Spencer, K. (2002) 'English spelling and its contribution to illiteracy: word difficulty for common English words', *Reading, Language and Literacy*, 36, 1: 16–25.

Sperling, R.A. (2006) 'Assessing reading materials for students who are learning disabled', *Intervention in School and Clinic*, 41, 3: 138–41.

Stafford A.M. (2005) 'Choice making: a strategy for students with severe disabilities', *Teaching Exceptional Children*, 37, 6: 12–17.

Stahl, K.A.D. and McKenna, M.C.(2006) *Reading Research at Work: Foundations of Effective Practice*, New York: Guilford Press.

Stahl, S. and Miller, P.D. (1989) 'Whole language and language experience approaches for beginning reading: a quantitative research synthesis', *Review of Educational Research*, 59: 87–116.

Stahl, S., McKenna, M.C. and Pagnucco, J.R. (1994) 'The effects of whole-language instruction: an update and reappraisal', *Educational Psychologist*, 29, 4: 175–85.

Stanford, P. and Reeves, S. (2005) 'Improving instruction through assessment', *Teaching Exceptional Children*, 37, 4: 18–22.

Stanovich, K.E. (1999) 'Foreword'. In R. Sternberg and L. Spear-Swerling (eds) *Perspectives on Learning Disabilities: Biological, Cognitive and Contextual*, Boulder, CO: Westview Press.

Steinberg, A.G. and Knightly, C.A. (1997) 'Hearing: sounds and silences'. In M.L. Batshaw (ed.) *Children with Disabilities* (4th edn), Sydney: Maclennan and Petty.

Steinman, B.A., LeJeune, B.J. and Kimbrough, B.T. (2006) 'Developmental stages of reading processes in children who are blind and sighted', *Journal of Visual Impairment and Blindness*, 100, 1: 3–46.

Sternberg, R. and Grigorenko, E.L. (2001) 'Learning disabilities, schooling, and society', *Phi Delta Kappan*, 83, 4: 335–8.

Stewart, D.A. and Kluwin, T.N. (2001) *Teaching Deaf and Hard of Hearing Students: Content, Strategies and Curriculum*, Boston, MA: Allyn and Bacon.

Stewart, E. and Ritter, K. (2001) 'Ethics of assessment'. In R.G. Beattie (ed.) *Ethics of Deaf Education*, San Diego, CA: Academic Press.

Swanson, H.L. (2000) 'What instruction works for students with learning disabilities?' In R. Gersten, E. Schiller and S. Vaughn (eds) *Contemporary Special Education Research*, Mahwah, NJ: Erlbaum.

Swanson, H.L. and Deshler, D. (2003) 'Instructing adolescents with learning difficulties: converting a meta-analysis to practice', *Journal of Learning Disabilities*, 36, 2: 124–34.

Swanson, H.L., Harris, K.R. and Graham, S. (eds) (2003) *Handbook of Learning Disabilities*, New York: Guilford Press.

Taylor, J. and Baker, R.A. (2002) 'Discipline and the special education student', *Educational Leadership*, 59, 4: 28–30.

Taylor, M. (2003) *Going Round in Circles: Implementing and Learning from Circle Time*, Slough: NFER Press.

Temple, C.M. (2001) 'Developmental dyscalculia'. In S.J. Segalowitz and I. Rapin (eds) *Handbook of Neuropsychology* (vol.7), Amsterdam: Elsevier.

Templeton, S. (2003a) 'Spelling: best ideas = best practices', *Voices from the Middle*, 10, 4: 48–9.

Templeton, S. (2003b) 'The spelling/meaning connection', *Voices from the Middle*, 10, 3: 56–7.

Therrien, W.J., Gormley, S. and Kubina, R.M. (2006) 'Boosting fluency and comprehension to improve reading achievement', *Teaching Exceptional Children*, 38, 3: 22–5.

Thibodeau, G. (2002) 'Spellbound: commitment to correctness', *Voices from the Middle*, 9, 3: 19–22.

Tomlinson, C.A. and Strickland C.A. (2005) *Differentiation in Practice: A Resource Guide for Differentiating Curriculum*, Alexandria, VA: Association for Supervision and Curriculum Development.

Tompkins, G.E. (2004) *Teaching Writing: Balancing Process and Product* (4th edn), Upper Saddle River, NJ: Pearson-Merrill-Prentice Hall.

Tompkins, G.E. (2006) *Literacy for 21st Century: A Balanced Approach* (4th edn), Upper Saddle River, NJ: Pearson-Merrill-Prentice Hall.

Topping, K., Nixon, J., Sutherland, J. and Yarrow, F. (2000) 'Paired writing: a framework for effective collaboration, *Reading*, 34, 2: 79–89.

Trezek, B.J. and Malmgren, K.W. (2005) 'The efficacy of utilizing a phonics treatment package with middle school deaf and hard-of-hearing students', *Journal of Deaf Studies and Deaf Education*, 10, 3: 256–71.

Tunmer, W.E., Chapman, J.W., Greaney, K.T. and Prochnow, J.E. (2002) 'The contribution of educational psychology to intervention research and practice', *International Journal of Disability, Development and Education*, 49, 1: 11–29.

Tuovinen, J.E. and Sweller, J. (1999) 'A comparison of cognitive load associated with discovery learning and worked examples', *Journal of Educational Psychology*, 91, 2: 334–41.

Turnbull, A., Turnbull, R. and Wehmeyer, M.L. (2007) *Exceptional Lives: Special Education in Today's Schools* (5th edn), Upper Saddle River, NJ: Pearson-Merrill-Prentice Hall.

Tweed, A. (2004) 'Direct Instruction: is it the most effective science teaching strategy?' *NSTA Reports 2004-12-15. National Science Teachers Association Web-News Digest.* Available at: http://www.nsta.org/main/news/stories/education_story.php?news_story_ID=50045 (accessed 19 May 2006).

UKLA/PNS (United Kingdom Literacy Association/Primary National Strategy) (2004) *Raising Boys' Achievements in Writing*, Royston, Hertfordshire: UKLA.

UNESCO (1994) *The Salamanca Statement and Framework for Action on Special Needs Education*, Salamanca: UNESCO.

UNESCO (2004) *Inclusive Education*. Available at: http://portal.unesco.org/education/en/ev.php-URL_ID=12078&URL_DO=DO_TOPIC&URL_SECTION=201.html (accessed 12 April 2006).

University of Hull (2006) *Research and Evaluation of Interactive Electronic Whiteboards*. Available at: http://www.thereviewproject.org/index.htm (accessed 16 May 2006).

US Congress (2002) *Individuals with Disabilities Education Act Amendments of 1997 (IDEA) (P.L. 105–17), 111 Stat. 37–157*, Washington, DC: Congress.

Vacca, J.A., Vacca, R.T. and Gove, M.K. (2006) *Reading and Learning to Read* (8th edn), Boston, MA: Pearson-Allyn and Bacon.

Van den Berg, R., Sleegers, P. and Geijsel, F. (2001) 'Teachers' concerns about adaptive teaching: evaluation of a support program', *Journal of Curriculum and Supervision*, 16, 3: 245–58.

Van der Kaay, M., Wilton, K. and Townsend, M. (2000) 'Word processing and written composition: an intervention for children with mild intellectual disability', *Australasian Journal of Special Education*, 24, 2: 53–9.

Van Garderen, D. and Whittaker, C. (2006) 'Planning differentiated, multicultural instruction for secondary inclusive classrooms', *Teaching Exceptional Children*, 38, 3: 12–21.

Vaughn, S., Gersten, R. and Chard, D.J. (2000) 'The underlying message in LD intervention research: findings from research synthesis', *Exceptional Children*, 67, 1: 99–114.

Vellutino, F.R., Scanlon, D.M., Small, S. and Fanuele, D.P. (2006) 'Response to intervention as a vehicle for distinguishing between children with and without reading disabilities: evidence for the role of kindergarten and first-grade interventions', *Journal of Learning Disabilities*, 39, 2: 157–69.

Vincini (2003) *The Nature of Situated Learning*. Available at: http://at.tccs.tufts.edu/pdf/newsletter_feb_2003.pdf (accessed 3 June 2006).

Vukovic, R.K. and Siegel, L.S. (2006) 'The double-deficit hypothesis: a comprehensive analysis of the evidence', *Journal of Learning Disabilities*, 39, 1: 25–47.

Walker, B.J. (2005) 'Thinking aloud: struggling readers often require more than a model', *The Reading Teacher*, 58, 7: 688–92.

Wall, K. (2004) 'The National Literacy Strategy and setting: an investigation in one school', *Curriculum Journal*, 15, 3: 233–46.

Wallace, C. (2005) 'Conversations around the Literacy Hour in a multilingual London primary school', *Language and Education*, 19, 4: 322–38.

Waterhouse, S. (2000) *A Positive Approach to Autism*, London: Jessica Kingsley.

Weaver, C. (2002) *Reading Process and Practice* (3rd edn), Portsmouth, NH: Heinemann.

Weeks, S., Brooks, P. and Everatt, J. (2002) 'Differences in learning to spell: relationships between cognitive profiles and learning responses to teaching methods', *Educational and Child Psychology*, 19, 4: 47–62.

Wehmeyer, M.L. and Agran, M. (eds) (2005) *Mental Retardation and Intellectual Disabilities: Teaching Students Using Innovative and Research-based Strategies*, Boston, MA: Pearson-Merrill-Prentice Hall.

Weisel, A. and Tur-Kaspa, H. (2002) 'Effects of labels and personal contact on teachers' attitudes toward students with special needs', *Exceptionality*, 10, 1: 1–10.

Wendon, L. (2006) *Letterland*, Barton, Cambridge: Letterland International. Available at: http://www.letterland.com/Teachers/Teachers_1.html (accessed 01 June 2006).

Westwood, P.S. (2001) 'Differentiation as a strategy for inclusive classroom practice: some difficulties identified', *Australian Journal of Learning Disabilities*, 6, 1: 5–11.

Westwood, P.S. (2003) 'Drilling basic number facts: should we or should we not?', *Australian Journal of Learning Disabilities*, 8, 4: 12–18.

Westwood, P.S. (2004a) 'Affective components of difficulty in learning: why prevention is better than attempted cure'. In B.A. Knight and W. Scott (eds) *Learning Difficulties: Multiple Perspectives*, Frenchs Forest, NSW: Pearson Educational Australia.

Westwood, P.S. (2004b) *Learning and Learning Difficulties*, Melbourne: Australian Council for Educational Research.

Westwood, P.S. and Graham, L. (2000) 'How many children with special needs in regular classes?', *Australian Journal of Learning Disabilities*, 5, 3: 24–35.

Wheatley, J.P. (2005) *Strategic Spelling: Moving Beyond Word Memorization in the Middle Grades*, Newark, DE: International Reading Association.

White, S. (2005) 'Education that works in the Milwaukee public schools: benefits from phonics and direct instruction', *Wisconsin Policy Research Institute Report*, 18, 4: 1–23.

Wiener, J. (2004) 'Do peer relationships foster behavioral adjustment in children with learning disabilities?', *Learning Disability Quarterly*, 27, 1: 21–30.

Wilen, W., Ishler, M., Hutchison, J. and Kindsvatter, R. (2000) *Dynamics of Effective Teaching* (4th edn), New York: Longman.

Wilson, L., Andrew, C. and Below, J. (2006) 'A comparison of teacher–pupil interaction within mathematics lessons in St Petersburg, Russia and the North-East of England', *British Educational Research Journal*, 32, 3: 411–41.

Wolraich, M.L. (2003) 'Disorders of mental development: general issues'. In M.L. Wolraich (ed.) *Disorders of Development and Learning* (3rd edn), Hamilton, Ontario: Decker.

Worthy, J., Broaddus, K. and Ivey, G. (2001) *Pathways to Independence: Reading, Writing and Learning in Grades 3–8*, New York: Guilford Press.

Wright, R. (2003) 'Mathematics Recovery: a program of intervention in early number learning', *Australian Journal of Learning Disabilities*, 8, 4: 6–11.

Wurst, D., Jones, D. and Luckner, J. (2005) 'Promoting literacy development with students who are deaf, hard-of-hearing, and hearing', *Teaching Exceptional Children*, 37, 5: 56–62.

Xin, Y.P. and Jitendra, A.K. (1999) 'The effects of instruction in solving mathematical word problems for students with learning problems: a meta analysis', *Journal of Special Education*, 32, 4: 207–25.

Xin, Y.P., Grasso, J.C., Dipipi-Hoy, C.M. and Jitendra, A. (2005a) 'The effects of purchasing skill instruction for individuals with developmental disabilities: a meta-analysis', *Exceptional Children*, 71, 4: 379–400.

Xin, Y.P., Jitendra, A.K. and Deatline-Buchman, A. (2005b) 'Effects of mathematical word problem-solving instruction on middle school students with learning problems', *Journal of Special Education*, 39, 3: 181–92.

Zentall, S.S. (2006) *ADHD and Education: Foundations, Characteristics, Methods, and Collaboration*, Upper Saddle River, NJ: Pearson-Merrill-Prentice Hall.

Zhou, L. (2001) 'Bridge the gap: reflections on whole-class interactive teaching'. Available at: http://www.people.ex.ac.uk/PErnest/pome17/bridge.htm.

Zirpoli, T.J. (2005) *Behavior Management: Applications for Teachers* (4th edn), Upper Saddle River, NJ: Merrill-Prentice Hall.

Index

mediated learning 20
memory: intellectual disability **21**;
 traumatic brain injury 38
mental retardation (*see* intellectual
 disability)
metacognitive strategies 24, 53. **59, 60**,
 193
milieu approach to language teaching **22,
 47**
mini lessons: for writing 147
miscues **117**
mnemonics 107, 108, 150, 154, 166, 192,
 197
mobility training **41**
modelling: as a teaching procedure 15, 58,
 61, 88, 108, 111, 139, 145, 149
moderate learning difficulties 6
modifications: curriculum 18, **200**;
 instruction **202–3**; resource materials
 197, **201**
morphemic approach to spelling **169**
motivation 1, 8, **12**, 30, 93, 124, 141, 145
motor memory: in spelling **165**
multisensory methods 25, **138–9**
multi-tiered intervention model **10**

National Literacy Strategy (UK) 124
National Numeracy Strategy (UK) 181
Neale Analysis of Reading Ability 118
No Child Left Behind Act (US) 93
non-readers: assessment of **116–17**
number facts: automaticity 178, 180;
 importance of 188; teaching of **187–8**
Numeracy Recovery 180
number sense 180, 181

objectives for learning 24, 28, 29, 68, 111,
 113–14, 138, 175, 196, 198, 199, 206,
 209
Old Way/New Way: for arithmetic errors
 190; for spelling **173**;
onset-rime units **132**, **137**, 171
oralism (oral-aural approach) **49**
orientation training **42**
orthographic memory **165**
orthographic units **95**, 113, 119, 13, 137,
 168
overlearning 21, 102, 151, 175, 222

paired writing **153**
parent involvement 5, 28, 29, 31, 125, 140,
 153, 189
parent tutoring 84, 125, **140**

patterned writing **154**
Pause, Prompt, Praise **140–1**
peer critiquing: in writing **149**
peer tutoring **85**, 8, 126, 142, 15, 199
perception 8, 21, 37, 130, 132: auditory 9,
 164; visual 9, 130, 132, **164**, 166
personalised instruction 161, **196**
Pervasive Developmental Disorders (PDD)
 26
phoneme blending 116, **133** (*see also*
 sound blending)
phonemic awareness (*see* phonological
 awareness)
phonetic stage in spelling **162**, 167
phonic dictation 170
phonic knowledge 100, 112, 11, 116, **117**,
 126, 166
phonics **95**, **132**, **134–5**, 144: analytic
 method 95, 134; instruction **134–5**;
 phonic skills 95, 98, 111, 118, 119,
 222, 132, 136; synthetic method 95,
 134; and spelling 162, **163–4**, **168–9**
phonological awareness 9, 11, 47, 112,
 115, 117, **131**
phonological training 117, **131–3**
physical disabilities **34–8**: cerebral palsy
 35–6; impact on learning 35, 40 spina
 bifida **37–8**; teaching and management
 36–7, 39, 40
pivotal response training **30**
place value: arithmetic 180, 185
Positive Behaviour Support (PBS) **64**
practice: importance of 13, 14, 15, 99, 10,
 111, 119, **126**, 137; insufficient 119,
 146
praise: descriptive 57, 70, 78, 86, 90, 149,
 203; importance of 57, 70
precision teaching 151
preference-based teaching **25**
pre-reading activities **129–30**
problem solving in mathematics 178, 185:
 difficulties with **191**; strategies for
 190–3; teaching of **190–3**
problem-based learning 214, **217–18**
process approach 14: mathematics 177;
 writing 146, **147–8**
project-based learning 14, **215**
proofreading 158, 163, **170**, 171
protective behaviours **23**
punishment 69, 71, **73**

readability of text 106, 109, 115, **120–1**
Reading Recovery **121–3**